U.S. Legal Practice Skills
for International Law Students

U.S. Legal Practice Skills for International Law Students

Anne M. Burr

Howard Bromberg

CAROLINA ACADEMIC PRESS

Durham, North Carolina

Library of Congress Cataloging-in-Publication Data

Burr, Anne M., author.
  U.S. legal practice skills for international law students / Anne M. Burr and
Howard Bromberg.
      pages cm
Includes bibliographical references and index.
ISBN 978-1-61163-108-1
  1. Practice of law--United States. I. Bromberg, Howard (Writer on U.S. legal
practice skills), author. II. Title. III. Title: United States legal practice skills for
international students.

KF300.B87 2014
347.73'504--dc23

2014022157

CAROLINA ACADEMIC PRESS
700 Kent Street
Durham, North Carolina 27701
Telephone (919) 489-7486
Fax (919) 493-5668
www.cap-press.com

Printed in the United States of America
2019 Printing

Dedication

To Dr. J. J. Liou, who has done so much to foster greater understanding globally, especially in the field of education.

HB

To Kenneth and Caitlin, for motivation, inspiration, and support in all things.

AMB

And to our law students who have taught us many things, not the least of which is the joy of sharing new ideas and the power of the law to shape them.

HB and AMB

Contents

Part Two
Introduction to U.S. Law and Legal Reasoning

Part Three
Writing Skills: Objective Legal Writing and the Office Memorandum

Part Four
Practice Skills: Professional Responsibility,
Client Communications, and Problem Solving

Part Five
Practice Skills: Interviewing and Counseling

Part Six
Writing and Practice Skills: Letter Writing
and Electronic Communications

Part Seven
Writing Skills: Transactional Drafting

Part Eight
Practice Skills: Alternative Dispute Resolution and Negotiation and Settlement

Part Nine
Practice Skills: Law Firm and
Courtroom Culture and Practice

Preface

We began to develop the ideas for this book when we were teaching the legal practice courses at the Peking University School of Transnational Law in Shenzhen, the first American-style law school in China. Even with the great talent of the student body, it was clear that effort had to be expended to familiarize our students with both the nature of the American common law system, and the specifics of practicing law in the U.S. Our experience teaching international law students in the LL.M. program at the University of Michigan Law School, Ann Arbor, confirmed that these challenges also existed with students from western and even common law countries.

Before their immersion in the American legal system, students must be initiated in the mysteries of common law. The Latin phrases that denote common-law reasoning, *ratio decidendi*, *obiter dictum*, *causa actio*, only highlight the medieval and British hallmarks of the common law, now pressed into service of the modern American regulatory state, replete with statutes, codes, and ordinances. The U.S. has a unique system of dual state and federal sovereignty. The 50 states retain the widest latitude in enacting laws for the health, welfare, and safety of their residents but almost paradoxically defer to limited yet supreme federal law. The state and federal structures were built from compromises over democratic and republican, elite and egalitarian principles that characterized the debates over the ratification and amending of the U.S. Constitution. These state and federal constitutions, the oldest continually operating such documents in the world, frame the laws of a nation that now projects its commercial interests, jurisprudential principles, and legal sensibilities across the globe.

The education of the international law student cannot end with an understanding, however thorough, of the structures of American law and its content. Law students go out to practice. The highly developed professional and courtroom culture of the U.S. is integral to the practice of law but without systematic and detailed explanation can be opaque to law students and foreign practitioners. The culture of American lawyers as expressed in film and fiction is almost a world-wide phenomenon. But the day-to-day skills of practicing lawyers can differ from their portrayal in the media and what emerges from law school casebooks. Even the most knowledgeable law student will be at a loss without learning such skills of modern communication as concise and to-the-point memo writing, counseling and negotiating, letter drafting and email-ing, in the manner these and other skills are utilized in the law office and court system.

We have concentrated in this book on the fundamental skills necessary for practice in the U.S.—the "tool kit" of an American lawyer—and the details of practicing law in a firm setting. We express our appreciation for the lawyers and scholars who exchange ideas across borders on explaining the rule of law and best practices for the legal profession. We hope that this textbook makes a small contribution in that direction.

Acknowledgments

We would like to thank all those whose knowledge and assistance helped us in forming the ideas for this book. We have learned much from our Legal Practice Program colleagues at the University of Michigan Law School. Intentional infliction of emotional distress ("IIED") has been a much-used area of law in the Program, and our examples benefitted from countless Michigan conversations on the development of IIED in Florida—and other topics—with colleagues Ted Becker, Margaret Cernak, Paul Falon, Margaret Hannon, Mark Osbeck, Tim Pinto, Thom Seymour, Nancy Vettorello, and Beth Wilensky.

We also benefitted from teaching in the University of Michigan LL.M. program, where we co-taught the legal practice course for international law students with Professors Grace Tonner and Phil Frost. We also thank Assistants to the Legal Practice Program, Kathi Ganz and Helen Ryan. Helen helped with the formatting of several of the documents. The excellent IT and AV staff of the University of Michigan Law School are always helpful, as is Liz Arnkoff of LexisNexis.

Many of our ideas for teaching U.S. legal practice skills for international students were developed while teaching People's Republic of China law students, both in China and in the U.S. We thank Jeffrey Lehman, chancellor and founding dean, for the opportunity to teach in Peking University School of Transnational Law in Shenzhen. For the opportunity to teach students from China University of Political Science and Law and Beijing Normal University, we thank Zhang Qing, Associate Professor, China University of Political Science and Law, and Edward Bruley, Secretary of the Board of the Macomb Cultural and Economic Partnership.

For advice and encouragement as we began this project, we thank Professor Mark Wojcik of the John Marshall Law School in Chicago, Illinois. For their support, patience, and consistent goodwill we thank our publishers at Carolina Academic Press, Linda Lacy and Keith Sipe. For editorial assistance, we thank Kenneth Munn, who tirelessly proofread and commented on the entire book, drawing on his expertise in law and business.

Most of all, we thank our law students for sharing their enthusiasm about the law and their visions for the future and the role of law in society.

U.S. Legal Practice Skills
for International Law Students

Part One

Introduction to Legal Practice and Civil Litigation

Chapter 1

Introduction to
U.S. Legal Practice Skills for International Law Students

Background

U.S. Legal Practice Skills for International Law Students is primarily intended for foreign students interested in learning about law practice and legal skills in the U.S. It may also be of interest to foreign lawyers and judges, as well as other professionals who interact with American law firms, corporations, judges, and clients.

The book aims to provide a description of the practice skills—the "toolbox"—of the successful U.S. lawyer. Think of it as a "global legal skills academy" for foreign students who have or are currently studying American substantive law, but desire a deeper understanding of legal practice basics such as problem solving, counseling, negotiation styles, law firm culture, and billing protocol.

The focus of the book is on readers who wish to become acquainted with U.S. legal culture and the practical ramifications of the common law system. Legal practice in common law countries, such as the U.S., differs from that in other jurisdictions. In common law countries, lawyers are trained by Socratic Method in the art of argument, rather than by lecture and the study of codes. Lawyers, rather than judges, shape the litigation process. Finally, lawyers' ethical duties to their clients result in unique attorney-client relationships. Foreign students of the U.S. legal system should be knowledgeable about the manner in which lawyers solve client problems, as well as legal doctrine.

This chapter is divided into five sections: (1) U.S. legal practice skills, (2) common law culture and its impact on legal skills, (3) the goals of the book, (4) the organization of the book, and (5) important legal concepts in the American common law system.

Legal Practice Skills in the U.S.

The toolbox of the American lawyer includes many skills. Foremost among them are: written and oral communication, problem solving, logical reasoning, organization, time management, and relationship building.

Written communication is an integral function of the legal profession. It involves the ability to draft legal memoranda, contracts, correspondence, and a multitude of legal documents. Oral communication includes the ability to convey information in a clear, concise, and logical manner. It also involves the ability to be an active listener. Problem solving involves analyzing the client's legal issues to produce a variety of possible solutions. Logical reasoning requires lawyers to assimilate complex information, draw inferences, make connections among legal authorities, and structure legal arguments. Organization requires a lawyer to identify client objectives and create a cohesive structure from unrelated information. Time management is crucial in a profession based on billable hours, where productivity determines financial gain. Successful time management involves an ability to juggle competing priorities, and a commitment to meeting deadlines while producing a quality legal product. Relationship building requires the ability to share knowledge and collaborate with others to reach a common goal.

Legal Culture in the U.S.

Lawyers in the U.S. have a unique perspective on addressing client problems. In many countries, codes are the primary source of law. Legal reasoning is primarily deductive; the lawyer applies the law set forth in the codes to a particular case. In the U.S., judicial opinions are a primary source of the law and prior opinions govern later ones. Lawyers engage in a combination of deductive, inductive, and analogical reasoning. The synthesis of individual cases interpreting specific factual situations creates a body of legal doctrine.

Such differences affect the way the law is taught and, ultimately, practiced. In many other countries, lecturing is the primary teaching style. Conversely, in the U.S., the teaching is interactive and based on a reading of judicial opinions. The professor encourages the students to interpret the cases and make arguments about what the law should be. Hence, in the U.S., the emphasis is on examining the development of the law through judicial decisions and on using that flexibility to solve a specific client problem.

Further differences exist in the roles of judges and lawyers. In the common law system, lawyers shape the litigation process. Judges respond to pleadings filed by the attorneys. Where a case proceeds to trial, judges play a neutral role ruling on evidentiary questions and objections, charging the jury, and entering the verdict. In contrast, judges in other legal systems frequently dictate the timing of the case, determine what evidence is necessary, control which witnesses should be examined, and perform the examinations.

The differences in the roles of judges and lawyers impact the attorney-client relationship. In the common law system as practiced in the U.S., a lawyer's primary duty is to the client. In contrast, in other jurisdictions lawyers may be perceived as having rights and duties independent from the client. As a result, rules regarding conflicts of interest are more flexible.

Goals of *U.S. Legal Practice Skills for International Law Students*

The foremost goal of *U.S. Legal Practice Skills for International Law Students* is to assist you in gaining competency in, and an appreciation of, the skills used in practice by American attorneys. Specifically, the goals include gaining an understanding of:

- the civil litigation process
- U.S. court systems
- U.S. legal concepts, such as jurisdiction and common law
- methods of legal reasoning used in analyzing legal issues for a specific client
- the rules of professional responsibility and the ethics related to legal practice
- the lawyer's obligation to assist the client in problem solving
- the application of verbal and non-verbal client communication styles
- methods of client interviewing necessary to discover legally relevant facts
- methods of client counseling necessary to assist a client in selecting legal options
- writing skills used in memoranda, contracts, and correspondence
- methods of alternative dispute resolution
- the practice of negotiation and settlement
- law firm culture and practice
- courtroom culture and practice

As indicated by the goals, the focus of *U.S. Legal Practice Skills for International Law Students* is on the practice of civil, as opposed to criminal, law within the U.S. common law system. Likewise, the book focuses on the details of the private practice of law; it does not review areas of substantive law. Nor does it cover the rapidly changing world of U.S. legal research, which in many countries is performed exclusively online. Finally, *U.S. Legal Practice Skills for International Law Students* focuses on those practice skills necessary to perform the tasks common to foreign law students and lawyers working with American corporations, law firms, and individual American clients: drafting memoranda, contracts, and correspondence. It does not cover the advanced techniques of written or oral advocacy practiced in the U.S. Studies show that most International law students use their degree to open doors to top employers of a variety of nationalities, but are generally placed in offices outside the U.S. Hence, skills focused on advocacy in an American courtroom are beyond the scope of this book. For those readers who wish more information, we have included a list of resources on a number of legal practice subjects in the Appendix.

Organization of *U.S. Legal Practice Skills for International Law Students*

U.S. Legal Practice Skills for International Law Students is divided into nine parts. Part One introduces legal practice and civil litigation in the U.S. Part Two provides an introduction to U.S. law and legal reasoning. Part Three presents objective writing skills and the office memorandum. Part Four discusses the practice skills inherent in representing a client, including a knowledge of professional ethics, client communication skills, and problem solving. Part Five discusses the practice skills of client interviewing and counseling. Part Six concerns the practice and writing skills involved in letter writing and electronic communications. Part Seven presents transactional writing skills. Part Eight discusses the practice skills involved in alternative dispute resolution, as well as negotiation and settlement. Lastly, Part Nine concerns law firm and courtroom culture and practice.

The chapters in Parts Three through Nine of the book are each dedicated to a specific skill. In addition, Parts Three through Eight are designated as relating to "writing skills" or "practice skills." The practice skills chapters are intermixed with those dedicated to writing, to emphasize that such skills are necessary irrespective of whether you are writing a memorandum, a contract, or correspondence.

Within Chapters 2 through 19 there is a uniform format. Each chapter begins with the chapter "highlights" to assist you in organizing the material as you encounter it for the first time. The highlights are followed by an introduction, describing the contents of the chapter.

The introduction is followed by a client hypothetical. Each hypothetical exposes you to the type of client issues encountered by lawyers in the U.S. The hypotheticals cover issues on free speech in federal court and unethical attorney behavior before the attorney grievance commission. They also cover contract and employment issues, set in Arizona. Finally, they include a series of four infliction of emotional distress problems set in Georgia and Florida. The continuum of emotional distress hypotheticals allows you to apply a single area of law to a variety of practice skills and clients.

Each client hypothetical is followed by substantive instruction in the subject matter of the chapter. The instruction sections are followed by a discussion of the application of the substantive material to the client hypothetical. In this way, it is hoped that you not only learn about subjects such as interviewing or negotiation, but how the concepts would be applied in specific client situations. Lastly, each chapter ends with sample documents. We included cross-cultural discussions where we believe they add to an understanding of the subject.

Overview of U.S. Legal Concepts

Following is an overview of commonly understood legal concepts in the U.S. Each concept is discussed in a later chapter, but it is important to have a basic understanding of how the concepts work together to begin to understand legal practice in the U.S.

Federalism and the Dual System of Government

The U.S. has a dual system of government, composed of a federal and a state system. Each system derives its law from four sources: constitutions, statutes, judicial decisions, and administrative regulations. The federal and state constitutions provide a framework for governance at the federal and state levels. The framework calls for three branches of government: the legislative which enacts statutes, the executive which enforces statutes and promulgates administrative regulations, and the judicial which interprets and reviews statutes and creates law in situations not addressed by statute.

State and Federal Courts

Each state, as well as the District of Columbia and the federal government, has its own legislative, executive, and judicial branches. Each court system is a separate jurisdiction.

Jurisdiction

Simply stated, jurisdiction is the area over which the courts of a particular system have the power to resolve disputes and enforce judgments. Jurisdiction is determined by geographic area, but it is also based on subject matter.

Structure of the State and Federal Court Systems

All of the court systems in the U.S. are hierarchical. Most state court systems are composed of a three-tiered vertical hierarchy consisting of a trial court, an intermediate court of appeals, and the highest or "supreme" court. The state courts are considered courts of "general jurisdiction"; they may hear all matters not expressly reserved for the federal courts. The federal court system is composed of the U.S. Supreme Court, thirteen federal courts of appeal, and at least one trial or district court in each state. The federal courts are courts of "limited jurisdiction"; they may hear only those matters involving federal law, adverse parties of different states, or cases involving the federal government as a party.

Role of the Trial and Appellate Courts

Trials courts determine facts. The lawyers make opening and closing statements; witnesses are questioned under oath; exhibits are introduced. The judge and jury render a verdict. Appellate courts review the trial record for any errors of law. After hearing oral argument of the lawyers, they affirm or reverse the decision in the court below, usually setting out the rationale for the decision in a published opinion.

Common Law and Precedent

The U.S. legal system is known as a "common law" system; it relies heavily on judicial opinions. Judges interpret and apply statutes; they also create and develop legal principles in situations not addressed by statute. Courts rely on prior judicial opinions in deciding cases involving similar legal issues and facts. Such prior decisions are known as "precedent."

Stare Decisis

A court is required to reconcile a new decision with higher court decisions in the same jurisdiction involving similar legal issues and facts. This is known as "stare decisis." Prior court decisions that a court must follow when reaching a decision in a current case are known as "mandatory precedent." Prior court decisions that a court may be persuaded to follow are known as "persuasive precedent."

The Judicial System

The legal system in the U.S. is adversarial. The system assumes that lawyers—although officers of the court—will act as zealous advocates of their clients. Lawyers, also known as attorneys or counselors, fill many roles in meeting client needs. Lawyers examine clients' legal issues and counsel them on how to proceed with their affairs, whether such affairs involve a business transaction or litigation. Lawyers also act as negotiators, drafters of transactional and litigation documents, and as litigators representing the client before the courts.

Civil Litigation

Civil disputes in the U.S. may be resolved by private methods of alternative dispute resolution, such as arbitration or negotiation. They may also be brought to a state or, assuming proper jurisdiction, a federal court for decision. Civil disputes begin in the trial court. Once a final judgment is entered in the trial court, a party unhappy with or "aggrieved" by the decision may appeal.

Reporting and Citation of Judicial Opinions

Appellate courts publish their opinions. Federal and state trial courts may publish their opinions; publication is at the discretion of the judge. Opinions are published in hard and electronic copy. Hard copies are reproduced in books known as "reporters." Federal trial court opinions are published in the Federal Supplement or the Federal Rules Decisions. Federal intermediate appellate court decisions are published in the Federal Reporter. U.S. Supreme Court opinions are reported in U.S. Reports, Supreme Court Reporter, and U.S. Supreme Court Reports, Lawyers' Edition. State court opinions are published in reporters for the state and also regional reporters. Electronic copies are produced by Internet providers such as LexisNexis or Westlaw.

Every case has a citation. The citation consists of the reporter volume number, the name of the reporter, the page on which the case is found, the court deciding the case, and the year of the decision. Proper citation format varies slightly within the court systems but is generally found in the *Bluebook: A Uniform System of Citation*, compiled by the editors of the Columbia, Harvard,

University of Pennsylvania, and Yale law reviews. In either the hard copy or electronic systems, the easiest way to find cases is by their citation. In a common law system focused on precedent, such as the U.S., citation to cases is required to demonstrate the weight of authority and the credibility of a lawyer's position on a legal issue.

Chapter 2

Introduction to Civil Litigation

Highlights

- The procedures in a civil action filed in a U.S. federal court are governed by the Federal Rules of Civil Procedure.
- The court action is commenced by filing a complaint outlining the allegations the plaintiff is making against the defendant, identifying the causes of action, and requesting specific relief from the court.
- A defendant must respond to the complaint by filing an answer or a motion to dismiss, asserting that no legal basis exists for the plaintiff's claims.
- If the court grants the motion to dismiss, a judgment is entered dismissing the complaint. If the motion is denied, the defendant must answer.
- After the defendant answers the complaint, the parties begin discovery.
- Either party may use the information obtained through discovery to support a motion for summary judgment. If summary judgment is granted as to all claims, the court issues a judgment disposing of the case. If summary judgment is not granted as to all claims, the case proceeds to trial.
- Trial involves the presentation of evidence to the finder of fact.
- Following the trial, the court will enter the judgment. A judgment is the final determination of the parties' rights, absent an appeal.

Introduction

This chapter focuses on civil litigation in the federal courts. Civil litigation in the federal court system is governed by the Federal Rules of Civil Procedure. Each state also has its own procedural rules.

The civil litigation process begins when the client meets with a lawyer for the initial client <u>interview</u>. Interviewing is discussed in Chapter 10. After the initial interview, the lawyer or an associate will research the law and the facts to determine the legal issues and the strengths and weaknesses of the client's case. The lawyer or associate will usually prepare a memorandum of law discussing the client's situation. Memoranda are discussed in Chapter 7. The lawyer will also discuss the findings with the client and make recommendations for potential courses of action in a counseling session, discussed in Chapter 11, and/or a client letter, discussed in Chapter 12.

If the lawyer's research indicates that the client's case is appropriate for litigation, and the client wishes to sue, legal action may be commenced. Conversely, the client may decide to negotiate a settlement or engage in another form of alternative dispute resolution rather than proceeding to the courts. Alternative dispute resolution is discussed in Chapter 16; negotiation is discussed in Chapter 17.

If the client decides to proceed to the court system, the litigation process will include the filing of the complaint, filing of the response, discovery, pre-trial motions, scheduling conference, trial, post-trial motions, judgment, and appeal. The party bringing the lawsuit is known as the "plaintiff." The party defending the suit is known as the "defendant." In the event of an appeal, the party appealing is known as the "appellant" and the party defending the appeal is known as the "respondent" or "appellee."

This chapter has seven sections: (1) commencing the action, (2) defendant's response, (3) discovery, (4) summary judgment, (5) the pre-trial conference, (6) trial, and (7) appeal and standard of review.

The Client

As you read this chapter, consider our clients Plymouth Rock High School ("PRHS") in Plymouth, Michigan and its Principal William Diehl. PRHS and Principal Diehl have hired our firm to defend it in a First Amendment action filed by PRHS student Michael Thomas.

Our senior partner interviewed Principal Diehl and shared the following facts. PRHS has a dress code that prohibits students from wearing clothing with inappropriate writing or graphic depictions that are offensive or otherwise distract from or disrupt the educational experience. The policy specifically states that "inappropriate depictions include, but are not limited to, drug, alcohol and/or tobacco use."

On January 12, 20__, Thomas wore a T-shirt to school which said "Support Medical Marijuana" on the front and "Don't just survive, take a bong hit and thrive" on the back. Students commented on the shirt. Some students apparently appreciated the slogan "take a bong hit and thrive." Others responded with rhetoric such as "drugs suck." The shirt generated discussion in several of Thomas's classes. During lunch, Thomas was pushed and food was dumped on him in the cafeteria.

Principal Diehl reacted by asking Thomas to turn the shirt inside out or change it. Thomas refused. He explained to Principal Diehl that his mother was a cancer survivor and that he had a right under the First Amendment to express his support for medical marijuana. Thomas went home and did not return until the next day.

Principal Diehl viewed the T-shirt as promoting drug use in violation of the school's dress code. Principal Diehl also believed it was destructive to the learning environment. Several prior events contributed to this view. In the first week of January 20__, PRHS student Bill Burns was reprimanded for wearing a T-shirt bearing the phrase "Drugs Suck." Furthermore, the school has had a problem with illegal drug use, involving both marijuana and cocaine, for several years.

On March 16, 20__, Thomas filed a complaint with the U.S. District Court for the Eastern District of Michigan. The suit challenges the application of the dress code policy as violating his First Amendment rights to free speech. PRHS and Principal Diehl are named as defendants.

Principal Diehl has asked for our firm's advice; he has never been sued before. The paperwork he received with the complaint states he and PRHS must respond in 20 days. What sort of response is required? What happens after that?

Commencing the Action

Before filing a complaint, the lawyer and the client must determine where to bring suit. Deciding where to bring suit involves choosing the forum and the law. It also involves considering venue.

Choice of Forum

The court chosen must have jurisdiction. Subject matter jurisdiction refers to the court's power to adjudicate the subject of the lawsuit. State courts have the power to hear all cases not preempted by the federal courts. Federal courts are limited to hearing those disputes involving federal law, those disputes where the adverse parties are citizens of different states and the amount exceeds $75,000, and those disputes where the federal government is a party. Jurisdiction is discussed in Chapter 3.

Choice of Law

Also to be considered are the procedural and substantive laws the court will apply. A court applies the rules of its own forum to procedural matters. Federal courts will always apply the Federal Rules of Civil Procedure. Determining a court's application of the substantive law is more difficult. In a federal question case, federal courts will apply the federal substantive law from its own jurisdiction. In a diversity case, however, a federal court is required to apply state substantive law to questions arising under state law.

Venue

Venue concerns the location of the lawsuit. Even if it is determined that there is federal court jurisdiction, it must be determined in which district court the case should be brought. Considerations may include a court situated in a convenient location for the parties or the witnesses.

The Complaint

After the lawyer and client have agreed on the court, the pleadings must be drafted and filed. Pursuant to the Federal Rules of Civil Procedure, the party bringing the suit, the plaintiff, must file a complaint and a draft summons notifying the defendant of the lawsuit. The court signs the summons and the plaintiff delivers the complaint and the summons to the defendant.

The summons is a form which may be obtained from the court. The complaint outlines the allegations the plaintiff is making against the defendant. Complaints are in the form of numbered paragraphs, requiring the defendant to answer each assertion individually.

The U.S. engages in "notice pleading." The complaint includes only the basic facts to alert the defendant of the specific causes asserted. It begins by identifying the parties to the suit and establishing jurisdiction. After providing factual background, the complaint identifies the causes of action and requests specific relief from the court. In the U.S., alternative causes of action may be pled.

Defendant's Response

A defendant must respond to the complaint. The defendant may file an answer to the complaint, a motion to dismiss the complaint, or both. In federal court, if the defendant fails to respond within 20 days, the court will enter a default judgment.

The Answer

The answer is written in paragraph form responding to each allegation of the complaint. The defendant must admit, deny, or plead lack of knowledge to each allegation. The defendant may next raise affirmative defenses to the plaintiff's allegations. The defendant may also include counterclaims against the plaintiff.

Motions to Dismiss

The defendant may file a motion to dismiss the plaintiff's entire complaint or certain claims in the complaint. In a motion to dismiss, the defendant asserts that even if the facts alleged in the plaintiff's complaint are true, the complaint must be dismissed because there is no legal basis for the claim. The basis of the motion may be that: (1) the court lacks personal or subject matter jurisdiction, (2) the plaintiff failed to state a cause of action upon which relief could be granted, or (3) the suit was improperly served, among others.

All motions, including motions to dismiss, require the filing of four documents: the motion itself, a notice to the opposition indicating when the motion is scheduled for hearing, a memorandum in support of the motion, and a certificate of service showing that the moving party has mailed a copy of the documents to opposing counsel. The motion is generally a short document describing the relief requested and the legal basis for the request. A memorandum in support provides the legal and factual arguments in support of granting the motion.

If the court grants the defendant's motion to dismiss, a judgment is entered dismissing the entire complaint or the specifically challenged claims. If the judge denies the motion to dismiss, the defendant must respond to all of the allegations in the complaint.

Discovery

After the defendant has responded to the complaint, the parties begin the discovery process. Discovery in the U.S. is more liberal than in the rest of the world. The parties may investigate any matters related to the claims or defenses raised in the pleadings. The rationale is that liberal discovery assists the parties in preparing for trial and determining the strengths or weaknesses of their positions.

Several methods of discovery are provided by the Federal Rules of Civil Procedure. The most common are written interrogatories, requests for admission, oral depositions, and requests for production of documents. Interrogatories consist of written questions, which must be answered in writing by the opposing party. Interrogatories are generally utilized before depositions to obtain basic, non-sensitive information. Document requests, also submitted in writing, require the opposing party to produce copies of all documents relevant to specific inquiries. Requests for admission ask the opposing party to admit or deny written fact statements. Admitted statements are considered binding, or established, at trial.

The most liberal discovery method in the U.S. is the oral deposition. Lawyers may subpoena the opposing party or any of its witnesses to appear and give oral testimony. The "deponent" appears at the lawyer's office, with counsel, is sworn in, and is required to tell the truth under penalty of perjury. The lawyer may ask any question that might lead to relevant evidence, provided it does not violate one of the recognized privileges. A court reporter records the questions and answers, and prepares a transcript of the deposition for the parties.

In a transnational dispute, foreign law is itself discoverable. The Federal Rules of Civil Procedure provide that the party seeking to raise an issue of foreign law must give notice and produce the law at issue.

Summary Judgment

A motion to dismiss may dispose of a case prior to trial, but generally it is difficult to resolve a matter in its early stages because the factual allegations of the complaint are assumed to be true. After discovery, either or both of the parties may use the documents and information obtained in discovery to support a motion for summary judgment. Motions for summary judgment, together with their supporting briefs, must demonstrate that there are no genuine issues of material fact and the moving party is entitled to judgment as a matter of law. If granted as to all claims, this motion resolves the case prior to trial; the court issues a judgment in the moving party's favor.

The Pre-Trial Conference

Assuming denial of any motions for summary judgment, the Federal Rules of Civil Procedure provide for the court to schedule a pre-trial conference with the lawyers and, occasionally, their clients. Together with the judge, counsel discuss managing issues at trial and the possibility of settlement. The pre-trial order subsequently issued by the judge controls further proceedings in the case.

Trial

Cases not disposed of through "dispositive motions"—such as motions to dismiss or for summary judgment—or through settlement, proceed to trial. In most actions for damages in the U.S., the parties have a right to a jury trial. If neither party requests a jury, the judge hears the case. This is known as a "bench" trial.

Selection of the Jury

In those cases where the parties request a jury trial, the first task is to choose the jurors. The process of selecting the jury is known as "voir dire." Prospective jurors are questioned by the judge, and occasionally counsel, to determine if they are impartial. Counsel may challenge a juror "for cause" where there is evidence of bias. Counsel also have a limited number of "peremptory challenges" where they may ask the judge to dismiss a juror without specifying a reason. Depending on the nature of the case, a panel of between six and twelve jurors will be chosen.

The Trial

Trial involves the presentation of evidence to the finder of fact, either the judge or the jury. It begins with plaintiff's opening statement. Defendant may give an opening statement next or may reserve it until presenting the defense. Opening statements do not constitute evidence. Rather, they provide a roadmap of the case for the judge and the jury.

Following opening statements, plaintiff calls witnesses. Each witness is questioned first by plaintiff on "direct examination." Then defendant may question the witness. This is known as "cross examination." After cross examination of a witness, plaintiff may ask questions on "re-direct examination," and defendant may have the opportunity to "re-cross."

After all of the witnesses supporting plaintiff's case have been called, the plaintiff will "rest." Defendant may move for a judgment as a matter of law on the grounds that plaintiff has not presented sufficient proof. Such motions are rarely successful. If defendant does not move for judgment as a matter of law or if the judge denies the motion, the defense will present its case. The defense witnesses will be subject to the same process of examination as those of plaintiff. Once defendant rests, plaintiff may be allowed to introduce additional evidence to "rebut" that raised by defendant.

When both parties have rested, either may move for a judgment as a matter of law. Assuming the motions are denied or not made at all, the case is submitted to the jury. Plaintiff and defendant will make their closing arguments to the jury. Closing arguments review the evidence presented at trial; counsel are not allowed to present new evidence.

Following closing arguments, the judge gives the jury instructions on the law to assist them in reaching a decision or "verdict." The judge may also provide general instructions on determining the credibility of witnesses and state which party has the burden to prove a particular fact on each issue. This is commonly known as a "jury charge."

Following the jury charge, the jury returns to the jury room to reach a verdict. The most common type of verdict in the U.S. is a "general verdict." The general verdict requires the jury to decide who won the case and, if it is plaintiff, the amount of damages plaintiff should receive.

Post-Trial Motions

After the jury returns its verdict, the losing party may move the court for a "renewed motion for judgment as a matter of law." The moving party may also move for a new trial, on the grounds of serious error. Such motions are seldom granted.

Judgment

Assuming all post-trial motions are denied, the court will enter the "judgment." A judgment is the final determination of the parties' rights in a case, absent an appeal. Judgments may be entered upon the jury's verdict or the findings of fact and conclusions of law of the judge in a bench trial. Judgments may also be entered on default if the party does not appear, or after the court grants a motion to dismiss or a motion for summary judgment.

Appeal and Standard of Review

A party aggrieved with the judgment of the trial court may file an appeal. An appeal is commenced by filing a "Notice of Appeal" within the prescribed time limit. In the federal courts, and most state courts, the case is appealed as a matter of right to the intermediate appellate court.

The appellate court reviews a copy of the trial court record, or "transcript." Counsel for each party submit appellate briefs on the points of error that are alleged to have occurred in the trial court. The appellate court may decline to consider new issues that were not raised in the trial court. In most cases, the appellate court will schedule oral arguments to allow the judges to question counsel on the points made in their briefs. Appellate courts do not hear the testimony of witnesses.

The appellate court generally issues its decision as a written opinion. Such opinions explain the court's reasoning for affirming or reversing the trial court. The appellate court may also send the case back for retrial. This is known as "remand."

In determining if there is "reversible error," the appellate court applies one of several "standards of review." The appellate court defers to the factual findings of the trial court, because the trial court has the opportunity to see the witnesses and assess their credibility. The appellate court generally reverses findings of fact only if they are "clearly erroneous." Conversely, an appellate court will apply a more stringent standard of review to the trial court's legal findings. Legal findings are reviewed anew. This standard is known as "de novo" review.

Analyzing the Client's Legal Needs and Issues

Let us return to our clients, PRHS and Principal Diehl. Plaintiff has filed his complaint in the U.S. Federal Court for the Eastern District of Michigan. Free speech under the First Amendment to the U.S. Constitution is a federal question; hence, subject matter jurisdiction is established. Plaintiff and defendants are located in the Eastern District of Michigan, the events at issue occurred in the district, and defendants have been served with the complaint; hence, jurisdiction and venue are also proper. Our clients must answer or file a motion to dismiss.

As jurisdiction resides in the federal court and it is unlikely our firm could prove that the facts fail to state a claim this early in the proceedings, we advise our clients to file an answer. The answer responds to each paragraph of the complaint as well as raising several affirmative defenses. The complaint of

Michael Thomas and the answer prepared by our firm for the defendants are included in the sample documents below.

After the answer is filed, the parties will commence discovery. Our firm will begin by serving written questions in the form of interrogatories and requests for production of documents on Michael Thomas. After the firm has reviewed the information received as a result of these discovery requests, we will schedule the deposition of Michael Thomas, as well as teachers and students at the school who have knowledge of the factual claims alleged in the complaint. It is the responsibility of plaintiff to schedule the deposition of Principal Diehl. An excerpt from our deposition of Michael Thomas is included in the sample documents below.

Following discovery, our firm moves for summary judgment. The motion must be accompanied by a brief explaining why there is no genuine issue of material fact and PRHS and Principal Diehl are entitled to judgment as a matter of law, by a notice of hearing, and by a proof of service. The motion for summary judgment is included in the sample documents below.

If our motion is granted, judgment will be entered for our clients. If the judgment is denied, the case will be set for trial. Trial involves the presentation of evidence to the finder of fact. Assuming Michael Thomas has made a request for a jury trial, a jury will be chosen and serve as the trier of fact. Once the jury reaches its verdict, a judgment will be entered by the trial court.

If our clients are dissatisfied with the judgment, our firm may file a notice of appeal to the Sixth Circuit Court of Appeals. The Sixth Circuit Court of Appeals, located in Cincinnati, Ohio, is the intermediate appellate court for the Eastern District of Michigan.

Sample Documents

Document 1
Federal Rules of Civil Procedure Checklist

Federal Rules of Civil Procedure

Complaint	Rules 7, 8
Summons	Rule 55
Service of Summons	Rule 4(d)
Answer and Affirmative Defenses	Rules 7, 8
Counterclaims	Rule 13
Motion to Dismiss	Rule 12(b) (6)
Discovery	Rules 26–37
• Interrogatories	Rule 33
• Production of Documents	Rule 34
• Admissions	Rule 36
• Depositions	Rule 30
Summary Judgment	Rule 56
Other Pre-trial Motions	Rule 7b
Pre-trial Conferences	Rule 16
Voir Dire	Rule 47
Trial	Rules 38–53
Judgment as a Matter of Law	Rule 50
Jury Charge	Rule 51
Appeal	Rules 77–80

Document 2
Complaint

IN THE UNITED STATES DISTRICT COURT
FOR THE EASTERN DISTRICT OF MICHIGAN

MICHAEL THOMAS,

Plaintiff

Civil Action No. 00-CV-4567

v.   COMPLAINT

PLYMOUTH ROCK HIGH SCHOOL
AND WILLIAM DIEHL, Principal

Defendants
_____ /

COMPLAINT

Plaintiff, Michael Thomas, by and through his counsel, alleges the following:

PARTIES

1. During all times mentioned in this Complaint, Thomas was a senior at Plymouth Rock High School ("PRHS")

2. During all times mentioned in this Complaint, Thomas had obtained the age of legal majority.

3. During all times mentioned in this Complaint, William Diehl was the principal of PRHS.

4. During all times mentioned in this Complaint, PRHS was a public high school located in Plymouth, Michigan.

JURISDICTION AND VENUE

5. This is a civil action brought pursuant to 42 U.S.C. § 1983 against the Defendants' application of the school dress code policy to Thomas for wearing a shirt with a controversial but political message.

6. Jurisdiction is conferred upon this Court pursuant to 28 U.S.C. § 1331, as this is a civil action arising under the Constitution of the United States.

7. Venue is proper in this District Court pursuant to 28 U.S.C. § 1391(b), as PRHS is located within the jurisdiction of the Eastern District of Michigan and all events that gave rise to the claim occurred in this District.

BACKGROUND

8. Thomas has attended PRHS since the ninth grade.

9. Before January 12, 20__, Thomas had been subject to only minor disciplinary action during his three and one-half years of high school.

10. PRHS has a dress code policy in place that provides: "Students may not wear clothing with inappropriate writing or graphic depictions that are offensive or otherwise distract from or disrupt the educational experience. Inappropriate depictions include, but are not limited to, drug, alcohol and/or tobacco use."

11. On January 12, 20__, Thomas wore a T-shirt that displayed a controversial message advocating for the use of medical marijuana.

12. Medical marijuana use within the State of Michigan was approved by popular vote on November 4, 2008.

13. On January 12, 20__, Principal Diehl told Thomas that his T-shirt violated the PRHS dress code because it was inappropriate, disruptive and advocated drug use. Thomas was instructed to turn the shirt inside out or change it. Thomas went home and did not return until the following day.

CAUSE OF ACTION

14. Thomas alleges that the PRHS dress code, as applied to his T-shirt, violates his First Amendment right to free speech.

15. At all times relevant to this Complaint, Principal Diehl was acting under color of his authority as a public employee and within the scope of his duties as school principal.

16. Principal Diehl's actions deprived Thomas of his civil rights in violation of 42 U.S.C. § 1983.

RELIEF REQUESTED

WHEREFORE, Michael Thomas respectfully requests that this Court find that the PRHS policy as applied to his T-shirt violates the First Amendment and order all appropriate relief, including:

A. A declaration that the Defendants have violated the rights of Plaintiff under the First Amendment to the United States Constitution;

B. A manadatory injunction prohibiting Defendants from further violating the same rights or the rights of similarly situated persons;

C. An award of compensatory damages against all Defendants;

D. All other relief as the Court may deem proper.

Dated: March __, 20__

/s/ _____

Counsel's Name and ID Number
Law Firm Name
Law Firm Address
Law Firm Telephone Number
Attorneys for Plaintiff

Document 3
Answer

IN THE UNITED STATES COURT DISTRICT COURT FOR THE
EASTERN DISTRICT OF MICHIGAN

MICHAEL THOMAS,

Plaintiff

Civil No. 00-CV-4567

v.   Hon. George E. Woods

PLYMOUTH ROCK HIGH SCHOOL
AND WILLIAM DIEHL, Principal

Defendants

_____ /

ANSWER

Defendants, Plymouth Rock High School and William Diehl, by and through their counsel, offer the following Answer to the Complaint in the above-captioned case:

1.–11. Admit the allegations contained in paragraphs 1–11.

12. Neither admit nor deny the allegations of paragraph 12, as it is a matter of public record.

13. Admit the allegations contained in paragraph 13.

14. Deny the allegation that the application of the dress code to the T-shirt violates the First Amendment as alleged in paragraph 14.

15. Neither admit nor deny the allegations contained in paragraph 15, as they are conclusions of law.

16. Deny the allegation that Diehl's actions deprived Thomas of his civil rights as alleged in paragraph 16.

AFFIRMATIVE DEFENSES

In further answer to Plaintiff's Complaint, and by way of affirmative defenses, Defendants state that they will rely upon the following affirmative defenses, if applicable and if supported by the facts:

A. Plaintiff failed to mitigate the alleged damages.

B. Defendants have qualified immunity from any award of damages in that there is no settled rule of law prohibiting a high school principal from disciplining a student under his supervision for displaying messages that a reasonable person would understand to advocate use of drugs.

WHEREFORE, Defendants respectfully request that this Honorable Court enter judgment in their favor and award Defendants all costs and attorney's fees incurred in defending against Plaintiff's Complaint.

Dated: April __, 20__

/s/ _____

> Counsel's Name and ID Number
> Law Firm Name
> Law Firm Address
> Law Firm Telephone Number
> Attorneys for Defendants

Document 4
Thomas Deposition, Exhibit B to Motion for Summary Judgment

IN THE UNITED STATES COURT DISTRICT COURT FOR THE EASTERN DISTRICT OF MICHIGAN

MICHAEL THOMAS,

Plaintiff

Civil No. 00-CV-4567

v.

Honorable George E. Woods

PLYMOUTH ROCK HIGH SCHOOL
AND WILLIAM DIEHL, Principal,

Defendants

_____ /

SELECTED EXCERPTS FROM THE DEPOSITION OF:

Michael Thomas

Taken on behalf of the Defendants and held in the law offices of [Fill in name and address of Plaintiff's counsel] on June 23, 20__, commencing at 10:00 a.m. Taken by Natalie Maines, a Certified Shorthand Reporter and Notary Public of the State of Michigan.

REPORTING SERVICES ARRANGED THROUGH:
KEITH & MAINES, C.S.R.
350 MAIN STREET
ANN ARBOR, MICHIGAN
(734) 525-1400

APPEARANCES:

Counsel's Name and ID Number	Counsel's Name and ID Number
Law Firm Name	Law Firm Name
Law Firm Address	Law Firm Address
Attorney for Plaintiff	Attorney for Defendants

Defendants' Exhibit B to Motion for Summary Judgment

DEPOSITION OF MICHAEL THOMAS (EXCERPT)

DIRECT EXAMINATION BY [Name of Defendants' counsel]

Michael Thomas having been duly sworn, testified as follows:

Q Can you describe the shirt you wore to school on January 12, 20__?

A Sure. It was a green and gold shirt—those are the school colors—I made on the silk screen machine in school to support the use of medical marijuana. My mother is a cancer survivor. She learned she had cancer in the summer of 20__, and she subsequently had an operation, radiation, and chemotherapy. She wanted to take medical marijuana but the laws are so screwed up, she was afraid to. I wanted to support my mother and others like her. It said "Support Medical Marijuana" on the front, and on the back, it said "Don't just survive, take a bong hit and thrive."

Q Did you know the school had a policy against encouraging illegal drug use?

A Yes, but medical marijuana isn't illegal.

Q Please just answer the question. Did you know the school had a policy against encouraging illegal drug use?

A Yes.

Q As far as the wording on the shirt is concerned, why did you include the language "Support Medical Marijuana"?

A My mother had cancer, she wanted to take medical marijuana for her nausea but she was afraid to take it …

Q Mr. Thomas –

A And I wanted to advocate for the legality of medical marijuana.

Q   Why did you include the language "Don't just survive, take a bong hit and thrive"?

A   I thought it was clever.

Q   What is your understanding of what "a bong hit" is?

A   Smoking marijuana.

Q   Was that also your understanding at the time you put that on your shirt?

A   Yeah.

Q   Had you ever seen students at Plymouth Rock High School smoke marijuana?

A   Mr. Gilson, do I have to answer that?

[Name of Plaintiff's counsel]: Mike, he's entitled to ask it at this point.

A   Yeah.

Q   Every day?

A   Well, not every day. But fairly frequently.

Q   You didn't understand that these students all had prescriptions for medical marijuana, did you?

A   Nope.

Q   Had you ever smoked marijuana yourself?

[Name of Plaintiff's counsel]: Mike, you do not have to answer that one.

A   That's all right. My answer is "No." I don't even smoke cigarettes.

Q   Have you seen students use cocaine or other illegal drugs at your high school?

A   Yes, but I didn't hang around with those kids.

Q   Let's return to the day of the incident. What happened when you arrived at school on January 12th?

A   A lot of people stared, which is what I wanted. Some made comments, and most of them seemed, like, positive.

Q   What specific comments were made about your shirt?

A   Stupid stuff, mostly. Most of the kids focused on the back of the shirt. They liked the idea of taking a bong hit. Some started chanting, "bong hits, bong hits" and high fiving me.

Q   Did you get any negative comments about the shirt?

A   Yeah, a few. There is a group at school that a lot of the jocks belong to "Students Against Drug Use and Other Crimes." One of those students, Bill Burns, called me a loser and a pot head.

Q   Do you think your shirt caused a disruption?

A   Not really. I have never been a popular kid at school. People say weird things to me all the time, but it doesn't bother me. My whole purpose was to make people think about the importance of medical marijuana. I thought the shirt could do that. If it offends the jocks in the process, so be it. At least they had to think for a change.

Q   Did your shirt cause any disruption in the classroom?

A   Nah, not really. I mean Reynolds ended up talking about legalizing marijuana in my first period Class, Contemporary Social Issues, but that's no big deal. It's not like anyone pays attention to that class anyway.

Q   How was first period disrupted?

A   It wasn't really. I mean, someone asked her, "Why does Thomas want America hooked on drugs," just to get her going. And she started a discussion about how I was just expressing a view.

Q   So, was the whole class period lost to this disruption?

A   I think people got something out of the discussion, but we didn't talk much about any other social issues that day.

Q   Did your shirt cause any other discussions?

A   Well, third period is History. We talked about legalizing pot in there. Some of the burnouts like Ron Rope got a little out of hand, singing and stuff. Bill Burns and all the jocks started yelling and old Miller let us go early, but that's not unusual. Old Miller is always letting us go early.

Q   What other discussions did your shirt cause that day?

A   Well, phys ed was second period, and I wore my peace shirt for that class, because I didn't want to get the other one sweaty. No one seemed to be bothered by the peace sign. It's pretty innocuous.

Q   What did you have for fourth period?

A   Study hall. We're not supposed to talk in there, so the shirt wasn't really a problem. A few spitballs made it in my direction, but that was about it. I don't think the teacher even noticed. If he did, he didn't do anything.

Q   After that, you went to lunch?

A   Yeah, lunch was a little ugly. There was some shoving in the lunch line. Bill Burns kind of nudged me, but I ignored him. After I was sitting down, a couple of other people managed to bump into my chair muttering while I was eating and some pudding seemed to fall off of one of the trays into my hair. But that's no big deal.

Q   So, would you agree that your shirt caused a major disruption?

A   No, it's school. Kids sometimes say things, push each other, throw food, stuff like that. There was more of it that day, but it wasn't like education came to a screeching halt. Diehl did see me near the end of lunch and told me to follow him to his office.

Q   What happened in Principal Diehl's office?

A   Oh, he said my shirt promoted drug use and violated the dress code. "Blah Blah Blah." He said I would need to turn it inside out. I told him that I was merely exercising my constitutional right to free speech, and he told me that the constitution applies differently in his school. I told him again that I wasn't taking it off, and he told me I would need to go home. So I went home. Yes, a day of Dr. Phil and Judge Joe Brown—every bit as educational as a day at PRHS.

Q   And that was the end of it, then?

A   Ummm, no. I called a lawyer that day, and then we filed this lawsuit.

Document 5
Defendants' Motion for Summary Judgment

IN THE UNITED STATES COURT DISTRICT COURT FOR THE
EASTERN DISTRICT OF MICHIGAN

MICHAEL THOMAS,

Plaintiff

Civil No. 00-CV-4567

v.   Hon. George E. Woods

PLYMOUTH ROCK HIGH SCHOOL
AND WILLIAM DIEHL, Principal

Defendants

_____ /

DEFENDANTS' MOTION FOR SUMMARY JUDGMENT

Defendants, by and through their counsel, respectfully move for summary judgment pursuant to Rule 56 of the Federal Rules of Civil Procedure.

In support of this motion, Defendants have filed a separate memorandum of law in support and attached (Ex. A) "Policy on Dress and Personal Appearance" of Plymouth Rock High School and Deposition of the following persons: (Ex. B) Michael Thomas, (Ex. C) William Diehl, (Ex. D) Alicia Reynolds, (Ex. E) Martha Miller, and (Ex. F) J.D. James.

The essential facts of this case are not in dispute and the diminished free speech rights of students in a public school setting make it clear that Defendants are entitled to judgment as a matter of law.

WHEREFORE, Defendants respectfully request that this Honorable Court grant Defendants' Motion for Summary Judgment and dismiss Plaintiff's Complaint in its entirety.

Respectfully Submitted,

_____

Counsel's Name and ID Number
Law Firm Name
Law Firm Address
Law Firm Telephone Number
Attorneys for Defendants

Dated: September __, 20__

Part Two

Introduction to U.S. Law and Legal Reasoning

Chapter 3

Introduction to U.S. Law

Highlights

- The U.S. has a federal system and a state system of government.
- Both systems have four sources of primary law: their respective constitutions, statutes, judicial decisions, and administrative regulations.
- A dual system of state and federal courts flows from the dual law-making authority of the federal and state governments.
- A court's jurisdiction is its power to resolve disputes and enforce judgments.
- In both the federal and state systems, most cases are first heard in trial courts. Appellate courts review the trial record for errors of law.
- The judicial decisions from the various courts make up the common law. The U.S. derives much of its law from judicial opinions, also known as "precedents."
- Earlier judicial decisions govern later cases as mandatory or persuasive precedent; this is known as the doctrine of stare decisis.

Introduction

The distinctive characteristics of the U.S. legal system are federalism, and the related concepts of state and federal jurisdiction, and common law, and the related concepts of precedent and stare decisis. As a system based on federalism, both the federal government and the states are sovereign entities as to their own jurisdictional authority. As a common law system, law in the U.S. may be derived from judicial opinions. Both principles—federalism and common law—run through the U.S. legal system. Legal actions are initiated in trial courts which exercise jurisdiction over their geographical area. Appellate courts review the decisions of the trial courts and render opinions according to common law methods. Under the doctrine of stare decisis, these decisions form a body of law to guide future courts. As a result, U.S. courts have a fundamental role in shaping the law.

This chapter focuses on six concepts: (1) federalism, (2) jurisdiction, (3) common law, (4) stare decisis, (5) mandatory and persuasive precedent, and (6) the interaction between common law and other types of law. Chapter 4 focuses on common law methods of legal reasoning.

The Client

As you read this chapter, consider our client Mr. Ahmed Al-Shirazi. Mr. Al-Shirazi is a twenty-six-year-old resident of the U.S. His family emigrated from Iraq when he was a teenager. In April of last year, he was walking in a downtown park in Atlanta, Georgia, when he was surrounded by a gang of ruffians, led by Mr. Jeff Jones. The ruffians called him various names, many obscene, and chased him through the park. Mr. Jones was carrying a club and shouted at Mr. Al-Shirazi, "I am going to bash your head in." Mr. Al-Shirazi feared for his life. A policeman arrived at the scene and arrested Mr. Jones, who was known to the police as a local troublemaker. The others fled. The next day, all criminal charges against Mr. Jones were dropped.

Mr. Al-Shirazi claims that he has suffered great mental anguish as a result of this incident and wants to recover money damages from Mr. Jones. His claim of mental anguish has been corroborated by his physician, Dr. John Greene.

Mr. Al-Shirazi asks our firm about the possibility of bringing a civil suit against Mr. Jones for his mental anguish. This raises several preliminary questions. Where may the lawsuit be brought? And what law applies?

Federalism: A Dual System of Government and Courts

The U.S. has both a federal and state system of government. Within the federal government and each of the 50 states there are three branches of government: the legislative which enacts statutes, the executive which enforces statutes and promulgates administrative regulations, and the judicial which interprets and reviews statutes and creates and applies common law.

The federal system has four sources of primary law: the U.S. Constitution, federal statutes, federal court decisions, and administrative regulations. The state systems also have four primary sources of law: the constitution of the particular state, its statutes, its court decisions, and its administrative regulations.

The dual system of state and federal courts flows from the dual law-making authority of the federal and state governments. The federal and the state court systems consist of a hierarchy of courts, best envisioned as a pyramid. The trial courts comprise the base of the pyramid, followed by the intermediate courts of appeal, with the court of final appeal or "last resort," also known as the "supreme" court, at the apex.

The Federal Court System

In the federal system, the trial courts are known as "district courts." Each state has at least one district court. There are 94 federal districts and several hundred federal district courts in the U.S. and its territories. The federal courts are courts of limited power or jurisdiction; they may hear only those matters involving federal law or delegated to them by statute within their geographic boundaries. Generally, the federal courts hear: (1) disputes involving federal law, including those disputes arising from the U.S. Constitution, federal statutes, and federal regulations, (2) disputes where the United States is named as a party, and (3) disputes where the parties are citizens of different states and the dispute involves more than $75,000.

The intermediate courts of appeal in the federal system are known as "circuit courts of appeal." Congress has divided the U.S. into 13 circuits. Eleven of these are numbered and are comprised of several states. The other two are the District of Columbia Circuit covering Washington, D.C. and the Federal Circuit covering certain suits against the U.S. government and patent suits. The number of judges sitting in each circuit varies, but the judges hear cases in panels of three.

There is a right to appeal final judgments of district courts to the circuit courts of appeal of the appropriate circuit. In addition, the circuit courts have jurisdiction to hear appeals from decisions of certain administrative agencies. The circuit courts of appeal may disagree in their interpretation of federal law.

The U.S. Supreme Court, located in Washington, D.C., is the court of last resort for appeals in the federal system, as well as for appeals of state court decisions involving federal issues. The Court consists of nine judges who sit "en banc" to make decisions. The Supreme Court hears appeals by the discretionary grant of a writ of certiorari or "by leave." The Court hears only a limited number of cases, generally those requiring an interpretation of federal constitutional or statutory provisions or conflicting interpretations of federal law.

In addition to the federal district courts, circuit courts, and Supreme Court, there are several federal courts with specialized jurisdiction. Most prominently, the U.S. Claims Court handles claims against the federal government; the Tax Court handles matters involving federal taxes; the Court of International Trade handles civil matters related to tariff and trade agreements; the Bankruptcy Courts handle personal and corporate insolvencies. U.S. Military Courts decide cases under the Uniform Code of Military Justice. U.S. territorial courts hear cases in the U.S. territories. Tribal courts hear cases related to American Indian Affairs.

The State Court System

Each of the 50 states has its own court system. Most state court systems consist of a three-tiered hierarchy: trial courts, intermediate courts of appeal, and the court of last resort. The names of these courts vary from state to state.

Consistent with the plenary power of states over their internal matters, state courts are courts of general jurisdiction with authority to hear most disputes occurring within their boundaries. The trial courts' geographic jurisdiction generally corresponds to the county lines of the state. Similar to the federal system, certain state courts have specialized jurisdiction. These include small claim courts, probate courts, and juvenile courts. Also similar to the federal courts, most states allow a right of appeal to the intermediate appellate court and a discretionary appeal "by leave" to the highest or supreme court. The decision of the supreme court of each state is final and cannot be further appealed, unless it involves an issue of federal law.

Jurisdiction

Jurisdiction is the authority of courts of a particular system to resolve disputes and enforce judgments. Jurisdiction is determined by geographic area, but it is also based on subject matter. Subject matter jurisdiction is the authority of a court to resolve disputes in only a particular area of the law. As noted above, federal courts are considered courts of limited jurisdiction; state courts are considered courts of general jurisdiction.

The parallel state and federal jurisdictions are each sovereign as to their own law. In the matters where federal law applies, it is the supreme law of the land. The laws of a state encompass most matters that pertain to its residents. Although the realm of state law is broader than federal law, where the two intersect state law defers to federal law. This system of parallel laws between federal and state jurisdictions differs from the unitary systems of many nations, where law flows from the central government and applies to all lesser provincial and municipal units. Outside of legal authority delegated under the federal constitution, the states remain supreme in applying their laws.

When the U.S. was founded in 1776, the original 13 states retained the power to make general laws affecting the health, safety, morals, and general welfare of their residents. Under the U.S. Constitution, ratified in 1789, the realm of law that affects relations between residents of individual states, such as interstate commerce, and powers that were thought necessary for the people of all of the states to exercise collectively, such as foreign treaty-making powers, were entrusted to the federal government. Over the last two centuries the realm of federal law has grown. But the principle of federalism remains in the American legal system, with legal authority divided in any particular place between the state and the federal government.

Within the federal and state jurisdictions, a hierarchical system of authority prevails. The U.S. Congress, Supreme Court, and President oversee all subdivisions of the federal government and federal law. Likewise, the law of each state governs all lesser units of the state—counties, cities, towns, villages—which are considered creations of the state governments.

The Common Law

The U.S. legal system is known as a "common law" system because it relies on judicial opinions as a source of law. All jurisdictions in the U.S., with the exception of Louisiana, are common law jurisdictions. Unlike the norm in civil law systems, the judiciary not only interpret and apply statutes, they also develop rules and legal principles in circumstances not addressed by statutes. Accordingly, much of the law in the U.S. derives from prior judicial opinions. Such prior decisions are known as "precedent." A court in the U.S. is required to reconcile a new decision with higher court decisions—the precedent—in the same jurisdiction involving similar legal issues and facts.

Stare Decisis

The common law system of the U.S. comprises both its own structure and form of reasoning. Its structure is stare decisis, discussed in this section. Its method of reasoning involves drawing specific applications from general principles. Legal reasoning is discussed in Chapter 4.

In the common law system as practiced in the U.S., earlier cases provide governing principles for later ones. This system is referred to under the Latin phrase stare decisis, which stands for *stare decisis et non quieta movere*: "stand by a decision and do not disturb settled matters." Under this doctrine, judges look to prior cases with similar or analogous factual settings to derive the principles whereby they adjudicate the case before them.

Stare decisis allows great flexibility; cases may be resolved not just by statutory law but by the wealth of principles that support judicial decisions. Stare decisis also provides consistency, predictability, and fairness to the legal system as it mandates that like cases be treated alike. Further, it allows for the creation of law in an organic and comprehensive manner. Each dispute results in a judicial decision which concretizes the law around a specific set of facts. This decision then guides the resolution of the next legal dispute arising from similar facts. In this way, the system of stare decisis is often analogized to a brick wall. As judicial decisions are handed down another brick is added to the wall. Over time the wall grows and the common law becomes an imposing edifice with concrete legal principles applying to the greatest variety of factual situations.

Mandatory and Persuasive Precedent

Stare decisis best applies to cases decided by a higher level of court in the same jurisdiction involving similar legal issues and facts. Such decisions are known as mandatory or binding precedent, meaning that they must be followed. Courts may also follow decisions from other jurisdictions or lower courts. Such decisions are known as persuasive precedent.

Of the many prior cases that have been decided, it is the lawyer's job to find the most analogous precedents that resemble the case under consideration in ways that are outcome determinative. The primary factors that affect precedential value are jurisdiction, level of court, similarity of facts and issues, and cogency of reasoning.

Same Jurisdiction

The first precedents a lawyer will look for are those that are mandatory. Because only a court of the same jurisdiction is applying the same law, a mandatory precedent must derive from the same jurisdiction. For example, lawyers involved in cases in the state courts of Michigan are bound by Michigan precedents, but not those of Ohio. Where mandatory precedent is not available and the lawyer wishes to choose persuasive precedent, the choice of jurisdiction becomes more complicated. A number of factors determine which cases from an outside jurisdiction will be persuasive, depending on the nature of the client's problem.

Higher Level of Court

Only those opinions written by courts above the court hearing the case in the same jurisdiction are mandatory. Middle level appellate court decisions bind trial courts within the appellate court's jurisdiction; a jurisdiction's highest court binds the middle level appellate courts and the trial courts within that jurisdiction. As with jurisdiction, considerations of court level in choosing persuasive precedent are more complicated and will depend on the nature of the client's problem. In general, the higher the court the more persuasive its decisions are considered.

Similar Facts and Issues

After determining the jurisdiction and level of court that will provide mandatory precedent, the lawyer looks for cases that raise similar legal questions, or issues, upon analogous facts. The facts will never be identical, but the more similar the facts the more persuasive a case will be.

Cogency of Reasoning

The heart of the common law lies in analogizing the reasoning of precedent to the client's case. In order to be persuasive, the court's reasoning in the prece-

Torts → Agravios

dent case must not only be well written and organized, it must apply equally to the client's problem. The more similar the facts and issues, the easier it is for a lawyer to apply the reasoning.

Interaction between Common Law and Other Sources of Law

Primary sources of law are enacted by one of the three branches of government. Hence, primary law consists of constitutions, statutes, judicial opinions, and administrative regulations. Within the federal system, the following primary sources of law control in the following order: (1) the U.S. Constitution, (2) federal statutes, (3) federal judicial opinions, and (4) federal regulations. Within each state system, the following primary sources of law control in the following order: (1) the U.S. Constitution, (2) the constitution of the particular state, (3) the statutes of the particular state, (4) the judicial opinions of the state, and (5) the regulations of the state. Primary authority may be mandatory or, if promulgated outside the particular system in which the legal issue arises, persuasive precedent.

Legal encyclopedias, treatises, law journal articles, restatements of the law and similar sources are "secondary authority." Secondary authority is not considered "law" and is not mandatory authority. It is used primarily to gain information on a particular issue and as a case finding tool.

Analyzing the Client's Legal Needs and Issues

Let us now return to our client, Mr. Al-Shirazi. He has inquired about bringing suit against Mr. Jones for his mental anguish. The first issue any lawyer must decide is where to bring suit.

This action arises under the inherent legal authority of the state in which the parties reside and the incident occurred, in this case the state of Georgia. It is an action that arises under the general warrant of state law to protect the health and safety of its residents. Such a civil wrong that harms the health, safety, or welfare of an individual is called a tort. There is no jurisdictional mandate under the U.S. Constitution that governs torts (except as relates to the U.S. government). Therefore, it is not a question of federal law. Likewise, although the events took place in the city of Atlanta and the county of Fulton, the law of the state of Georgia governs, as all lesser entities of states, such as a city or a county, are governed by the general law of the state.

Of course with some variations, we could imagine both federal law and the municipal law of Atlanta entering the litigation. For example, if Mr. Jones's attack were racially based, it might fall under the category of a hate crime which would be covered by federal as well as any state anti-discrimination law and thus would add a federal issue to the lawsuit. In addition, there may be a unique municipal law pertaining to Atlanta, which could also apply to the litigation. But under the facts as presented, it is the general law of Georgia that governs torts and thus the lawsuit.

Having decided that suit should be brought in state court in Georgia, the lawyer must decide which state court. Lawsuits begin in the trial court, and so the case would be brought in the trial court that sits in the city of Atlanta. Civil claims over $15,000 are brought in the "superior court," as the trial court in Atlanta is known. This court would try the issue of what tortious wrong Mr. Jones committed under state law and what damages he owes Mr. Al-Shirazi as a result. At the end of the trial, any appeal would be taken to the intermediate appellate court of Georgia, known as the Court of Appeals. From there an appeal could be taken to the Georgia Supreme Court, the highest judicial authority on Georgia law.

Having decided that the suit should be brought in state court in Atlanta, the lawyer must determine what law will apply. Although Mr. Jones may have engaged in criminal conduct, the criminal charges have been discharged. But a civil lawsuit in tort may still arise from this matter. What is the applicable Georgia law that governs torts of this nature? Like all American jurisdictions, the highest legal authority in Georgia is the state constitution. But again, like most constitutions, the Georgia constitution outlines the fundamental composition of government and law without substantively setting out the law. Georgia does have statutes and codes, but none that exactly relate to this particular situation.

As with most jurisdictions in the U.S., Georgia is a common law jurisdiction. As such, much of its law is not contained in statutes but derives from previous judicial opinions. The central principle of common law is stare decisis; the decisions of earlier cases in the same jurisdiction from higher courts govern subsequent cases. Accordingly, we know that our mandatory precedents will come from prior cases of the Georgia Court of Appeals or the Georgia Supreme Court.

Assume that through research and application of the principles discussed above, we determine that there is one mandatory precedent that governs our case from the Georgia Court of Appeals. This is the 1944 precedent of *Beck v. Watson*, reproduced below. Please read this case carefully; it will be used as an example of legal reasoning in the next chapter.

Sample Documents

Document 1
Otto Beck v. John Watson

Otto BECK v. John WATSON.[1]
Georgia Court of Appeals, No. 33040.
May 5, 1944

SHIRVA, Chief Judge.

This was an action in Fulton Superior Court for damages for assault and battery, brought by Otto Beck against John Watson. The evidence at trial showed that on July 3, 1943, a gang of young men, including defendant Watson, approached plaintiff Beck, a German immigrant, who was walking in Zenith Central Park, and shouted insults and epithets at him. When the plaintiff ran away, the gang of youths pursued him for some distance, until they caught him in a vacant lot. The defendant, who seems to have been a leader of this gang, hit the plaintiff several times with a limb from an oak tree, resulting in a fracture to the plaintiff's right arm, left leg, and numerous lacerations. The jury returned a general verdict of $2,600 for the plaintiff, judgment was rendered accordingly, and the defendant moved for a new trial. The motion was overruled and defendant excepted.

The motion for a new trial was based on an alleged erroneous jury instruction, objection to which was duly noted at trial. In regard to damages, the judge charged that the plaintiff was entitled to compensation for the physical injuries he suffered and also for his mental anguish or mental pain and suffering as a result of the attack. The defendant contends that the instruction to the jury that the plaintiff could be compensated for his mental anguish or his mental pain and suffering was in error.

Error is assigned on a portion of the charge as follows: "Now in addition to the damages for the alleged physical injuries, the plaintiff seeks to recover damages for the mental anguish or mental pain and suffering which might be the result of the attack. I charge you, gentlemen, that in every intentional tort wherein physical injury is caused, the jury may also give damages for the mental anguish or mental pain and suffering caused to the plaintiff."

---

1. Drawn from a composite of Georgia cases.

The evidence at trial clearly established the extent of mental suffering to the plaintiff as the result of the assault and battery. At trial, the plaintiff testified as follows:

Q. [by plaintiff's attorney]. "What other repercussions were there?"

A. "I am terrified and do not want to leave my home. I see young men, I think, they will beat me because I am German. Also, many times, I cannot fall asleep. All the time, I am upset...."

This along with other portions of testimony established beyond question that the plaintiff had suffered great mental anguish and mental pain and suffering as a result of the defendant's battery upon him. The defendant does not dispute the force of this evidence and at trial put in no evidence or made any argument challenging it.

Rather the defendant argues that in all cases of intentional tort, a plaintiff is entitled only to compensation for physical damages (and where warranted, punitive damages, as a separate item in the verdict—or as a special verdict, as it is sometimes called—to deter wrongdoers). However, the defendant contends, compensation for mental injury should not be included in a general verdict. The defendant presents two arguments in favor of this legal contention. First, the defendant argues that a judicial forum is an inappropriate venue for deciding such an ambiguous and subjective question as to whether a tort victim has suffered mental injury, and that it is impossible for a court to trace or attribute the precise cause of such an evanescent concept as "mental distress." Second, the defendant points out the great difficulty of differentiating between genuine mental injuries and fictitious ones, as well as between those that are serious enough to warrant legal redress and those that are not. Thus, the defendant argues that an absolute distinction should be drawn in tort cases between physical damages, easily ascertained and compensable, and mental damages, which are not.

It is self-evident that there are a multitude of problems connected with assessing and assigning liability and damages for injuries to one's mental state that do not exist with physical injuries, and we acknowledge the defendant's arguments. Nevertheless, we fail to find the defendant's contention convincing here. First, the mental injury in this case grew out of a well-established tortious cause of action. In fact, at the very beginning of the civil law, Gaius in his *Institutes*, noted that the tort of "outrage is committed ... by striking a man with the fist or a stick or by flogging him," for which monetary compensation was provided. Gaius' Institutes, lib. III, c. 220, 224. Of course, this tort of assault and battery was one of the very first causes of action established in the English common law (and it bears reminding that when this nation became independent, most states adopted the common law of England as the rule of decision in all state courts so long as it was not repugnant to or inconsistent with the Constitution of the United States or the constitution or laws of the particular state). Thus there can be no thought of an inappropriate judicial forum or remedy, when the defendant's actions would inevitably subject him to civil action, and perhaps criminal as well.

Second, there seems little danger of being unable to differentiate between genuine and fictitious injuries when, as is the case here, the mental trauma follows so closely from the grievous physical damage, that they are linked together, so to speak, by a chain which cannot be broken. Indeed, it is entirely to be expected that one who suffers an assault and battery as shocking as this one, with such serious physical injuries in its attendance, will suffer grave mental injuries as well.

It is a fundamental principle of natural justice that a victim of a tortious cause of action is entitled to compensation for his injuries from the tortfeasor. We will not allow this defendant, in this particularly vicious and disgusting battery, resulting in the maiming of the plaintiff, both physically and mentally, to escape liability for the injuries he inflicted.

The trial judge did not err in overruling the motion for a new trial.

Judgment affirmed.

AFELCK and BURNESS, JJ., concur.

Chapter 4

Introduction to Legal Reasoning

Highlights

Legal Reasoning and Statutes

- Although the U.S. is a common law country, its laws increasingly consist of state and federal legislation.
- Where a statute applies, the lawyer begins his reasoning with the language of the statute applied according to common law methods.
- A vast array of common law decisions guide the application and interpretation of statutes; when interpreting statutes, courts use tools of statutory construction.

Legal Reasoning and Cases

- Judicial decisions are important in understanding common law areas such as contracts and torts, as well as understanding how statutes should be applied.
- Most published judicial opinions contain the following sections: (1) a heading, (2) editorial notes, (3) the name of the judge, (4) the legal opinion, and (5) any concurrences or dissents.
- The legal opinion itself will generally include: (1) a statement of the issues, (2) the facts and any relevant procedural history, (3) the holding of the case, (4) the law of the case, including the application of the precedent to the present case and rationales, and (5) the disposition.

Introduction

Lawyers in the U.S. must analyze and apply constitutions, statutes, judicial opinions, and regulations. Their goal in each instance is to discover the law relevant to their client's legal problem and apply that law to the client's problem in a manner which benefits the client. The specific language of constitutional provisions, statutes and regulations must be analyzed, but cannot be understood in a vacuum. In a common law system, such language may best be understood where interpreted by the courts.

Likewise when no constitutional provision, statute, or regulation applies and judicial opinions alone control, a lawyer must prove the case by demonstrating the manner in which the client's position conforms to the mandatory authority within the jurisdiction, or lacking mandatory authority, persuasive authority.

In either case, the ability to read and analyze judicial opinions is crucial to effective lawyering. In authoring an opinion, a judge addresses the parties to the suit and the lawyers and judges who will rely on the opinion as precedent. In reviewing prior precedent the judge chooses cases with similar facts and raising similar issues, analyzes the similarities and differences between the precedent and the case before the court, and renders a decision. Hence, a judicial opinion not only relies on and contributes to precedent, it models effective legal reasoning.

This chapter focuses on two concepts: (1) legal reasoning and statutes, and (2) legal reasoning and cases, including the case method analysis.

The Client

We first met Mr. Al-Shirazi in Chapter 3. Mr. Al-Shirazi is a young man in his twenties who immigrated to the U.S. from Iraq as a teenager. He was recently "attacked" by Jeff Jones. Mr. Jones chased him with a stick and threatened to "bash his head in," but never physically harmed him due to police intervention. Mr. Al-Shirazi has been unable to eat, sleep, or leave his home without fear since the incident. He wants our firm to sue Mr. Jones for the mental anguish he has suffered. We considered two questions on Mr. Al-Shirazi's behalf. First, where the lawsuit may be brought. Second, what law is to be applied. We determined that suit would be brought in the state trial court in Atlanta, Georgia. We further decided that the law of Georgia applied and that there was one mandatory precedent: *Beck v. Watson*.

How will you utilize *Beck v. Watson* to determine the law of Georgia and how it applies to our client? How does legal reasoning work in a common law system? And, does that method of reasoning change if a statute applies?

Legal Reasoning and Statutes

Interaction with Case Law

Although the U.S. is a common law country, its laws increasingly consist of state and federal legislation. Where a statute applies, the lawyer begins the process of reasoning with the language of the statute. The lawyer then applies the statutory provisions according to common law methods. Statutes — as well as constitutional provisions and administrative regulations — have a vast array of common law decisions guiding their application. Because most legislation in the U.S. consists of codification of the common law, the myriad of cases decided both before and after legislative enactment represent an authoritative guide to statutory interpretation.

Statutory Construction

The first step courts utilize in applying statutes is to follow the plain meaning — the ordinary meaning of the words in the text, according to everyday dictionary definitions and rules of grammar. However, often application of the statute requires going beyond the plain meaning of the text. In that case, there are three chief avenues of statutory construction under the common law: statutory intent, statutory context, and canons of construction.

Intent

In applying statutes, courts attempt to realize the intent of the legislation. They consider the purpose of the statute and the goals and policies it is trying to achieve. The broad language of the statute indicates its intent as well as the circumstances of its enactment. Legislative history reveals the purpose of the legislators. The timing and content of legislative debates, proposed amendments, and repealed provisions all shed light onto statutory intent.

Context

The meaning of the statute can also be derived from its context. Courts look to related provisions in the code. The statute as codified is likely to have a preamble, a title, section headings, and provisions defining key terms. All of these indicate how the statute is to be construed.

Canons of Construction

Canons of construction are an integral part of common law, helping to determine how statutes are read. Canons are summary rules of grammar and logic that guide statutory interpretation. All 50 states have codified canons. The most basic canon of construction is that statutory terms are to be taken in their ordinary meaning unless they are terms of art and that statutory language is to be read according to its commonly understood grammatical structure.

Some canons clarify open-ended or ambiguous language. *Expressio unius est exclusio alterius*, "expression of one thing excludes others," states that where a statute names particular items, items not mentioned are implicitly excluded. For example, a statute that authorizes "police vehicles, fire-trucks, and ambulances to exceed the speed limit in the course of duty," implicitly excludes public utility vehicles from doing so. *Ejusdem generis*, "of the same kind," indicates that a general term should be interpreted according to the specific items that describe it. For instance, *ejusdem generis* has been applied to determine that the National Motor Vehicle Theft Act—which makes interstate theft of "an automobile, ... truck, automobile wagon, motorcycle, or any other self-propelled vehicle" a federal crime—does not include aircraft, for the reason that airplanes, unlike the specific vehicles listed, do not run on land. *In pari materia*, "as to the same matter," harmonizes statutes by stating that ambiguous terms in a statute should be interpreted consistently with other statutes that deal with similar matter. Finally, some statutes go to the underlying structure of law, such as the *rule of constitutional construction*, that a statute should be interpreted so as to render it constitutional if at all possible.

It is important to note that canons are rarely dispositive by themselves as most canons can be answered by other canons that suggest a different result. For example, the fundamental canon that statutory terms are to be interpreted according to their grammatical meaning can yield to the canon that grammatical rules are to be disregarded if adherence would defeat the purpose of the statute.

Illustration

A well-known hypothetical in American jurisprudence illustrates the various modes of statutory construction. A state legislature, concerned with noise and smog pollution, enacts a statute prohibiting "vehicles" in a state park. The plain language indicates that vehicles ordinarily defined as transportation units are banned. But which ones specifically? Statutory intent dictates the prohibition of automobiles, the chief source of air and noise pollution in society. Both statutory intent and context can indicate what other types of vehicles are included. Clearly there was no intent to ban a child's tricycle or a toy car, even if motorized. How about bicycles? Plain meaning indicates they are vehicles but they are certainly non-polluting. A court might look into legislative history to see if the legislators discussed bicycles. As to the legislative context, the preamble might state that the purpose of the bill is to reduce pollution in all its forms, suggesting that bicycles were not meant to be prohibited. If the preamble suggested pedestrian safety was a concern, bicycles would more likely be included in the ban.

If the statute provides a list followed by the general term "vehicles" such as a ban on "automobiles, motorcycles, radio-controlled miniature aircraft, and other vehicles," application of *ejusdem generis* would indicate that skateboards are not included under the general term "vehicles," as the specific entities listed are all motor powered. A motorized wheelchair falls within the plain meaning of the statute but under *the rule of constitutional construction* it should be allowed in the park, at the very least so as not to offend the federal Americans with Disabilities Act. If the statute prohibited "automobiles, trucks, boats, bicycles, motorcycles, mopeds, and mechanized carriages," push scooters are presumably allowed under *expressio unius,* as not expressly prohibited. "Carriages" are specifically mentioned in the statute, and plain meaning would indicate motor carriages are prohibited but baby carriages are not. What about a horse-drawn carriage? *In pari materia* looks to other parts of the code—how is a horse-drawn carriage classified in laws regulating taxi service, recreational use in the park, and driving while intoxicated laws.

Most importantly, as the courts decide the particulars as to which "vehicles" are excluded, a body of general rules for interpreting this statute develops. A court facing a new question no longer reasons from the statute *ab initio* but can compare with the cases of automobiles, motorized wheelchairs, bicycles, tricycles, and the like, already adjudicated. Suppose a local, patriotic association wants to install a World War II truck on a pedestal as a park memorial. The court examines the precedents and generates helpful rules, for example, that motorization is a common element of banned vehicles. Is the World War II truck engine in working order or has it been disabled? The previous cases may have focused on the intent and purpose of the legislation as to noise and air pollution. Would the proposed truck memorial in a pristine park be an eyesore, analogous to a form of visual pollution? The process of statutory construction through harmonization of precedents makes statutory interpretation a collective enterprise of the courts.

Legal Reasoning and Cases

Judicial decisions are crucial in understanding common law areas such as contract, tort, and property and, as noted above, they play an important role in understanding how statutes—as well as constitutions and administrative regulations—should be applied. Judicial opinions also demonstrate methods of legal analysis used throughout practice. In authoring an opinion, a judge addresses the parties to the suit and the lawyers and judges who will rely on the opinion as precedent. In reviewing prior precedent the judge chooses cases with analogous facts and issues, analyzes the similarities and differences between the precedent and the case before the court, and reaches a decision. Careful analysis of such opinions is crucial to effective lawyering in a common law system.

Analyzing Cases

Most published judicial opinions contain the following sections: (1) a heading, (2) editorial notes, including a synopsis and headnotes, (3) the name of the authoring judge, (4) the legal opinion, and (5) any concurrences or dissents. The legal opinion itself will generally include: (1) a statement of the issues, (2) the facts and any relevant procedural history, (3) the holding of the case, (4) the law of the case, including the application of the precedent to the present case and rationales, and (5) the disposition or decision.

The Heading

The heading, or style, of the case includes the parties, the court, and the date of the decision. Because judicial opinions are either mandatory or persuasive, the lawyer must note the court and to a lesser degree the date to evaluate the case as precedent.

Editor's Notes: The Synopsis and Headnotes

The synopsis, or summary, is a description of the case prepared by the publisher to assist the reader. The summary is not law, because it is not promulgated by a court. Headnotes are also prepared by the publisher to assist the reader. Each headnote concerns a specific point of law and corresponds to a numbered paragraph in the judicial opinion. As with the summary, the headnotes do not constitute law.

The Judge

Following the headnotes are the names of the lawyers involved in the case and the name of the judge authoring the opinion. All of the material following the judge's name constitutes the judicial opinion and is considered legal authority.

The Judicial Opinion

Although they are usually not labeled, and may appear in any order and combination, the following components can be extrapolated from most judicial opinions.

Statement of the issues: The issues are the legal questions the court must answer to resolve the dispute between the parties. The issues frame the context for the opinion.

The facts and procedural history: The procedural history recounts the manner in which the case has moved through the courts and its current disposition. The recitation of facts focuses on the events that led to the parties' disputes relevant to the issues before the court. It is important to note that in the U.S., judges must decide the specific case brought by the parties. Judges may not issue "advisory" opinions based on abstract concepts. Accordingly, a judge must interpret the law in the context of the factual dispute.

The holding: The court's holding, traditionally referred to as *the ratio decidendi*, answers the legal issue. Each issue is generally analyzed separately. As a result, the number of holdings corresponds to the number of issues.

The law and reasoning: This portion of the opinion describes and applies the legal principles that the judge used to decide the case. First, the judge will discuss the general principles of law that are relevant to the case given its facts and issues. Next, the court will apply the law to the facts and reach its decision. The rules or legal principles may arise from any combination of the sources of American law. The application of the law to the facts involves the court's reasoning. In generating the legal rules and explaining its analysis, the court often moves from general to specific. The court's reasoning is the most useful part of an opinion to a practicing lawyer looking to analogize the court's ruling to the client's case.

The disposition: The disposition describes the action the court is taking with this case. An appeals court may affirm or uphold a lower court, it may reverse it or overturn it, or it may remand it—sending the case back for further proceedings.

Concurrences and Dissents

Concurrences and dissents are opinions of judges assigned to hear the case who wish to express a different view from the judge writing the opinion. A judge who reaches the same result, but for different reasons, will author a concurring opinion. Dissenting opinions are written by judges who disagree with the majority. Concurrences and dissents are never mandatory precedent but they are often found to be persuasive.

A Note on Holdings versus Dicta

A court may decide only the issue the parties bring before it. As noted above, the court's holding is its answer to the legal issue. Courts, however, often make additional statements beyond what is strictly necessary to resolve the parties' specific problem. Such statements are known as "dicta," an abbreviation of *obiter dicta* meaning a comment to which "a party is not bound." As with concurrences and dissents, dicta is not mandatory precedent but is often found to be persuasive.

The Importance of Reasoning

Courts engage in a wide variety of reasoning formats. The most common forms of legal reasoning are deductive and inductive.

Syllogisms and Deductive Reasoning

Deductive reasoning provides the organizational structure for much of the legal analysis in the U.S. The Greek philosopher Aristotle provided the most famous syllogism, reasoning:

1. All men are mortal.
2. Socrates is a man.
3. Therefore, Socrates is mortal.

Today, this syllogism is familiar as a principle of mathematics:

1. $A = C$
2. $B = A$
3. Therefore, $B = C$

A syllogism has a major and a minor premise, both of which are true, and a conclusion that follows assuming both premises are true. In legal reasoning, the legal rule is the major premise. The application of the facts to the rule is the minor premise. Assuming that both premises are true, a logical conclusion is reached. The general rule leads to the specific conclusion resolving the legal issue.

Analogical and Inductive Reasoning

In inductive reasoning, the specific leads to the general. Inductive reasoning uses examples to develop general principles. The courts decide particular cases which lead to general rules. Courts may author opinions by comparing and contrasting the cases before them with other similar cases, ultimately deciding to follow the earlier cases because of those similarities. This is a form of inductive reasoning known as analogical reasoning. Analogical reasoning satisfies stare decisis by connecting a current decision to precedent.

The Case Brief or Matrix

In order to appreciate the reasoning of a court's opinion, a lawyer must do more than merely read the opinion. The lawyer must utilize an organizational structure to retain the information obtained from the many cases read. Most first year law students in the U.S. are taught to brief cases. Typical case briefs include a section on facts, issue, holding, reasoning, disposition, any concurring or dissenting opinions, and thoughts or comments relevant to the use of the case. Practicing lawyers may brief cases, but more often chart or diagram the relevant portions of opinions to assist them in analyzing cases. In either event, the process of reviewing issues, facts, the holding, and legal principles and reasoning of an opinion models the basic paradigm of objective legal writing, discussed in Chapters 6 and 7.

Analyzing the Client's Legal Needs and Issues

Legal Reasoning and Cases

Let us return to our client, Mr. Al-Shirazi. How will you utilize *Beck v. Watson* to determine what the law of Georgia is and how it applies to your client? How does legal reasoning work?

You should begin by briefing or charting the case of *Beck v. Watson*. A sample of both a case brief and a case chart for *Beck* are included below. Were you to chart out the premises and conclusions in *Beck* that underlie your case brief or chart, it might look like this:

Tortious conduct
1. Major premise: Compensable physical injuries are caused by tortious conduct.
2. Minor premise: The mental injuries in *Beck* were caused by physical injuries.
3. Conclusion: Therefore, Beck's mental injuries were caused by tortious conduct.

Compensation for that conduct
1. Major premise: All injury caused by tortious conduct is compensable.
2. Minor premise: The mental injuries in *Beck* were caused by tortious conduct.
3. Conclusion: Therefore, Beck's mental injuries are compensable.

You will note that the premises in a legal argument are not as obvious as they are in classical reasoning. It is your job, as the lawyer, to demonstrate the credibility of the premises and the resulting conclusion.

You will also note that the analysis above describes the judge's reasoning in *Beck*, but does not automatically answer the issues raised by our client. *Beck* allowed recovery for certifiable emotional as well as physical damages arising from a tortious cause of action, in that case the assault and battery. Does this mean that Mr. Al-Shirazi can recover emotional damages as well? The answer depends on how you apply the holding of *Beck* to the client's facts.

Most judicial holdings are capable of being applied in either a strict or an expanded manner, and such application will alter the precedential value of the opinion. A strict reading tends to closely relate the legal principle to the particular facts of the precedent. An expanded reading not only takes a more general view of the underlying legal principle, but also often makes wider use of dicta in the opinion.

For example, a strict reading of *Beck* holds that when emotional damages arise directly from physical damages, they are so expected and ascertainable that the legal system can provide compensation. This reading suggests that Mr. Al-Shirazi would not be able to recover compensation for mental anguish, as his emotional damages did not arise from physical injury; the police intervened before he could be physically harmed.

However, an expanded reading of *Beck* supports a different result. Although the holding indicates that in this particular case physical contact gave rise to emotional damages, it does not explicitly require physical contact to be present for recovery. Further, the dicta in *Beck* supports the proposition that a wrongdoer is responsible for all damages inflicted on a victim including emotional damage, if such damages are certified and arise from an established cause of action, such as assault and battery. Under this expansive construction, Mr.

Al-Shirazi a victim of assault—which does not require physical contact—would be entitled to collect recovery from Mr. Jones for the emotional damages certified by Dr. Greene.

Legal Reasoning and Statutes

So far, we have assumed that Mr. Al-Shirazi's problem is governed only by case law. Now, however, assume that Georgia recently passed the following statute:

> It shall be unlawful for any person maliciously and with specific intent to intimidate or harass another person because of that person's race, color, religion, ancestry, or national origin to: (a) cause physical injury to another person; or (b) damage or destroy any real or personal property of another person; or (c) to threaten, by word, to do the acts prohibited if there is reasonable cause to believe that any of the acts described in subsections (a) or (b) will occur.

Further, on close questioning of Mr. Al-Shirazi, you learn that Mr. Jones called him a "terrorist" and similar insulting slurs while he was chasing him with a stick and threatening to "bash his head in." What reasoning would you apply in this situation?

You would, of course, research the statute to determine how it had been interpreted by the courts. But as a new statute, there may be little information. In any event, deductive reasoning is most often used in the application of statutes.

Your reasoning might take the following form:

1. Under the statute, it is actionable to maliciously intend to harass someone on account of their national origin by threatening to physically injure them with probability to do so;
2. Jones maliciously intended to harass Mr. Al-Shirazi based on his Iraqi origin as evidenced by his ethnic slurs;
3. And threatened to physically injure Mr. Al-Shirazi, by chasing him with a stick and shouting that he would bash his head in;
4. And would have carried out this physical injury but for the fortuitous intervention of the police;
5. Therefore Jones acted unlawfully, violating the statute.

This process of proving the premises for issues by rule application—whether from statutes or cases—is discussed in more detail in Chapters 5 through 7.

Sample Documents

Document 1
Case Brief of Beck v. Watson (1944)

Beck (Plaintiff-Appellee) v. Watson (Defendant-Appellant)
Court of Appeals of Georgia (1944)

Facts: Defendant (D) led a gang that chased and beat Plaintiff (P), a German immigrant, while shouting insults and epithets. D hit P several times with a tree limb, resulting in a fractured arm, a fractured leg and numerous lacerations. In addition to physical injuries, P testified: "I am terrified and do not want to leave my home. I see young men, I think, they will beat me because I am German. Also, many times, I cannot fall asleep. All the time, I am upset...."

Procedural History: Cause of action is assault and battery.
1. *Trial Court*—jury returned a verdict for P in amount of $2,600; D made motion for a new trial claiming that the jury instruction was erroneous, because it stated that damages may be awarded for mental pain and suffering (in addition to the physical injuries). D's motion for a new trial was overruled.
2. *Appeal*—To Ct. of Appeals.

Issue: Is mental pain and suffering a compensable damage when it is linked to physical injury?

Holding: Yes. Mental pain and suffering is a compensable damage when accompanied by physical injury.

Reasoning: D made two arguments: (1) that a court is not qualified to determine whether and how a P has suffered mental distress and; (2) it is difficult to differentiate between genuine and fictitious mental injuries.

The court reasoned: (1) A court of law is the proper forum in which to assign liability and determine damages arising from tortious conduct. This is evident from both the common law received in the United States from England and the Civil Law influences stretching back to Gaius' *Institutes*. (2) The court also reasoned that there is little difficulty in determining genuine mental injury when it is so closely related to the obvious physical harm.

Judgment: Affirmed.

Comments: *Policy*—"Natural Justice" requires that a tort victim be compensated for his injuries, including mental injuries when they flow from the physical harm.

Further Questions—Can mental injuries/suffering be compensated even if they are not related to a physical injury?

Document 2 Case Law Matrix

Case	Yr/Ct	Issue	Facts	Holding	Rule/Standard used	Reasoning	Disposition/Policy
Beck	GA 1944	Is mental anguish linked to physical injury compensable?	A German immigrant is taunted with insults and hit with a tree limb.	Yes. Mental anguish is compensable when accompanied by physical injury.	A court of law is the proper forum to assign liability and damages arising from tortious conduct.	The mental injury in this case grew out of a tortious cause of action: assault and battery. And, there is little difficulty in determining genuine mental injury related to physical harm.	Affirmed. Justice requires a tort victim to be compensated for his injuries.

Part Three

Writing Skills: Objective Legal Writing and the Office Memorandum

Chapter 5

Synthesis and the Evolving Common Law

Highlights

- A cause of action is a basis in law that allows for a legal remedy; an advantage of the common law is its flexibility in developing new causes of action.
- The process of reconciling the ever-growing volume of evolving case law to create workable legal principles which can be applied to similar cases is known as synthesis.
- In many instances, judicial opinions provide a basis for synthesis. It is necessary for the lawyer to build on the court's work, adding later cases or those closely related to the client's facts or issue.
- The process of synthesizing is inductive. The lawyer begins with the specifics of individual cases and works towards the general of a unified, provable legal principle.

Introduction

A cause of action is a claim in law that allows for a legal remedy. Constitutional provisions and statutes explicitly provide for causes of action. In the U.S., the common law provides the basis for causes of actions as well. Not every harm that occurs in social interactions rises to the level of a legally cognizable claim. Over time, however, as new social norms develop calling for different perspectives, a new cause of action may be created in case law to respond to the needs of society.

Prior chapters have assumed the existence of one applicable case. In reality, however, a lawyer researching the law will find multiple cases relevant to the client's problem. These precedents will address different factual situations and different interpretations of legal principles. Before the lawyer can use the legal principles and reasoning from these cases to solve the client's problem, the lawyer must relate these cases to one another. This process of reconciling diverse cases to create workable legal principles which may then be applied to resolve the client's problem is known as synthesis.

This chapter provides for the synthesis of two cases. Chapter 6 builds on that synthesis to organize a legal analysis. Chapter 7 utilizes the analysis in a legal memorandum. This chapter specifically addresses: (1) the evolving common law, (2) synthesis, and (3) common law in action—an examination of the process of creating a new cause of action and synthesizing cases in practice.

The Client

Assume a new client, Veruca Salt, has come to your office with her mother Angina Salt, inquiring into a lawsuit against William Wonker, Inc. Angina alleges that Arthur Wilkinson, manager of the William Wonker Chocolate Factory, made frightening remarks to Veruca during a factory tour in Miami, Florida. These are the facts you learn from Angina and Veruca.

Veruca is a ten-year-old girl living with her parents in Miami, Florida. William Wonker, Inc., is a Florida corporation. Recently, Veruca and her mother attended a tour conducted by the manager, Mr. Wilkinson, at the Wonker Chocolate Factory in Miami. Wilkinson was filling in as tour guide on an emergency basis.

Veruca incessantly asked questions of Mr. Wilkinson. Wilkinson responded in an increasingly agitated manner and a couple of times berated her, saying words to the effect of, "Little girl, I told you, no questions until the end of the tour!" At one point, Veruca swiped a prototype grape-flavored candy, the Everlasting Gobstopper, from the display table and popped it into her mouth. Wilkinson exploded with anger. He ordered her to open her mouth and showed her the color of her tongue in a mirror. "I warned you, runt," he said ominously, "now your tongue will be purple for the rest of your life. You'll be known as little Miss Blueberry." Veruca screamed and ran out of the room, sobbing hysterically, "I don't want a purple tongue!" Angina spent the entire night scrubbing the grape color off of Veruca's tongue, while Veruca cried, "See, it will never come off."

Since the incident, Veruca's behavior has been characterized by loss of appetite, anxiety, inability to concentrate, and sleeplessness. She still has nightmares of the incident and expresses fear that her tongue will turn purple again. Her teachers have noticed that she has become even more withdrawn in class. A physician diagnosed Veruca as suffering from extreme emotional trauma as a result of her experience during the factory tour.

What advice can you give Veruca and her mother? There is no statute in Florida establishing a cause of action for insulting and frightening language, yet medical professionals have certified that Veruca has suffered real harm. Does Veruca have a cause of action that would permit her to proceed to trial? If so, what are its elements? **Before reading the rest of this chapter, please read and brief or complete the case matrix for two cases: *Slocum* and *Korbin*. *Slocum* and *Korbin* and a blank case matrix are reproduced in the sample documents below.**

The Evolving Common Law

The genius of the common law is its flexibility in developing new causes of action. A judge can take note of a particular situation, evaluate the facts, apply legal principles, and incrementally reach a solution. Over time, as new situations call for different judicial perspectives, a new cause of action arises to respond to the needs of society.

The common law is capable of adapting to new social circumstances. Many causes of action in common law systems originate with a court's effort to fairly resolve a concrete dispute. As similar disputes are resolved, new legal claims and remedies—new causes of action—grow organically. Eventually these new causes of action may be codified by statute, but remain closely allied to the accumulated experiences of the community.

This is not to say that the common law system is without difficulties. The effort to extrapolate common law rules and principles can be laborious, causes of action can proliferate beyond sober bounds, and the measured discourse of social interaction can be overwhelmed. But, despite its challenges, the common law continues to contribute to a flexible and organic growth of legal doctrine.

A cause of action presents a set of facts for which the law provides relief. It represents a claim for a violation of a legally protected right of the plaintiff, based on a legal wrong or breach of legal duty committed by the defendant. As explained in Chapter 2, pleading practice requires a complaint to describe the factual and legal basis for relief. The legal basis can arise from the violation of a legal right or interest secured by the constitution, statute, or common law. If there is no legally protected right or interest, the complaint is dismissed. To determine whether a cause of action exists a lawyer must examine the relevant legal theories. And to do so, the lawyer must have available the primary skill for dissecting a pattern of cases—synthesis.

Synthesis

As discussed in Chapter 4, where an answer to a client's problem involves an analysis of statutes it also generally requires a review of judicial opinions. Alternatively, the answer to the client's problem may not involve a statute at all and may only be governed by judicial opinions. In either circumstance, a lawyer will find multiple cases relevant to the client's problem within the applicable jurisdiction. Furthermore, these cases will address different factual situations and, as noted above, evolving interpretations of a legal principle. To effectively use the legal principles and reasoning from these cases to solve the client's problem, the lawyer must relate these cases to one another. This process of reconciling diverse cases to create workable legal principles which may then be applied to resolve the client's problem is known as synthesis.

In many instances, the judges authoring the opinions will provide a basis for synthesis. For instance, they may provide the definition of a cause of action and the elements necessary for its application. In formulating the definition, the judges will have analyzed the relevant precedents and harmonized them into a rule reconciling their respective holdings.

Even where judicial opinions provide a basis for synthesis, it is necessary for the lawyer to build on the court's work, adding later cases or those closely related to the client's facts or issue. Synthesis is the step between reading and analyzing cases, discussed in Chapter 4, and writing an objective, predictive analysis of the client's problem, discussed in Chapters 6 and 7.

For the most part, the process of synthesizing is inductive. The lawyer begins with the specifics of individual cases and works towards the general of a unified, provable legal principle. The written work product of the lawyer providing an objective analysis of the client's problem is deductive, however. The lawyer begins with the legal principle so painstakingly synthesized and only then provides the rule proof that resolves the client's legal problem.

Common Law Synthesis in Action

The process of synthesis is best understood by its actual practice. The client problem currently at issue is set in the jurisdiction of Florida and involves emotional trauma resulting from frightening remarks to a child. In order to decide whether there are valid grounds for filing a lawsuit, the lawyer needs to synthesize Florida case law to determine: (1) whether the behavior complained of is actionable, (2) and if so, what elements must be proven, such that the client may maintain a cause of action. The two previously briefed precedents, *Slocum* and *Korbin*, illustrate the process of synthesis for the purpose of answering the client's inquiries.

Slocum

The first case, *Slocum*, is from the Florida Supreme Court, the highest judicial authority on questions of Florida law. The facts of *Slocum* are relatively clear. The plaintiff asked a clerk the price of an item and the clerk replied: "You stink to me." As a result, the plaintiff suffered extreme emotional distress although no physical contact or other wrongful activity had occurred. The plaintiff sued in trial court and the case was dismissed at the outset—without a trial or examination of the evidence—because the plaintiff failed to make out a cause of action, that is, a legally cognizable harm. The case was appealed to the highest court in Florida which affirmed the decision of the trial court. Plaintiff's complaint was dismissed—no trial, no recovery.

Understanding the *Slocum* court's reasoning, or rationale, for its decision is paramount in proceeding with the process of synthesis. First, the court looked at the question of whether the deliberate disturbance of "emotional equanimity" violated a legally protected right and thus stated an independent cause of action. The court acknowledged that the previous decisions allowed for emotional damages to be recovered without direct physical injury, but only where they arose from an existing tort. The *Slocum* court considered the question of whether there can be recovery for emotional distress without this independent tort as one of first impression. It declined to answer this question, although it did acknowledge a trend in the law nationwide to recognize such an independent tort.

Second, the court considered, if such a cause of action existed in Florida, what elements would be needed to prove it. Here, the court stated that such a cause of action could only be established by actions "calculated to cause 'severe emotional distress' to a person of ordinary sensibilities," absent special knowledge that the victim was hypersensitive, in a manner that "exceeds all bounds which could be tolerated by society."

Third, the court considered whether the elements it set forth had been met in the case before it. The court concluded that the comments of the clerk to plaintiff were "mere vulgarities" and not calculated to cause severe emotional distress. There would be no purpose in a trial to assess facts, for even if proven, defendant's actions were too innocuous to present a legal violation. Thus, the court reasoned, it need not address the question of whether the deliberate disturbance of emotional equanimity existed as an independent cause of action as its elements could not be satisfied in any event.

Korbin

The second precedent, *Korbin*, is a later case from the intermediate appellate court of Florida. Again, the facts are fairly straightforward. An adult woman made the following statements to a six-year-old girl: "Do you know that your mother took a man away from his wife? Do you know God is going to punish them? Do you know that a man is sleeping in your mother's room?" It was alleged the statements were knowingly false and made "for the purpose of causing the plaintiff-child undue emotional stress, mental pain and anguish."

Korbin raised the same initial question as *Slocum*: whether a cause of action exists for inflicting emotional distress through hurtful words alone. As with *Slocum*, the trial court dismissed the cause of action at the outset under the theory that there can be no recovery for mere insulting language.

The appellate court reached a different decision: it allowed for recovery for the emotional damage to the victim. The court held that the words were slanderous and were calculated to cause emotional distress to a child of ordinary sensibilities, the six-year-old girl, who was distressed by the accusation. On the question of the necessary elements to support a cause of action for emotional distress, the *Korbin* court followed *Slocum* in applying an objective standard of harm. The principle evolved, however, as the court's language was calibrated towards the standard of what would objectively cause harm to a child—rather than an adult—of ordinary sensibilities. The court reversed the dismissal of the complaint and sent the case to trial on the basis of plaintiff's cause of action.

Synthesis

A lawyer faced with these two mandatory precedents—one of which dismissed the cause of action for emotional distress and the other which allowed the cause of action to proceed to trial—must synthesize the cases before advising the client. Recall that the process of synthesizing is inductive. The lawyer begins with the specifics of individual cases and works towards the general of a unified, provable legal principle. This synthesis of case law will include both explicit rules and principles announced by the courts and concrete facts illustrated through case-by-case reasoning.

As to the specifics of the individual cases, lawyers will often follow the reasoning of the courts. In this circumstance, the first inquiry is whether intentional infliction of emotional distress constitutes an independent cause of action. The court in *Korbin* appears to have found a common law cause of action for inflicting emotional distress exists—the question of first impression which the *Slocum* court declined to answer. Although not explicitly stated in the opinion, there are no other grounds on which the court could have sustained the cause of action. Although *Korbin* does mention slander of the mother, this could not be the basis of recovery; no suit was brought by the plaintiff's mother for slandering her reputation. This conclusion is supported by the dicta in *Slocum*, which suggests that an independent cause of action for emotional distress could be sustained in Florida if caused by acts exceeding all bounds which can be tolerated by society.

As to the second question, the nature and required elements of the cause of action, *Slocum* and *Korbin* use similar language: the tort is made out by actions "calculated to cause 'severe emotional distress' to a person [child] of ordinary sensibilities." The different results of *Slocum* and *Korbin* are explained by their distinguishable facts. In *Slocum*, the clerk's comment was merely gratuitous and not calculated to cause severe emotional distress to the plaintiff, whose susceptibility to emotional distress was not known to the defendant. Conversely in *Korbin*, the false and malicious comments concerning the adultery of a young girl's mother were calculated to, and reasonably capable of, harming the child.

The lawyer next utilizes the analysis of the individual cases to produce unified, provable legal principles. In the present case, the lawyer should reach the following conclusions. First, Florida probably recognizes a cause of action for the infliction of mental suffering, even if there is no other tort involved, when the action by the defendant is "calculated to cause emotional distress" but not if the action or words constituted "mere vulgarities" or other acts not likely to cause harm to the ordinary victim. Second, although the harm is measured by what likely would cause harm in a person of ordinary sensibilities, that standard is lower for the ordinary child, whose sensibilities are easily shocked.

As with a case holding, this synthesis is capable of both a strict and expansive reading. The strict reading would require that defendant act with actual malice and deliberate purpose to cause the emotional distress. Likewise the victim must be someone almost certain to be hurt by such actions, such as a six-year-old child. The expansive reading would require only that defendant acted intentionally, with the probability that emotional distress would result to adults or children of ordinary sensibility.

Analyzing the Client's Legal Needs and Issues

Let us now return to our clients, the Salts. Does Veruca have a cause of action? If so, what is its nature and what elements must be satisfied?

As this is a matter of state law, you will look for Florida precedents that address the question of whether there can be damages for inflicting emotional harm. You may recall that you already dealt with a question of recovering emotional damages with your client Mr. Al-Shirazi in Chapters 3 and 4. However, you should realize that *Beck v. Watson*, the case used to analyze Mr. Al-Shirazi's problem, is not valid precedent for the Salts' problem for two reasons. First, *Beck* is a Georgia rather than a Florida case and hence not mandatory precedent. Second, Mr. Al-Shirazi was the victim of assault, an independent tort from which emotional damages resulted. Veruca, however, was the victim only of frightening words; there was not an independent tort. Thus the facts, issue, reasoning and holding of *Beck* are too easily distinguished to be useful even as persuasive precedent.

You therefore turn to the synthesis of the Florida precedents, *Slocum* and *Korbin*, to answer the inquiries of your clients. Your synthesis established that a cause of action appears to exist in Florida for the infliction of emotional distress. You were also able to determine both an explicit rule as to the elements of the cause of action and examples of how the elements would be satisfied under specific facts. The explicit rule is that conduct that satisfies the independent cause of action must be "calculated to cause 'severe emotional distress' to a person or child of ordinary sensibilities" and thus beyond the bounds which can be tolerated by society. The examples that illustrate the rule are that gratuitous words that show mere annoyance are not beyond the bounds which can be tolerated by society, but words of a false and malicious nature are. With this synthesis of legal principles, you can complete the analysis of the Salt's legal problem, as demonstrated in Chapter 6.

A Final Note on Synthesis and the Evolving Common Law

It is worthwhile to note that the Florida appellate courts in the cases of *Dominguez v. Equitable Life Assurance Society*, 438 So. 2d 58 (1983), and *Metropolitan Life Insurance v. McCarson*, 467 So. 2d 277 (Fla. 1985), did confirm our synthesis of *Slocum* and *Korbin* and found that Florida does have a common law independent cause of action for the intentional infliction of emotional distress, a ruling that has been echoed in the courts of most states. This raises the question of why this tort was only recognized in the common law in the latter half of the twentieth century when similar tortious causes date back to early English common law. The answer brings us to the very heart of the common law system. The common law was originally an outgrowth of the customs of medieval England. As such, it retains its reliance on cultural traditions. The emotional and psychological damage caused by many human interactions only became part of social understanding with twentieth-century advances in psychology. The common law absorbed these new cultural norms, first by allowing recovery for emotional damages when accompanying physical damages, then by allowing for emotional damages even when there was no direct physical injury, and finally by elevating the infliction of emotional damage into its own cause of action.

Sample Documents

Document 1

Julia SLOCUM and Homer V. Slocum, her husband, Appellants,

v.

FOOD FAIR STORES OF FLORIDA, INC., a Florida corporation, Appellee.

Supreme Court of Florida.

February 14, 1958.

DREW, Justice.

This appeal is from an order dismissing a complaint for failure to state a cause of action. Simply stated, the plaintiff sought money damages for mental suffering or emotional distress, and an ensuing heart attack and aggravation of pre-existing heart disease, allegedly caused by insulting language of the defendant's employee directed toward her while she was a customer in its store. Specifically, in reply to her inquiry as to the price of an item he was marking, he replied: "If you want to know the price, you'll have to find out the best way you can * * * you stink to me." She asserts, in the alternative, that the language was used in a malicious or grossly reckless manner, "or with intent to inflict great mental and emotional disturbance to said plaintiff."

No great difficulty is involved in the preliminary point raised as to the sufficiency of damages alleged, the only direct injury being mental or emotional with physical symptoms merely derivative therefrom. <u>Kirksey v. Jernigan</u>, Fla., 45 So.2d 188, 17 A.L.R.2d 766. While that decision would apparently allow recovery for mental suffering, even absent physical consequences, inflicted in the course of other intentional or malicious torts, it does not resolve the central problem in this case, i.e. whether the conduct here claimed to have caused the injury, the use of insulting language under the circumstances described, constituted an actionable invasion of a legally protected right. Query: does such an assertion of a deliberate disturbance of emotional equanimity state an independent cause of action in tort?

Appellant's fundamental argument is addressed to that proposition. The case is one of first impression in this jurisdiction, and she contends that this Court should recognize the existence of a new tort, an <u>independent cause of action for intentional infliction of emotional distress.</u>

A study of the numerous references on the subject indicates a strong current of opinion in support of such recognition, in lieu of the strained reasoning so often apparent when liability for such injury is predicated upon one or another of several traditional tort theories....

A most cogent statement of the doctrine covering tort liability for insult has been incorporated in the Restatement of the Law of Torts, 1948 supplement, sec. 46, entitled "Conduct intended to cause emotional distress only." It makes a blanket provision for liability on the part of "one, who, without a privilege to do so, intentionally causes severe emotional distress to another," indicating that the requisite intention exists "when the act is done for the purpose of caus- ing the distress or with knowledge * * * that severe emotional distress is sub- stantially certain to be produced by [such] conduct." Comment (a), Sec. 46, supra. Abusive language is, of course, only one of the many means by which the tort could be committed.

However, even if we assume, without deciding, the legal propriety of that doc- trine, a study of its factual applications shows that a line of demarcation should be drawn between conduct likely to cause mere "emotional distress" and that causing "severe emotional distress," so as to exclude the situation at bar. Illus. 5, sec. 46, supra. "So far as it is possible to generalize from the cases, the rule which seems to be emerging is that there is liability only for conduct exceed- ing all bounds which could be tolerated by society, of a nature especially cal- culated to cause mental damage of a very serious kind." Prosser, Mental Suffering, 37 Mich.L.R. 889. And the most practicable view is that the functions of court and jury are no different than in other tort actions where there is at the out- set a question as to whether the conduct alleged is so legally innocuous as to present no issue for a jury. Wade, p. 91, supra. See also 7 Miss.L.J. 390.

This tendency to hinge the cause of action upon the degree of the insult has led some courts to reject the doctrine in toto. Wallace v. Shoreham Hotel Corp., D.C. Mun.App., 49 A.2d 81. Whether or not this is desirable, it is uniformly agreed that the determination of whether words or conduct are actionable in character is to be made on an objective rather than subjective standard, from common acceptation. The unwarranted intrusion must be calculated to cause "severe emotional distress" to a person of ordinary sensibilities, in the absence of special knowledge or notice. There is no inclination to include all instances of mere vulgarities, obviously intended as meaningless abusive expressions. While the manner in which language is used may no doubt determine its ac- tionable character, appellant's assertion that the statement involved in this case was made to her with gross recklessness, etc., cannot take the place of allega- tions showing that the words were intended to have real meaning or serious ef- fect....

Affirmed.

TERRELL, C.J., and THOMAS, HOBSON and ROBERTS, JJ., concur

Document 2

**Wendy KORBIN, a minor, by and through her guardian and next friend,
Lill Korbin, Appellant,**

v.

Muriel BERLIN, Appellee.

District Court of Appeal of Florida. Third District.

July 6, 1965.

CARROLL, Judge.

This appeal is from an order dismissing an amended complaint in an action brought by a six year old girl through her guardian and next friend. It was alleged in the amended complaint that at a certain time and place the defendant "Willfully and maliciously approached the said plaintiff * * * and made the following statement to her: 'Do you know that your mother took a man away from his wife? Do you know God is going to punish them? Do you know that a man is sleeping in your mother's room?' She then again repeated, 'God will punish them.'" It was alleged the statements were knowingly false, "made maliciously, willfully and with utter disregard to the feelings of the six-year-old Plaintiff," and it was further alleged that the statements were made "for the purpose of causing the plaintiff-child undue emotional stress, mental pain and anguish." Resultant injuries were alleged, and damages were sought.

In our opinion the trial judge was in error in holding that a cause of action was not stated, and we reverse on the authority of <u>Kirksey v. Jernigan</u>, Fla. 1950, 45 So.2d 188, 17 A.L.R.2d 766, and <u>Slocum v. Food Fair Stores of Florida</u>, Fla. 1958, 100 So.2d 396....

The complaint in the instant case met the requirements for validity.... The alleged tortious injury did not occur incident to violation of a contract obligation, but in the course of a tortious act, which, if the facts so established, was a slander of the plaintiff's mother.

In the later <u>Slocum</u> case, the Supreme Court showed readiness to apply the rule discussed and quoted there from the Restatement and Prosser, to allow recovery for words or conduct which are intended or calculated to cause "severe emotional distress." However, in the <u>Slocum</u> case it was held the words used were not of such consequence.

Therefore, the determinative question here is whether what was said to the child was intended or reasonably calculated to cause the child "severe emotional distress." The alleged statements and the manner and circumstances under which they were communicated to the child leave little room to doubt they were made with a purpose and intent to shame her, and to shock the sensibilities of this child of tender years. Relating, as they did, to the child's mother, the content and import of the statements were such that it cannot be said as a matter of law that this alleged deliberately harmful act was not one "calculated to cause 'severe emotional distress' to a person [child] of ordinary sensibilities." See Slocum v. Food Fair Stores of Florida, supra.

Accordingly, the order dismissing the amended complaint is reversed and the cause is remanded for further proceedings.

Reversed and remanded.

SWANN, Judge (dissenting).

I dissent on the authority of Slocum v. Food Fair Stores of Florida, Inc., Fla. 1958, 100 So.2d 396, and Mann v. Roosevelt Shop, Inc., Fla. 1949, 41 So.2d 894.

Document 3 Case Law Matrix

Case	Yr/Ct	Issue	Facts	Holding	Rule/Standard	Reasoning	Disposition/Policy

Chapter 6

Organization of an Objective Legal Analysis

Highlights

- Legal analysis is organized by issues and sub-issues.
- The first step, Issue Formulation, requires framing the questions that need to be answered to resolve the client's legal problem.
- The second step, Issue Resolution, requires applying the law to the facts to answer the question raised in the particular issue or sub-issue.
- The most common document employing objective legal analysis is the office memorandum.
- The tone of the analysis in an office memorandum is formal, but it should be easily understood by its target audience: other lawyers.
- Legal analysis in an office memorandum is supported by citation to legal authority.

Introduction

Chapter 5 explained the process of synthesizing case law to create legal principles. This chapter considers the method of organizing legal principles to create an objective legal analysis. This analysis may be communicated in writing, or orally, and provides the basis for a number of legal documents. Chapter 7 discusses the most common of these documents: the office memorandum.

As explained in Chapter 5, a lawyer may spend hours synthesizing cases. This process is done analogically. The cases must be individually analyzed before they can be synthesized into general rules. After the process is completed, the end result must be explained deductively. The information must be organized around the issues raised by the general principles, rather than the individual cases. Treating the analysis as a summary of cases is like serving guests raw food; it is the lawyer's job to do the hard work and cook the cases into an easily digestible format.

Objective legal writing has a large scale organization, which may be thought of as "Issue Formulation," and a small scale organization, which may be thought of as "Issue Resolution." Issue Formulation requires organization around the points that must be analyzed to resolve the client's legal problem. In Issue Resolution, each issue or sub-issue is resolved by analyzing the law and applying it to the facts of the client's problem related to the particular issue or sub-issue.

This chapter is divided into six sections: (1) a formulistic approach to legal writing, (2) Issue Formulation, (3) Issue Resolution, (4) audience and tone, (5) outlining, and (6) citation.

The Client

In Chapter 5, our clients Veruca and Angina Salt sought advice regarding a lawsuit against William Wonker, Inc. Angina alleges that Arthur Wilkinson, manager of the William Wonker Chocolate Factory, made frightening remarks to Veruca during a factory tour in Miami causing her mental distress. In Chapter 5, you analyzed and synthesized several cases, *Slocum* and *Korbin*, related to Veruca's problem. How would you organize a formal legal discussion of her problem?

A Formulistic Approach

Legal writing in the U.S. often follows a formulistic approach. The approach allows the busy lawyer to read and evaluate written work product as efficiently as possible. In a system where most work is billed on an hourly basis and lawyers handle many matters simultaneously, both discussed further in Chapter 18, such an approach saves the client money and allows the lawyer to manage a substantial workload.

The formula for objective legal writing is known by a series of acronyms, IRAC and CREAC are two of the most common. The various formulas all require the same thing. First, the discussion of the client's legal problems is separately organized by each legal issue and sub-issue the lawyer is analyzing. This may be considered Issue Formulation. Second, the discussion of each issue or sub-issue is internally organized according to the IRAC /CREAC formula requiring identification of the issue, statement and explanation of the rule, and application of the client's facts to reach a conclusion. This may be considered Issue Resolution.

Issue Formulation

The first step in legal analysis is to formulate the issues and sub-issues that need to be answered to resolve the question. This is the macro-organization of the problem. These issues are derived from the law itself as it pertains to the particular controversy under review, whether that law is based on a constitution, statutes, or judicial decisions. Issue Formulation generally has three steps. First, the lawyer identifies all of the issues or claims. Second, the issues are arranged in logical order. Third, each issue is broken down into sub-issues, and occasionally — based on the nature of the law — into further subdivisions.

Issue Resolution

Issue Resolution refers to micro-organization, the structure of the legal analysis presented for each issue and sub-issue. Although there are various ways of internally organizing an issue or sub-issue, there are a few fundamental points. First, the lawyer begins the discussion of each issue or sub-issue with a topic sentence that identifies the issue. Second, the legal analysis follows the deductive reasoning pattern of first stating what the law is and then applying it. In this regard, the IRAC/CREAC formulas provide for: (1) the identification of the particular issue, (2) a statement of the rule, (3) an explanation of the rule through case law, (4) application of the rule to the client's problem, supported by case illustration, and (5) a conclusion.

Identification of the Issue

A lawyer begins each section or sub-section by identifying the issue or sub-issue—the "I" in IRAC—or identifying the issue by also stating the conclusion of the issue analysis—the first "C" in CREAC. Issues are the legal questions that are applied to the factual situation to reach the predicted result. They are derived from the legal authority that governs the factual situation, whether that is construing a statute or synthesizing a line of cases. The issue is often presented in the format of a sub-heading.

General Statement of the Rule

The issue is followed by a statement of the relevant law or rule. This is the "R" in IRAC and CREAC. For a common law problem, the lawyer will often be required to synthesize legal principles from a series of cases. Where a statute applies, the statutory terms may serve as the basis of the rules. A statute should be quoted or paraphrased before the discussion of related case law principles.

Explanation of the Rule

In the section on rule explanation, the lawyer explains the manner in which courts have interpreted the relevant law. This is the "E" in CREAC. In choosing the cases, the lawyer looks for mandatory precedents with similar issues and facts. In discussing the cases, the lawyer seeks to provide every relevant aspect of each case, without distracting the busy supervising lawyer with irrelevant information. The lawyer will generally include the facts, holdings, and reasoning of each case relevant to the legal principle under discussion.

Application of the Rule

In the section on rule application, the lawyer evaluates how the law affects the client's situation. This is the "A" in IRAC and CREAC. Application is most often accomplished by comparing and contrasting the facts of the client's problem with analogous cases. A lawyer first discusses the likely resolution of the issue. After discussing the most likely resolution, the lawyer then evaluates any counterpoints. This counteranalysis addresses significant legal arguments that suggest a resolution of the issue contrary to the one that has been reached. After presenting the counteranalysis, the lawyer discusses the reasons it is unlikely to prevail. As will be discussed in Chapter 8 on professional responsibility, a lawyer in the U.S. has an affirmative duty to advise a client about negative as well as positive aspects of a case.

Conclusion

The analysis of each issue or sub-issue should end with a brief conclusion. This is the "C" in IRAC and CREAC. The conclusion supplies an answer to the issue or sub-issue, in one or two sentences.

The Writing Process

The formulistic requirements of objective legal writing bear an intrinsic relationship to the writing process. Issue Formulation and Issue Resolution are signaled by judicious use of paragraphs and topic sentences. Each issue and sub-issue should be stated in a topic sentence. A new paragraph is usually begun with each of the IRAC/CREAC components. Thus, for example, a new paragraph signals the transition from rule statement to rule explanation, or from analytical comparison with an illustrative case to the presentation of the counteranalysis.

Audience and Tone

In all types of legal writing, the goal is to understand and communicate with the audience. The tone should be formal, but the document should be easily understood. Simple English should be used and unnecessary legal language avoided. U.S. lawyers focus on what the intended audience needs to know and how best to communicate that information. They also consider the secondary audience to whom the document may ultimately be forwarded such as clients, opposing counsel, and judges. Finally, all lawyers should seek to generally understand the culture and experience of the audience. This may include gender, race, religion, national origin, and a number of other factors. Communication across cultural lines is discussed in Chapter 9.

Outlining

The process of organizing a legal discussion is complicated. Creating an outline before beginning to write is recommended. In the outline, each main point heading should relate to an issue. Within each of the main point headings, the outline should then set out the sub-points which support an answer to the main question. This provides the Issue Formulation structure for the discussion. Each sub-point should then set out legal and factual support. This information provides the Issue Resolution portion of the analysis.

The Importance of Citation

In a common law system focused on precedent, such as the U.S., citation to cases and statutes is necessary to demonstrate the weight of authority and the credibility of a lawyer's position on a legal issue. In many forms of objective writing, citation is provided for legal arguments which are quoted or paraphrased, irrespective of whether they are taken from statutes, cases, or secondary authorities such as law reviews. Citations are so important in the practice of American law that they are inserted directly into the text, and not footnoted, as in other professions. It is not unusual for every statement of a legal proposition to be followed by a citation indicating the legal source on which the lawyer is relying. Citation format is provided in *The Bluebook*, discussed in Chapter 1.

Analysis of the Client's Legal Needs and Issues

Let us return to our clients, the Salts. Veruca Salt has inquired about bringing a lawsuit against a corporation whose employee made frightening comments to her causing emotional distress. In Chapter 5, you synthesized two cases— *Slocum* and *Korbin*—and concluded that she should be able to bring suit against the company. How will you organize an objective analysis of your conclusions?

Issue Formulation in the Salt case follows the questions that have been derived from a synthesis of *Slocum* and *Korbin*. First, is intentional infliction of emotional distress ("IIED") an independent cause of action? Second, if it is, is it satisfied in this case? Issue two may in turn be subdivided into two sub-issues: the elements of the cause of action and whether they are met. Finally, the sub-issue of whether the elements of the cause of action are met may be divided into the questions of whether the defendant's actions were "calculated to cause" and did "cause severe emotional distress" to a person of "ordinary sensibilities."

After the issues are formulated, we move to Issue Resolution. The first issue, whether IIED is an independent cause of action in Florida, was addressed in Chapter 5. After synthesizing the cases of *Slocum* and *Korbin*, we concluded that IIED is an independent cause of action.

The second issue is whether a cause of action for IIED may be sustained under the present facts. First, we must address the elements of IIED. The nature of IIED is also derived from the synthesis of *Slocum* and *Korbin*. A cause of action exists when a defendant causes severe emotional distress to a plaintiff of ordinary sensibilities, and does so by acts in a manner beyond that which can be tolerated by society.

Having identified the elements of IIED, the IRAC/CREAC formula may be employed to organize the analysis. Did Wilkinson cause severe emotional distress to Veruca Salt? This element was satisfied in *Korbin* when it was alleged that the child was caused "undue emotional stress, mental pain and anguish." Applying this rule to the Salt case, it is apparent that her distress was both severe and caused by Wilkinson; her physician corroborated that her nightmares and anxiety were the result of Wilkinson's frightening words.

This brings us to the central issue in the case: whether Wilkinson acted in a manner calculated to cause emotional distress in a manner beyond that which can be tolerated by society. This rule is also explained by *Slocum* and *Korbin*. Acting in a manner beyond that which can be tolerated by society was exemplified by telling a young child that her mother is an adulterer, but not by mere vulgarities or insults, such as a clerk expressing annoyance at the questions of a customer. Inductive reasoning allows us to formulate two rule statements to resolve this issue. First, the words must not be innocuous in content, but must have a serious meaning and malicious purpose. Second, they must be directed to a person of ordinary sensibility who is likely to be hurt.

As to the first rule, Wilkinson's words do seem to have real and serious meaning and they were malicious. Like the words in *Korbin*, they were false but designed to shame and shock. The fear of permanent physical impairment may be as damaging as words that disparage one's parents. A counteranalysis might point to the fact they were also spoken in irritation at incessant questioning, as was the "you stink to me" comment in *Slocum*, and that perhaps Wilkinson was trying to teach Veruca a lesson in behavior. But whereas the clerk's irritation in *Slocum* led him to make a harmless aside, Wilkinson acted in anger and carried out a plan to frighten Veruca.

The second rule as to intolerable conduct is that the words must be directed to a person of ordinary sensibility who is likely to be injured by them. Whereas there was no reason to think that the adult in *Slocum* would suffer the severe distress that she did upon hearing the clerk's remark, it was apparent that the six-year-old in *Korbin* could be devastated by the shocking words about her mother. A counteranalysis might suggest that Veruca was a sensitive girl, and while this may be true, it is hardly enough to distinguish her from a child of ordinary sensibility.

As we concluded as to each issue that the element of IIED is most likely satisfied, the conclusion of the analysis is that it is very probable that Wilkinson's acts frightening Veruca would make out a valid cause of action and a complaint that can be sustained. An outline for the Salts' legal problem and a checklist for writing a legal discussion are included in the sample documents below.

Sample Documents

Document 1
Outline of the Salt Analysis

Issue: Whether Veruca Salt may state a cause of action to recover damages for comments Wilkinson made to her during the factory tour.

- Is IIED an independent cause of action?
  - In *Korbin*, the Florida Court of Appeals allowed recovery where distress was caused by language alone.
  - In dicta in *Slocum*, the Florida Supreme Court acknowledged nation-wide support for IIED as an independent cause of action, and suggested that it would be recognized under the proper facts.
  - Conclusion: IIED is an independent cause of action.
- If so, are its elements met in this case?
  - What are the elements of the cause of action?
    - A cause of action exists when a defendant causes severe emotional distress to a plaintiff of ordinary sensibilities and does so in a manner beyond that which can be tolerated by society.
  - Are they satisfied here?
    - Defendant must cause severe emotional distress to the plaintiff. This element is met here as Salt's physician corroborated that her distress was the result of Wilkinson's words.
    - Defendant's conduct must be calculated to cause severe emotional distress, beyond the bounds that could be tolerated by society.
      - The words must have real and shocking meaning, motivated by malice.
        - In *Korbin*, the court found the words had real and shocking meaning, motivated by malice.
        - In *Slocum*, the court found the words to be a gratuitous insult.
        - In the present case, Wilkinson calling Veruca a "runt" was a gratuitous insult, similar to the words "you stink to me" in *Slocum*. However, suggesting to Veruca that she would be permanently impaired with a purple tongue was shocking and malicious, similar to the malicious words disparaging the mother in *Korbin*, and thus intolerable.
        - Counteranalysis: Although Wilkinson was also motivated by irritation and perhaps the desire to teach Veruca a lesson in behavior, his words were still frightening and not a mere aside.
      - The words must be directed to a person of ordinary sensibility who is likely to suffer distress upon hearing them.

- ○ In *Korbin,* the court found the six-year-old girl vulnerable to words accusing her mother of adultery.
- ○ Here, the ten-year-old girl was similarly vulnerable. A child of that age is likely to believe the words of an adult acting in an official capacity and would not know that her tongue was not permanently stained.
- ○ Counteranalysis: Although Veruca may be very sensitive, the words were such that they would have shocked the ten-year-old child of average sensibilities.
- ○ Conclusion — Wilkinson's frightening words which were maliciously designed to, and did cause, severe emotional distress in a child of ordinary sensibility, satisfied the elements of an independent cause of action in Florida for the infliction of emotional distress.

Document 2
Analysis Checklist

Issue Formulation

Organize discussion logically, so that:
- Separate issues and sub-issues are treated distinctly
- The discussion begins with the issue that logically should come first

Issue Resolution

For *each* issue and sub-issue:
- Set forth the issue or sub-issue in a topic sentence and/or sub-heading
- State or analyze the rule
- Explain the rule using appropriate illustrative cases
- Include facts, holding, reasoning
- Apply the law to the client's facts
  - First, make fact specific analogies and distinctions between the client's case and the illustrative cases
  - Second, evaluate counteranalysis
- Reach a conclusion

Citation Format
- Cite authority where appropriate

Writing:
- Objective
- Accurate

Chapter 7

The Office Memorandum

Highlights

- Lawyers often communicate their legal analysis to supervising lawyers by an office memorandum.
- A traditional office memorandum is generally long and time-consuming. Many clients and legal employers have begun requesting short form memoranda where more limited analysis is required.
- A traditional long form office memorandum includes a heading, facts, issues, brief answers, a discussion, and a conclusion.
- A short form memorandum includes a heading, an introduction, a discussion, and a conclusion.
- The discussion section of long and short form memoranda utilize the Issue Formulation/Issue Resolution format discussed in Chapter 6, on organization of a legal analysis.

Introduction

Chapter 5 explained the process of synthesizing case law to create legal principles and Chapter 6 explained the method for organizing legal principles to create an objective legal analysis. This chapter focuses on communicating the analysis in the form of an office memorandum, or "memo."

An office memorandum is generally written to communicate a lawyer's research and analysis on a client's legal problem to another member of the firm or organization. It is written from a neutral point of view; its purpose is to predict an outcome rather than advocate one. It also memorializes a legal analysis of the problem for future reference.

A traditional long form office memorandum includes facts, issues, brief answers, a discussion, and a conclusion. A short form memorandum includes an introduction, a discussion, and a conclusion. Both long and short form memoranda utilize the Issue Formulation / Issue Resolution format discussed in Chapter 6, in the discussion section.

This chapter has four sections: (1) purpose of the office memorandum, (2) format of the office memorandum, (3) the traditional office memorandum, and (4) the short form office memorandum.

The Client

In Chapter 5 our clients Veruca and Angina Salt sought advice regarding a lawsuit against William Wonker, Inc. Angina alleges that Arthur Wilkinson, manager of the William Wonker Chocolate Factory, made frightening remarks to Veruca during a factory tour in Miami, Florida causing her mental distress. In Chapter 5 you analyzed and synthesized several cases, *Slocum* and *Korbin*, related to Veruca's problem. In Chapter 6, you organized a formal legal discussion of her problem. Now, a supervising lawyer has requested that you write an office memorandum addressing the issue of whether Veruca Salt can maintain a cause of action in the Florida courts for the distress she suffered during the factory tour.

Purpose of an Office Memorandum

An office memorandum is the most common form of objective legal writing. It is written with other lawyers as its intended primary audience. It is not a court document and is therefore not dictated by court rules, unlike the documents discussed in Chapter 2 on civil litigation.

The supervising lawyer may ask for a memorandum on any topics which advance the work of the law office. Therefore, the first requirement of the lawyer receiving the assignment to write an office memorandum is to understand the purpose of the memorandum and what it should address. The process of obtaining this information is discussed more fully in Chapter 18 on law firm practice. The lawyer receiving the assignment should also clarify whether the supervising lawyer wishes a formal office memorandum, which can be lengthy and time consuming, or a short form memorandum. Both forms are discussed below. The supervising lawyer may request a memorandum that addresses one specific issue, in which case the short form memorandum may be most appropriate, or one that analyzes a complete cause of action, in which case the longer formal office memorandum would be preferred.

The lawyer as audience allows the writer to make certain assumptions. The senior lawyer will be knowledgeable about the law generally, but very busy. Therefore, the memorandum: (1) must be concise and straightforward, presenting conclusions and important points sooner rather than later, (2) should follow the accepted paradigms for legal writing, including the Issue Formulation and Issue Resolution formulas for the discussion section as well as the overall memo format discussed below, (3) need not address common legal knowledge, but (4) must point out everything that is specific to this case. In addition, the lawyer must remember that the memorandum may end up in the hands of a secondary audience: lawyers, judges, and perhaps even clients unfamiliar with the facts, issues, or relevant law of this particular case. The memorandum should be a self-contained document; if it relies on information outside its scope, it should refer to those documents.

Format of an Office Memorandum

As discussed in Chapter 6, legal writing in the U.S. follows a formulistic approach. Chapter 6 concerns the formula used for analysis in most objective writing, including the discussion section of the office memorandum. The office memorandum has an overall format as well. The components of a traditional office memorandum are: (1) heading, (2) facts, (3) issues also known as "questions presented," (4) short or "brief" answers, (5) discussion, including a thesis paragraph and the Issue Formulation / Issue Resolution analysis discussed in Chapter 6, and (6) a conclusion. The components of a short form memorandum are: (1) heading, (2) introduction, (3) discussion, and (4) conclusion.

In either case, the basic structure follows that of judicial opinions discussed in Chapter 3 on legal reasoning: facts, issue, reasoning, and conclusion.

The Traditional Office Memorandum

Heading

The heading or caption identifies the recipient, author, subject, and date of the memorandum. "Memorandum" is printed in capital letters and centered at the top of the page. The identifying information is flush with the left-hand margin. It is important to capture the proper name for client billing purposes, discussed in Chapter 18. It is necessary to properly describe the nature of the subject matter so that the memorandum may be electronically retrieved by other lawyers in the future.

MEMORANDUM

To: Partner
From: Associate
Re: Veruca Salt; sufficiency of claim for IIED
Date: September 16, 20__

Facts

The statement of facts section conveys the legally relevant facts in a straightforward, concise manner. The legally relevant facts are those necessary to resolve the legal problem. Therefore, this section should recite all of the facts which will be discussed in later sections of the memorandum as well as background information and the procedural history of the case. Facts should be cited to their sources, as appropriate. The facts section should be written objectively, with no analysis or argument. The facts section usually begins with a short introduction to the memorandum identifying the client and the legal problem being addressed.

Facts
Our client, Veruca Salt, seeks to recover damages for intentional infliction of emotional distress (IIED) against William Wonker, Inc. for distress
she suffered during a factory tour in Miami, Florida.

Although the facts may be derived from disparate sources, they need to be
rearranged in an organization that is easy to understand, such as chronologically or topically.

The Plaintiff, Veruca Salt ("Veruca"), is a ten-year-old girl residing in
Miami, Florida. The Defendant, William Wonker, Inc., ("Wonker"), is a
Florida corporation located in Miami, Florida. (Wonker Corporate papers,
filed 2/24.)

Recently Veruca and her mother Angina Salt attended a tour conducted
by manager Mr. Wilkinson at the Wonker Chocolate Factory. (Interview
with A. Salt, September 7.) At one point, Veruca, grabbed a new grape
candy, the Everlasting Gobstopper, from the display table and popped it
into her mouth. Wilkinson exploded with anger. He ordered Veruca to open
her mouth and showed her the color of her tongue in a mirror. "I warned
you, runt," he said ominously. "Now your tongue will be purple for the rest
of your life." (Interview with A. Salt, September 7; Interview with S. Beauregarde, September 9.)

Veruca has been diagnosed by her physician as suffering from emotional
trauma as a result of the incident. (Medical report from Dr. Hofstedder,
August 25.)

The narration of what happened is usually followed by the procedural history of the litigation.

On September 5, Angina Salt inquired with this law firm as to the pos-
sibility of filing a civil suit against Wonker. On September 7, Angina and Veruca
Salt were interviewed by Georgina Bucket, a senior partner at our firm. On
September 9, Bucket interviewed Scarlett Beauregarde, another parent who

> was on the tour. The Salts will return on September 27 for counseling as to this matter.

Finally, the facts section may conclude with a short description of the scope of the memorandum.

> This memorandum addresses whether Veruca can maintain an action for IIED against Wonker as a matter of Florida law.

Question Presented

The question presented identifies the legal issue which the memorandum discusses and answers. It usually includes the governing jurisdiction, the parties, the cause of action or legal category, and some mention of the salient facts. A common but not required format for a question presented has three parts beginning with "Under" [jurisdiction], "does/can" [legal theory], "when" [significant facts].

Ideally the question presented should be a single sentence. Although this sentence may well be complex, it should not be cumbersome. The questions presented should correlate to the issues, with a question for each major issue. For example, as the Veruca Salt memorandum has two basic issues—whether IIED is an independent cause of action; and if so are its elements satisfied in this case—it has two separate questions presented.

> <u>Questions Presented</u>
> I.   Do Florida courts recognize an independent tort for intentional infliction of emotional distress (IIED)?
> II.   Under Florida law, can ten-year-old Veruca Salt maintain a cause of action against Wonker, when its employee, in the course of giving her a tour, berated her and frightened her into believing that her tongue was permanently discolored?

Short Answer

The short answer resolves the question presented. It usually consists of a brief one sentence answer, followed and supported by a summary of the legal doctrine and application of the legal doctrine to the facts of the case. The short answer usually consists of a one or two word answer—"yes," "no," "probably," "perhaps"—followed by a reason stated in one or two sentences. Note that the reason should do more than state the relevant law in the abstract. Like the question presented, it should tie in with the legally relevant facts. However as this is a *short* answer, there is no space for analysis, which is saved for the discussion section.

Short Answer

I.   Yes. A Florida court has applied IIED as an independent cause of action.

II.   Probably yes. Wilkinson's comment frightening Veruca that she would be permanently disfigured was intended to shock and shame a child and was motivated by anger and unprofessional demeanor. That Wilkinson may have also believed that his actions were necessary for tour decorum and to improve the behavior of an unruly child does not render his comment less hurtful.

If the question presented is a purely legal one—for example, whether IIED is a cause of action in Florida—both the question and answer will be devoid of facts. Usually, however, both the question and answer will raise the relevant law in terms of the legally significant facts. There may be a certain amount of repetition between the question presented, short answer, and thesis paragraph, discussed below. This repetition is not undesirable as it offers the reader several opportunities to grasp the fundamental essence of the case at the beginning of the memorandum. In addition each section presents the conclusion of the analysis in a slightly different context.

In some memo formats, the question presented and short answer precede the fact section. In that format, it is usual to refer to the parties in general terms rather than by name, as they have not yet been introduced in the fact section.

Discussion

The discussion section is the heart of the memorandum. It sets out the relevant legal doctrine and applies it to the facts of the controversy so as to resolve the problem. It includes a thesis paragraph and the Issue Formulation/Issue Resolution method of legal analysis discussed in Chapter 6. The discussion must always be organized around the relevant issues and each issue and sub-issue must address the law before applying the facts.

Thesis Paragraph

The thesis paragraph, also known as the "umbrella" paragraph, presents an overview or roadmap of the discussion section. Its primary purpose is to present a prediction of the outcome of the discussion section—the thesis—in a manner easily comprehended by the reader.

The first sentence of the thesis paragraph generally presents the "bottom line" conclusion of the analysis. The first sentence is followed by a road map of the discussion section that identifies—in order—the issues and sub-issues that will be discussed. Lastly, the paragraph provides the basic reasons for the conclusion stated in the first sentence, succinctly framed.

If the discussion section revolves around a particular statute or a critical case, the lawyer may quote or paraphrase it in the thesis paragraph. Otherwise, the thesis paragraph does not include any case references. An example of a thesis paragraph is below; note that the thesis paragraph is not separately labeled.

Discussion

Veruca can probably maintain a claim for IIED against Wilkinson. Florida most likely recognizes an independent cause of action for IIED. To succeed in such an action, a plaintiff must demonstrate that the challenged conduct "exceed[s] all bounds which could be tolerated by society" and was "calculated to cause" and did cause "severe emotional distress" to another person. The conduct at issue in this case—Wilkinson's frightening comments to Veruca—seems to have exceeded those bounds, and the context in which the conduct occurred demonstrates that they were calculated to cause Veruca severe emotional distress. That Wilkinson was reacting to Veruca's provocations or that he hoped to teach her a lesson in good behavior will probably not suffice to show that his behavior was privileged.

After the thesis paragraph, the discussion section proceeds with a sustained analysis—issue by issue. Major issues are treated in their own sections which are identified by topic headings. Topic headings are "signposts" rendering the organization immediately clear to the reader. The Salt discussion has two major issues.

Analysis of Issue I: A Purely Legal Issue

The first section of the Salt memorandum discussion concerns the cause of action. The heading may simply identify the issue, as below, or it may state a conclusion, as in the sample memo reproduced in the sample documents.

I.	**IIED as an Independent Cause of Action**

The first issue in the Salt problem is a purely legal one; no facts specific to the Salt case are discussed. This is a classic threshold issue; it must be decided before a court can move on to the next question of whether a claim for IIED has been established. The holding of *Korbin* is presented as a binding precedent to demonstrate that there can be recovery for IIED in Florida. Dicta from *Slocum* is utilized to support this conclusion.

Florida courts recognize IIED as an independent tort. The Third District Court of Appeal in <u>Korbin v. Berlin</u>, allowed a plaintiff to pursue a cause of action for IIED, even though the defendant had committed no other tort against the plaintiff. Although <u>Korbin</u> was the first Florida case to allow a cause of action for this tort and is only an intermediate-level court opinion, it is fully consistent with the Florida Supreme Court's opinion in <u>Slocum v. Food Fair Stores</u>.

After this analysis, two points of counteranalysis are offered and rejected, which allows the conclusion of issue one to be restated.

> While the <u>Slocum</u> court conceded that no Florida court had recognized an independent cause of action for IIED, it clearly signaled its willingness to do so, where the defendant's conduct was more egregious. Likewise, while dicta in <u>Korbin</u> mentions the independent tort of slander, the mother did not bring a cause of action for slander. Thus, even if she has no other claim against Wonker or Wilkinson, Veruca can assert an IIED claim.

Analysis of Issue II: Application of Elements Analysis

The second issue addresses whether the elements of IIED have been made out in the Salt case.

> II.   Veruca Can Likely Maintain A Claim for IIED

Because this section is fairly complicated it begins with its own thesis paragraph.

> Assuming an independent claim for IIED may be brought, does Veruca Salt's claim satisfy the elements of IIED. Because Wilkinson's actions seemed to grow out of a desire to hurt a young child and were likely to do so, such actions were calculated to cause severe emotional distress, and went beyond the bounds of conduct that could be tolerated by society. Accordingly, Wilkinson's actions, as alleged in Veruca Salt's complaint, are probably sufficient to support an action for IIED.

Several preliminary sub-issues are next discussed. Because these questions are relatively straightforward, they are disposed of quickly. To speed the analysis, efficient use is made of a "parenthetical." Parentheticals are singular points a case illustrates. Such points are included in parentheses following the case citation, hence their name.

> As preliminary matters, it should be noted that there is no bar that the suit was brought by her mother, Angina, on behalf of Veruca as her guardian and next friend. Such a vicarious lawsuit is permitted by Florida and in fact when a minor is the named party, as here, is mandated. <u>Korbin</u>. Likewise, Wonker is clearly liable for the actions of its employee under the theory of respondeat superior, <u>Slocum</u> (supermarket chain responsible for the actions of its employee clerk), especially as Wilkinson is the high ranking manager of the factory. Finally, it is clear that Florida law allows for recovery of mental damages, even when they are the sole direct injury and physical symptoms are only derivative therefrom. <u>Slocum</u> (citing <u>Kirksey v. Jernigan</u>).

With the preliminary matters disposed of, the discussion section moves on to the logical points that must be considered before addressing the question of whether Wilkinson's conduct was intolerable: What is the nature of an IIED tort and what aspect is in question in this case? These points are synthesized from *Slocum* and *Korbin*.

> As to the substance of the claim, a cause of action for IIED lies when a person's conduct "exceed[s] all bounds which could be tolerated by society" and is "calculated to cause" and does cause "severe emotional distress" to a person of ordinary sensibilities. <u>Slocum</u>; <u>Korbin</u>.
>
> There is no dispute that Veruca's emotional damage in this case was severe, and that it resulted from the incident at the factory. During the tour, Veruca sobbed hysterically and after she returned home she began suffering nightmares and was anxious that her tongue would once again turn purple. Her physician, Dr. Hofstedder, <u>diagnosed her as suffering from extreme emotional distress as a result of the incident.</u>

With the basic rule of IIED stated, the discussion section now addresses the central question. The next sub-issue, concerning whether Wilkinson's conduct is intolerable, is the most important one. This issue is further divided into two sub-issues: <u>the meaning and purpose of the words used and the vulnerability of the victim.</u> Each of the sub-issues is handled according to the model of Issue Resolution discussed in Chapter 6. Throughout the discussion, the writer contrasts *Slocum*, an example of gratuitous insult, and *Korbin*, an example of intolerable abuse. The complete discussion is included in the formal memorandum reproduced in the sample documents below.

Each issue in the discussion section concludes with a short summary of the answer. The audience expects to receive a definite conclusion on each issue and sub-issue. It is important to not merely raise the arguments for each side on each issue, hitting them back and forth like ping-pong balls. Rather, the lawyer must draw a conclusion on each of the issues and sub-issues and reach a reasoned final conclusion supported by the law.

A Note on the Analysis of a Statute in the Discussion Section

The discussion section of a memorandum based on a statute follows the same format of a memorandum based on case synthesis. However, because a statute takes precedence over case law, as explained in Chapter 4, a statutory memorandum gives primary emphasis to the terms of the statute. For example, the thesis paragraph in the discussion section might cite the entire statute and each Issue Formulation section then refer to the particular term of the statute. The Issue Resolution section for each term of the statute would follow the IRAC/CREAC methodology, utilizing judicial opinions to analyze the terms of the statute.

Conclusion

The conclusion section to an office memorandum states the predicted outcome, supported by the chief legal reasons. It generally consists of one paragraph, summarizing the key points previously addressed.

CONCLUSION

Veruca Salt's cause of action against Wonker will likely be sustained, as she suffered severe emotional distress caused by Wilkinson's intolerable conduct.

Short Form Memoranda

Lawyers are often asked to a draft short memorandum rather than, or in addition to, the traditional office memorandum. The formal office memorandum described above includes a heading, statement of facts, issues, short answers, discussion, and conclusion. In contrast, the short memorandum generally follows a simplified format: (1) heading, (2) introduction, (3) discussion, and (4) conclusion. Such a memorandum usually omits the statement of facts, the issues, and the brief answers. In addition, the discussion is more concise.

Heading

As in the formal memorandum, at the top of the first page the word "Memorandum" is printed in capital letters and centered. Flush with the left-hand margin, the recipient's name, the writer's name, the client name and matter, and the date are provided.

Introduction

The introduction to the short memorandum will state what the client or supervising lawyer asked to be done and confirm that it has been accomplished. If the memorandum is being written at the request of the client, it may include an abbreviated version of the major facts to ensure that they were accurately understood. When writing to a supervising lawyer, it is generally unnecessary to include the facts. If the factual summary is unnecessary, the introduction should identify: (1) the question asked by the supervising lawyer, (2) the rule of law providing the answer to the question, and (3) the conclusion.

Discussion

The discussion section of the short memorandum follows a concise version of the Issue Formulation/Issue Resolution formula discussed above and in Chapter 6. The discussion should include the rule which answers the inquiry identified in the introduction, an explanation of the rule through case law, and the application of the rule to the client's facts. As with the formal memorandum, the discussion section of the short memorandum is written deductively beginning with the general legal principle or rule.

Only important cases are discussed during the explanation. Factually analogous cases should include the holding and the essential parts of the court's reasoning and, where applicable, the facts that support the holding. Any other necessary cases should include only the point the case illustrates. Such points may often be included in parentheses following the case citation.

In the rule application, the manner in which the cases illustrate the client's factual situation is discussed. The application should include the important factual arguments, both favorable and unfavorable, as in the formal memorandum. Unlike the formal memorandum, however, such arguments should include only the most basic points necessary for the reader to understand the argument.

The structure of the short memorandum will depend on the inquiry of the client or assigning attorney. If two questions are asked, or if the question has two parts, the discussion section must follow the Issue Formulation/Issue Resolution format and be divided into two main sections each of which state, explain, and apply the rule. Further, as with the long memorandum, topic headings should be used as "signposts."

Conclusion

After the heading, introduction, and discussion are completed, the conclusion is added at the end of the short memo. The conclusion restates the assignment, the legal conclusion, and argument in one or two sentences.

Analyzing the Client's Legal Needs and Issues

A supervising lawyer has requested that you write an office memorandum on whether Veruca Salt can maintain a cause of action in the Florida courts for the distress she suffered during the chocolate factory tour. The supervising lawyer gives you one week to complete the task, reasoning that it should be easy since you have already read *Slocum* and *Korbin*, the only cases to be addressed in the memorandum. After ascertaining that you understand exactly the purpose and format of the memorandum and have been given all of the relevant facts, you review your outline and begin your analysis. You write a draft of the memorandum and then revise it several times so that it is well organized, well written, to the point, and the citations are correct. A traditional office memorandum on the Salt problem is included below. After reviewing your work, the supervising lawyer asks you to revise it into a short memorandum to be forwarded to the client. A short form memorandum is also included in the sample documents.

Sample Documents

Document 1
Formal Office Memorandum

MEMORANDUM

TO: Partner
FROM: Associate
DATED: September __, 20__
RE: Veruca Salt; Sufficiency of claim for intentional infliction of emotional distress

Statement of Facts

Our client, Veruca Salt, seeks to recover damages for intentional infliction of emotional distress (IIED) against William Wonker, Inc. for alarming comments Arthur Wilkinson, manager of its Chocolate Factory, made to Veruca during a factory tour in Miami, Florida.

The Plaintiff, Veruca Salt, is a ten-year-old female who attended the public tour of the chocolate factory on August 14 of this year with her mother Angina Salt. Veruca is a sensitive young girl, who has had some difficulty making friends in her sixth-grade class. Her parents report that she gets distressed at perceived slights or rejections at her school and cries easily. A. Salt interview, September 7, at 2. Veruca was very excited to go on the factory tour, as the popular tour had a long waiting list and Veruca obtained two spots by means of a promotional invitation that had been hidden in Wonker chocolate bars. There were approximately fifteen people on the hour-long tour; the other children on the tour were older teenagers. Although the group stayed together during the tour, at various points individual members left to go to the restrooms. Id. at 2–3.

The Defendant, William Wonker, Inc., ("Wonker"), is a Florida corporation located in Miami, Florida. (Wonker Corporate papers, filed 2/24.) Arthur Wilkinson, the manager of the William Wonker Chocolate Factory, conducted the tour on August 14, as Ms. Slugworth, the usual tour guide, was indisposed. Veruca, as is her disposition, interrupted Wilkinson's presentation at numerous points with questions, despite Wilkinson's request to hold all questions until the final talk in the Factory gift shop. According to Angina and another parent, Wilkinson grew more agitated with Veruca's questions and a couple of times berated her, saying words to the effect of, "Little girl, I told you, stop with the questions!" Id. at 3; S. Beauregarde interview, September 9, at 4.

About thirty minutes into the tour, Veruca began touching each candy bar that was exhibited, despite the instructions given by Wilkinson at the beginning of the tour for the guests not to touch anything and await their goody bags from the gift shop. Every time Veruca touched a candy bar, Wilkinson shouted, "Don't touch it!" or "Put it back!" in increasingly angry tones. Salt interview at 4. At one point, Veruca lifted a Scrumdiddlyumptious candy bar that was on display and began to unwrap it. Wilkinson walked over, grabbed it from Veruca, and angrily returned it to the shelf, shouting, "What have I told you!" Wilkinson then turned around to lead the tour, while Veruca left the tour in the direction of the restroom. Angina went to Wilkinson and apologized, explaining that Veruca was an inquisitive girl. Wilkinson replied, "I am sorry but we can never complete the tour if the children keep grabbing the candy; she's not a baby." Id. at 3–4.

Angina then headed to the restroom where she found Veruca sobbing. Angina said, "I know that he's rude, but you have been waiting a year for this tour and you shouldn't let him ruin our experience." Angina helped Veruca wash up so that her tears were no longer visible and the two rejoined the tour, having missed only a few minutes. Id.

Towards the end of the tour, Wilkinson brought the group into the famous chocolate laboratory and showed them a newly invented grape-flavored candy called an Everlasting Gobstopper. The prototype label described the Everlasting Gobstopper as candy that "lasts in your mouth longer than you can remember and whose yummy taste you can never forget." When the tour group began walking to the exits, Veruca grabbed the Everlasting Gobstopper from the display table, unwrapped it, and popped it into her mouth, chewing vigorously. Id. at 4. Wilkinson turned red with anger. "That's bad news for you, runt," he said. He took a small mirror from the table and walked slowly to Veruca. "Open your mouth, like a doctor's office," Wilkinson said. When Veruca extended her tongue, purple from the candy, Wilkinson showed Veruca her reflection in the mirror. "I warned you," he said ominously, "now your tongue will be purple for the rest of your life. You'll be known as Little Miss Blueberry." Id. Veruca screamed at the top of her lungs and ran out of the room. Angina turned to Wilkinson and said, "Now you've done it, you jerk." Wilkinson replied, "Listen lady, you should be thanking me; perhaps now your daughter has learned there are consequences to her behavior." Id. at 5.

Angina ran to the restroom but Veruca was not there. She returned to Wilkinson and told him that Veruca was missing. Wilkinson seemed concerned and made a call with his cell phone. A few minutes later, a female employee walked into the room with Veruca, who was sobbing hysterically, exclaiming, "I don't want a purple tongue!" Angina took Veruca out of the factory. When they reached home, Angina spent the entire night scrubbing Veruca's tongue, while

Veruca cried, "See, it will never come off." Angina was able to quiet Veruca only by washing the grape flavoring completely off her tongue. <u>Id.</u> at 6–7.

Since the incident, Veruca has become increasingly anxious. Her behavior is characterized by loss of appetite, depression, inability to concentrate, and sleeplessness. She still has nightmares about the incident and sometimes asks her parents if what Wilkinson said was true and will her tongue turn purple again. Her teachers have noticed that she has become even more withdrawn in class. Her physician, Dr. Hofstedder, diagnosed Veruca as suffering from extreme emotional trauma as a result of her experience during the factory tour. <u>Id.</u> at 9.

On September 5, Angina Salt inquired with this law firm as to the possibility of filing a civil suit against Wonker. On September 7, Angina and Veruca Salt were interviewed by Georgina Bucket, a senior partner at our firm. On September 9, Bucket interviewed Scarlett Beauregarde, another parent who was on the tour. The Salts will return on September 27 for counseling as to this matter.

This memorandum addresses whether, applying Florida law, Salt can maintain an action for IIED against Wonker as a matter of law or whether Salt's complaint would be dismissed under Florida Rule of Civil Procedure 1.140(b)(6) for failing to state a claim upon which relief can be granted.

Questions Presented

I.   Do Florida courts recognize an independent tort for intentional infliction of emotional distress (IIED)?

II.   Assuming the Florida courts do recognize an independent tort for IIED, can Veruca Salt maintain a claim against Wonker for the actions of its employee, Arthur Wilkinson, who in the course of giving Veruca a tour of the factory, berated her, and frightened her into believing that her tongue was permanently discolored?

Short Answers

I.   Yes. A Florida court has applied IIED as an independent cause of action.

II.   Probably yes. Wilkinson's comment frightening Veruca that she would be permanently disfigured was intended to shock and shame a child and was motivated by anger and unprofessional demeanor. That Wilkinson may have also believed that his actions were necessary for tour decorum and to improve the behavior of an unruly child does not render his comment less hurtful.

Discussion

Veruca can probably maintain a claim for IIED against Wilkinson. Florida recognizes an independent cause of action for IIED. To succeed in such an action, a plaintiff must demonstrate that the challenged conduct "exceed[s] all bounds which could be tolerated by society" and was "calculated to cause" and did cause "severe emotional distress" to another person. The conduct at issue in this case— Wilkinson's frightening comments to Veruca—seems to have exceeded those bounds, and the context in which the conduct occurred demonstrates that they were calculated to cause Veruca severe emotional distress. That Wilkinson was reacting to Veruca's provocations or that he hoped to teach her a lesson in good behavior will probably not suffice to show that his behavior was privileged.

I. Florida state courts recognize an independent tort for IIED.

Florida courts almost certainly recognize IIED as an independent tort. The Third District Court of Appeal in Korbin v. Berlin, 177 So. 2d 551, 553 (Fla. Dist. Ct. App. 1965) allowed a plaintiff to pursue a cause of action for IIED, even though the defendant had committed no other tort against the plaintiff. Id. at 553. Although Korbin was the first Florida case to allow a cause of action for this tort and is only an intermediate-level court opinion, it is fully consistent with the Florida Supreme Court's opinion in Slocum v. Food Fair Stores, 100 So. 2d 396, 398 (Fla. 1958). Indeed, the Korbin court relied extensively on Slocum to justify its decision. Korbin, 177 So. 2d at 552–53.

While the Slocum court conceded that no Florida court had recognized an independent cause of action for IIED, it clearly signaled its willingness to do so, recognizing "the strong current of opinion in support" of IIED as an independent tort in both the scholarly literature and in the law of other states. Slocum, 100 So. 2d at 397. It quoted at length the Restatement of Torts § 46 (Supp. 1948), which summarized this new tort. Id. It even delineated the elements needed to establish such a tort. Id. at 397–98. It is true that the Slocum court did not take the final step of explicitly recognizing the tort of IIED, because the frivolous nature of the comment "you stink to me" did not meet the delineated elements. However, as the court in Korbin noted, the Slocum court showed that it was ready to apply the IIED doctrine in a case where the defendant's conduct was more egregious. Korbin, 177 So. 2d at 553.

It may be possible that <u>Korbin</u> did not actually permit an independent cause of action for IIED since the plaintiff's lawsuit—an action by a young girl against a woman who accused her mother of adultery—was connected with slander of the girl's mother. <u>Id.</u> at 552–53. This analysis, however, is unpersuasive. The mother did not bring a cause of action for slander; and even if she had, that slander would only have constituted a tort *against the mother*, not the plaintiff. Thus, the child's claim of IIED must be considered as independent from the mother's separate claim for slander. <u>Id.</u> at 553. Accordingly, the <u>Korbin</u> decision cannot be interpreted to have linked the IIED to the slander of the mother. Thus, even if she has no other claim against Wonker, or Wilkinson, Veruca can assert an IIED claim.

II.   Assuming, as is likely, that Florida does recognize an independent tort for IIED, Veruca Salt, a ten-year-old child, can probably maintain such a claim against Wilkinson who falsely made her fear that her looks were permanently impaired.

Assuming that a claim for IIED may be brought even when unconnected to any other tort, the question remains whether Veruca Salt's claim satisfies the elements of IIED. Because Wilkinson's actions seemed to grow out of a desire to hurt a young child and were likely to do so, such actions were calculated to cause severe emotional distress, and went beyond the bounds of conduct tolerated by society. Accordingly, Wilkinson's actions, as alleged in Veruca Salt's complaint, are probably sufficient to support an action for IIED.

As preliminary matters, it should be noted that there is no bar that the suit was brought by her mother, Angina, on behalf of Veruca as her guardian and next friend. Such a vicarious lawsuit is permitted by Florida and in fact when a minor is the named party, as here, is mandated. See <u>Korbin</u>, 177 So. 2d. at 551. Likewise, Wonker is clearly liable for the actions of its employee under the theory of respondeat superior, see <u>Slocum</u>, 100 So. 2d at 399 (supermarket chain responsible for the actions of its employee clerk), especially as Wilkinson is the high ranking manager of the factory. Finally, it is clear that Florida law allows for recovery of mental damages, even when they are the sole direct injury and physical symptoms are only derivative therefrom. <u>Slocum</u>, 100 So. 2d at 397 (citing <u>Kirksey v. Jernigan</u>, 45 So. 2d 188).

As to the substance of the claim, a cause of action for IIED lies when a person's conduct "exceed[s] all bounds which could be tolerated by society" and is "calculated to cause" and does cause "severe emotional distress" to a person of ordinary sensibilities. <u>Id.</u>; <u>Korbin</u>, 177 So. 2d. at 551.

There is no dispute that Salt's emotional damage in this case was severe, and that it resulted from the incident at the factory. During the tour Veruca broke into tears on two occasions, sobbing hysterically until consoled by her mother. Salt's mother would testify that Veruca's overall demeanor, school habits and personality have changed and that she suffers nightmares and daily fears connected to the incident. Her physician, Dr. Hofstedder, diagnosed her as suffering from extreme emotional distress as a result of the incident. The fundamental question then is whether the defendant's conduct "exceeded all bounds which could be tolerated by society," and was "calculated to cause 'severe emotional distress' to a person of ordinary sensibilities." Slocum, 100 So. 2d at 397, 398; Korbin, 177 So. 2d at 553.

There is no question that words alone can constitute conduct intolerable in society, if they have both serious meaning and are directed at a person whom the defendant knows to be vulnerable to them. See Slocum, 100 So. 2d at 398; see generally Korbin, 177 So. 2d at 552–53. "[M]ere vulgarities" are not actionable because they are not "intended to have real meaning or serious effect." Slocum, 100 So. 2d at 398. Deliberately false and malicious statements, however, can be actionable. Korbin, 177 So. 2d at 553.

In Korbin, for example, when a woman told a girl that her mother was committing adultery and that God would punish her, such words were deemed actionable because the false comments had real "content and import," and were objectively likely to "shame" a young girl and "shock her sensibilities." 177 So. 2d at 553. In Slocum, on the other hand, the court concluded that a store clerk's comment to a customer, "you stink to me," 100 So. 2d at 397, was a mere vulgarity which had no "real meaning" and was not likely to cause "a person of ordinary sensibilities" severe emotional distress. Id. at 398. Thus, the customer had no cause of action for IIED. Id.

In this case, Wilkinson's statement that Veruca's tongue was permanently disfigured can be viewed as false and malicious, as it was untrue and motivated by the desire to strike alarm in a young girl. Certainly the other comments made by Wilkinson for most of the tour do not fall into this category. At several points, Wilkinson berated Veruca for grabbing candy, calling her "little girl." These comments, while rude and insensitive, are virtually indistinguishable from the meaningless "you stink" comment in Slocum, and are unlike the statements about a mother's adultery found actionable in Korbin. Likewise, when Wilkinson wrested the Gobstopper from Veruca, and called her a "runt," his comment was no more than a meaningless vulgarity, especially as Wilkinson was entitled to keep decorum and protect the guests from injury and the factory from disruption.

Although a tour guide might be held to a higher duty of courtesy to patrons, akin to the duty owed by an employee of a carrier, hotel, or theater, see

Slocum, 100 So. 2d at 399, Wilkinson's initial comments were so innocuous that even this heightened duty was not breached.

However, Wilkinson's final action of the tour was clearly calculated to cause extreme emotional distress to Veruca. Wilkinson frightened Veruca into thinking that her tongue would remain purple for a long time, perhaps the remainder of her life, and that she would be perennially humiliated. The fear of permanent disfigurement, even if only cosmetic, could be devastating. Such a scare could certainly be expected to cause distress to any person, much less a child.

Unlike with his earlier comments, Wilkinson cannot claim his conduct was privileged by the need to keep the tour orderly or to corral an unruly child. Although privilege may exempt from liability an actor who acts from necessity, Slocum, 100 So. 2d. at 397 (quoting Restatement of Torts §46 cmt. e (1948)), Wilkinson was not obligated to act as he did. To maintain order, it was sufficient for him simply to remove the candy with a reprimand, as he had been doing throughout the tour. This is especially so as the tour was nearing completion. As for his attempt to teach Veruca a lesson, as he claimed to Angina, first, it was not the duty of Wilkinson, a tour guide and neither a parent nor a teacher, to do so. Secondly, there was little instructive value in this threat. In fact as it was made with the seeming desire to hurt Veruca, it "exceeded all bounds which could be tolerated by society." 100 So. 2d at 397–98.

Closely related to the content of the words is their intended impact. To be actionable, words must be calculated to cause severe emotional distress to a person of ordinary sensibilities. Slocum, 100 So. 2d. at 397. Thus, words must be directed at a person who is likely to suffer severe emotional distress upon hearing them. Korbin, 177 So. 2d at 551–53. In Korbin, the court found that the defendant's comments were intolerable not only because of their content, but also because they were directed at a "child of tender years" whose "sensibilities" would inevitably be "shocked" by the remarks. Id. at 553. In Slocum, by contrast, there was no allegation of such intended effect. 100 So. 2d at 398.

Here, as in Korbin, the comments were directed at a child of tender years. Although an adult may have realized that there was no truth in Wilkinson's alarm that Veruca's tongue would be permanently discolored, a child could not have been expected to realize the falsity of the threat. In fact, it was Veruca's young age that made Manager Wilkinson's comment credible and hence hurtful. Although Veruca is four years older than the plaintiff in Korbin, she is similarly a "child of tender years" whose "sensibilities" would inevitably be "shocked" by the remarks. 177 So. 2d at 553.

It is true that the egregiousness of Wilkinson's conduct must be viewed *from an objective standpoint*, Slocum, 100 So. 2d at 397–98, and Wilkinson was not aware that Veruca was a particularly sensitive child. Although she did break into tears during the tour this fact was apparently unknown to Wilkinson. Nevertheless he should have known the effect that his frightening comment would have on any young child. And Veruca's sensitivity and difficulty making friends hardly distinguish her from a child of ordinary sensibilities, the objective standard that <u>Korbin</u> indicates should be applied to this case.

For all of these reasons, Wilkinson's actions against Veruca most probably support a cause of action for IIED.

CONCLUSION

Veruca Salt's independent cause of action for IIED against Wonker will likely be sustained, as she suffered severe emotional distress as the result of Wilkinson's comments, which were calculated to frighten and alarm her and were thus intolerable. Therefore a motion filed by Wonker to dismiss a complaint pursuant to R.1.140 of the Florida Rules of Civil Procedure would likely be denied.

Document 2
Short Form Memorandum

MEMORANDUM

TO: Partner
FROM: Associate
DATED: September __, 20__
RE: Veruca Salt; claim for intentional infliction of emotional distress

Introduction

You asked me to research whether our client, Veruca Salt, may maintain a claim against William Wonker, Inc. ("Wonker") for the actions of its employee, Arthur Wilkinson, who, in the course of giving Veruca a tour of the company's chocolate factory in Florida frightened her into believing that her tongue was permanently stained purple. I have completed the research and concluded that the answer is probably yes. Florida recognizes a cause of action for IIED when a person's conduct exceeds all bounds which could be tolerated by society and is calculated to cause and does cause severe emotional distress.

Discussion

A cause of action for IIED exists when a person's conduct "exceed[s] all bounds which could be tolerated by society" and is "calculated to cause" and does cause "severe emotional distress" to a person of ordinary sensibilities. Korbin v. Berlin, 177 So. 2d 551, 553 (Fla. Dist. Ct. App. 1965); Slocum v. Food Fair Stores, 100 So. 2d 396, 398 (Fla. 1958). There is no dispute that Veruca's emotional damage resulting from the incident at the factory was severe. The question is only whether the defendant's conduct "exceeded all bounds which could be tolerated by society," and was "calculated to cause 'severe emotional distress' to a person of ordinary sensibilities."

Intolerable Conduct

Words alone can constitute conduct intolerable in society, if they have a serious meaning and are directed at a person known to be vulnerable. See Slocum, 100 So. 2d at 398. In Korbin, when a woman told a girl that her mother was committing adultery and that God would punish her, such words were deemed actionable because the false comments had real "import," and were objectively likely to "shame" a young girl. 177 So. 2d at 553. In Slocum, on the other hand, the court concluded that a store clerk's comment to a customer, "you stink to me," was a mere vulgarity with no "real meaning" and hence not actionable. 100 So. 2d at 397–98. In this case, Wilkinson's statement that Veruca's tongue was permanently disfigured can be viewed as false and malicious, as it was untrue and motivated by the desire to strike alarm in a young girl.

Intended to cause severe emotional distress

To be actionable, words must be calculated to cause severe emotional distress. Slocum, 100 So. 2d. at 397. In Korbin, the court found that the defendant's comments were actionable not only because of their content, but also because they were directed at a "child of tender years" whose "sensibilities" would inevitably be "shocked". Id. at 553. In Slocum, by contrast, there was no allegation of such intended effect. 100 So. 2d at 398. Here, as in Korbin, the comments were directed at a child of tender years. It was Veruca's young age that made Wilkinson's comment credible and hence hurtful. Although Veruca is four years older than the plaintiff in Korbin, she is similarly a child who could be expected to be shocked by the remarks.

Conclusion

Veruca Salt may maintain a claim against Wonker for the actions of its employee, Arthur Wilkinson, who, in the course of giving Veruca a tour of the company's chocolate factory in Florida frightened her into believing that her tongue was permanently stained purple. Florida recognizes a cause of action for IIED when a person's conduct exceeds all bounds which could be tolerated by society and is calculated to cause and does cause severe emotional distress.

Part Four

Practice Skills:
Professional Responsibility,
Client Communications,
and Problem Solving

Chapter 8

Professional Responsibilities of Lawyers in the U.S.

Highlights

- An American lawyer's primary duty is to provide responsible and effective client representation.
- Lawyers practicing in the U.S. should be aware of two major ethical areas relating to the attorney-client relationship: the attorney-client privilege and the rules of professional responsibility.
- The attorney-client privilege protects communications between lawyer and client made in confidence for the purpose of obtaining legal advice.
- Rules of professional responsibility exist in all jurisdictions in the U.S. and govern lawyers' ethical behavior.
- Under the rules of professional responsibility, a lawyer must render competent representation, communicate regularly with clients, maintain client confidentiality, and avoid client conflicts.

Introduction

In the U.S., lawyers have a duty to provide ethical and effective client representation. The attorney-client privilege protects communications between a lawyer and a client from disclosure, where the purpose of the communication is obtaining legal advice. Further, in all jurisdictions in the U.S., rules of professional responsibility govern lawyers' behavior. Many states have adopted the American Bar Association's Model Rules of Professional Conduct. These rules impose upon lawyers a duty to be competent, diligent, and communicative while representing clients. They also limit a lawyer's ability to divulge client confidences or represent clients with conflicting interests.

This chapter is intended as an introduction to the attorney-client privilege and select rules of professional responsibility. It has four sections: (1) the delivery of legal services, (2) the attorney-client relationship, (3) the duties that lawyers owe to the judicial system, and (4) the duties that lawyers owe to third parties.

The Client

As you read this chapter, consider the duties raised by the representation of our firm's new client, Stephen Mathews. Stephen Mathews is an attorney with another firm. He has been charged by the attorney grievance commission for the State Bar of Michigan with commingling, or combining, client funds with his own. The firm has asked you to represent Stephen in his disciplinary hearing.

At your first meeting with Stephen, you discuss strategy. Stephen acknowledges that commingling client funds is in violation of the rules of professional responsibility. He says he will testify that: (1) he is a disorganized person, (2) he intended to deposit the client funds in his client trust account as required by the disciplinary rules, but (3) he mistakenly deposited the money in his own account.

At a subsequent meeting, however, Stephen tells you "confidentially" that he is guilty of the charge. He admits that he purposefully put the client funds in his own account. He explains that he purchased a boat and needed the extra money for "a short time" to cover the payments. He intended to move the money back into the client account when he "could afford it."

What advice do you have for Stephen? Should you continue to represent him? Regardless of whether you continue to represent him, should you disclose his confession to the state bar?

The Delivery of Legal Services

The rules of professional responsibility govern the manner in which lawyers practice law. The rules are intended to protect the public by ensuring the independence and competence of lawyers.

Independence

Lawyers practicing in the U.S. must exercise independent professional judgment. The rules prohibit a lawyer from sharing legal fees with a non-lawyer. The rules also prevent lawyers engaged in the practice of law from forming partnerships with non-lawyers. The concern is that the non-lawyer partners in a multidisciplinary practice might exercise economic control of the lawyer to the detriment of the client. Finally, the rules prohibit lawyers from practicing in a firm for profit if any non-lawyer owns any interest in the firm, is an officer or director of the firm, or otherwise controls the activities of the lawyer.

Competence

Only licensed lawyers are permitted to practice law in the U.S. Further, lawyers may only practice law in the states in which they are licensed. Lawyers are admitted to the bar on a state-by-state basis. Because the laws of the states vary, lawyers may not utilize a license issued in one state to establish an office in another. However, lawyers may be granted permission to engage in certain temporary activities in other states.

In addition, lawyers may not assist non-lawyers in the unauthorized practice of law. Further, the rules prohibit lawyers from allowing non-lawyer staff members from assuming responsibilities requiring formal legal training.

The Attorney-Client Relationship

The rules of professional responsibility specify the duties owed by lawyers to clients, the manner in which authority is divided between lawyer and client, and the circumstances under which lawyers should withdraw from the representation of a client.

Competent Representation and Diligence

The rules compel a lawyer to render competent representation to a client. Competence includes knowledge, skill, thoroughness, and preparation. Accordingly, a lawyer lacking sufficient knowledge to adequately represent a client must decline representation or associate with a more experienced lawyer.

Lawyers must also act with reasonable diligence and promptness in representing clients. Delay is to be avoided; client matters must be actively pursued.

Communications and Advice

Lawyers have a duty of communication that includes: (1) consulting with the client on preferred methods of achieving objectives, (2) keeping the client informed regarding the status of the matter, and (3) promptly complying with client requests for information. Lawyers in the U.S. are required to inform clients about all major developments in a case or transaction.

Lawyers in the U.S. also owe clients their independent judgment and candid advice, irrespective of whether the advice is acceptable to the client. Lawyers are permitted, but not required, to advise clients about non-legal aspects of the client's problem.

The Division of Authority

The rules specify that some decisions belong exclusively to the client. As noted above, the client decides the objectives of the representation and also has the power to decide whether to settle a matter. Other decisions are shared by the lawyer and the client. A lawyer is required to consult with the client on the means by which the client's objectives are reached. It is anticipated that a client will defer to the lawyer on matters within the lawyer's area of expertise.

Finally, a lawyer is not permitted to assist a client in the perpetration of a crime or fraud. The lawyer may caution the client on the consequences of such action, but may not render assistance. The lawyer must also withdraw from representation if continuation of representation will require perpetration of a fraud, crime, or violation of the rules of professional responsibility.

Fees

The rules require lawyers to charge reasonable fees. The rules list a number of factors to be considered in the evaluation of "reasonableness." Included are the time and labor required for the services, the novelty and difficulty of the matter, the customary fee for such services, the result, the experience and reputation of the lawyer, and whether the fee is fixed or contingent. The details surrounding fees and billing are discussed in Chapter 18.

Confidentiality

Lawyers owe clients a duty of confidentiality. A lawyer may not disclose any information relating to the representation of a client, unless the client consents following consultation or disclosure is required to enable the lawyer to carry out the representation.

The duty of confidentiality includes, but is broader than, the "attorney-client privilege." The attorney-client privilege protects communications between lawyer and client made in confidence for the purpose of obtaining or giving legal advice. The duty of confidentiality protects these communications, as well as all information relating to the representation.

The lawyer's duty of confidentiality contains several exceptions. First, lawyers are permitted to reveal the confidential information of clients with their express, informed consent or with implied authorization. Informed consent requires that the lawyer explain to the client the risks of, and alternatives to, the proposed course of conduct. Implied authorization allows lawyers to routinely share a client's confidential information where necessary to assist the client. Second, the lawyer is permitted to reveal confidential client information if reasonably believed to be necessary to prevent death or serious bodily harm. Third, the lawyer is permitted to reveal confidential information if the client has used the lawyer's services to cause financial injury to another through a crime or a fraud and if revealing the information can prevent, mitigate, or rectify the harm. Fourth, lawyers are permitted to reveal confidential client information to obtain advice about compliance with the rules of professional conduct, to defend themselves, to collect a fee, or to comply with other laws or court orders.

In addition to the generally recognized exceptions above, there are several other circumstances where a lawyer may, or must, reveal confidential information. First, lawyers who represent entities such as corporations are expected to act to protect the entity. If the lawyer learns that someone within the entity is acting in an illegal manner that will cause substantial injury to the entity, the lawyer is expected to bring the matter to the attention of the corporate officers. If the officers refuse to act, the lawyer has the option to reveal the confidential information if reasonably believed to be necessary to prevent the injury. Second, a lawyer may be required to reveal fraud in order to avoid assisting in it. Third, a lawyer may be required to reveal the falsity of evidence or criminal or fraudulent activity related to a judicial proceeding to a court or tribunal.

Loyalty

A lawyer is prohibited from representing a client where the lawyer has conflicting interests. Such conflicts of interest may arise out of concurrent conflicts, former client conflicts, or imputed conflicts among members of a firm.

A lawyer has a concurrent conflict of interest if the representation of one client will be directly adverse to another client. A lawyer also has a concurrent conflict of interest if there is a significant risk that representing a client will be materially limited by obligations to another client, a former client, a third person, or personal interests. A lawyer cannot represent a client if the lawyer has a concurrent conflict of interest, without obtaining the client's informed consent. When permitted by the rules to seek consent, the lawyer must explain the risks involved in the representation as well as any alternatives—such as retaining other counsel.

A lawyer has a former conflict where the new representation would be materially adverse to the interests of the former client and the new matter is the same as, or is substantially related to, the matter for which the lawyer represented the former client. The purpose of this limitation is to ensure that the lawyer does not use the former client's confidential information in the new matter.

A lawyer may have an imputed conflict of interest as a result of actions taken by other lawyers in the same firm. The general rule is that concurrent conflicts and former client conflicts are imputed to all lawyers in the firm.

Termination of the Attorney-Client Relationship

Lawyers must withdraw, with the permission of the court if the matter is in litigation, if they are fired, are physically or mentally incapable of continuing representation, or if representation would violate the rules of professional responsibility. Lawyers are permitted to withdraw for a variety of reasons, including failure of the client to pay for legal services.

Duties to the Judicial System

Candor

As an officer of the court, a lawyer is prohibited from presenting evidence known to be false. A lawyer must discourage a client from committing perjury. If perjury takes place, it should be disclosed to the court or tribunal. In addition, lawyers have the obligation to cite legal authority to a court or tribunal. If there is adverse mandatory precedent on point, and opposing counsel does not cite it, the lawyer must do so.

Avoiding Frivolous Claims

A lawyer is prohibited from frivolously defending a proceeding or asserting or controverting an issue. It is permissible to assert a position that might currently be contrary to legal authorities, but it must be based on a good faith argument for a modification of existing law.

Impartiality

The rules also forbid lawyers from seeking to improperly persuade a judge or juror. Accordingly, any unauthorized ex parte conduct is forbidden. Ex parte conduct generally involves communications with a judge or juror without opposing counsel present.

Duties to Third Parties

Truthfulness

Lawyers are prohibited from making a false statement of material fact or law to a third person. However, negotiators from outside of the U.S. should be aware that these rules do not always apply to negotiations. In the U.S., negotiators may "huff and puff" or exaggerate. Statements regarding value or a party's intentions regarding settlement may not be found to be "statements of fact" covered by the duty of truthfulness. Negotiation is more fully discussed in Chapter 17.

Avoiding Contact with Represented Parties

A lawyer who knows that the opposing party is represented by counsel is prohibited from having contact with the party. The rule applies even where the opposing party initiates the contact. A lawyer contacted by a represented opposing party must terminate the conversation. Only the other party's lawyer has the authority to waive the rule.

Where the opposing party is an entity, such as a corporation, the rule is more complicated. The rule permits contact with all corporate personnel involved in a matter, except those: (1) who supervise, direct, or regularly consult with the entity's counsel, (2) who have the authority to obligate the organization, or (3) whose acts or omissions may be imputed to the organization for purposes of liability.

If the other party is not represented, a lawyer cannot imply disinterest. Further, a lawyer who has reason to believe that the unrepresented party misunderstands the lawyer's role must correct the misunderstanding.

Analyzing the Client's Legal Needs and Issues

Let us return to Mr. Mathews. Should you continue to represent him? Regardless of whether you continue to represent him, should you disclose his confession to the state bar?

First, recall the lawyer's ethical duty of confidentiality. With certain exceptions, the rules require lawyers to keep all information relating to the representation of a client confidential. This is particularly the case with Rule 1.6, reproduced below. Rule 8.3, also reproduced below, concerns professional misconduct. It provides that a lawyer who knows that another lawyer has committed a violation of the rules shall inform the appropriate authorities. Nevertheless, Rule 8.3(c) provides that the rule does not require disclosure of information otherwise protected by Rule 1.6. Hence, where the information of another lawyer's misconduct is obtained in the course of a confidential attorney-client relationship, the information may be protected from disclosure.

Nevertheless, if Mr. Mathews does actually lie under oath to the attorney grievance commission you may be required to report it. Rule 3.3, reproduced below, provides that an attorney may not permit fraud on a tribunal. This duty takes priority over a lawyer's duty of confidentiality to a client. Where a lawyer knows that a client has provided false testimony, the lawyer must take reasonable remedial measures, including disclosure of the perjury to the court or tribunal.

The best course of action is to urge Mr. Mathews to tell the truth at the hearing. Perjury is a serious criminal offense and will only increase his problems. You should remind him that while you may not be able to disclose his intention to commit perjury ahead of time, you will be obligated to report the perjury to the attorney grievance commission if in fact he testifies that commingling funds was an innocent mistake. For your own benefit, be aware that the failure to take action to remedy known perjury would violate Rule 1.2, reproduced below, which prohibits a lawyer from assisting a client in fraudulent conduct. Subornation of perjury is also a crime.

Sample Documents

Document 1
Select ABA Model Rules of Professional Conduct
abanet.org/cpr/mrpc/mrpc_toc.html

Client-Lawyer Relationship

Rule 1.1 Competence

A lawyer shall provide competent representation to a client. Competent representation requires the legal knowledge, skill, thoroughness and preparation reasonably necessary for the representation.

Rule 1.2 Scope Of Representation And Allocation Of Authority Between Client And Lawyer

(a) Subject to paragraphs (c) and (d), a lawyer shall abide by a client's decisions concerning the objectives of representation and, as required by Rule 1.4, shall consult with the client as to the means by which they are to be pursued. A lawyer may take such action on behalf of the client as is impliedly authorized to carry out the representation. A lawyer shall abide by a client's decision whether to settle a matter. In a criminal case, the lawyer shall abide by the client's decision, after consultation with the lawyer, as to a plea to be entered, whether to waive jury trial and whether the client will testify.

(b) A lawyer's representation of a client, including representation by appointment, does not constitute an endorsement of the client's political, economic, social or moral views or activities.

(c) A lawyer may limit the scope of the representation if the limitation is reasonable under the circumstances and the client gives informed consent.

(d) A lawyer shall not counsel a client to engage, or assist a client, in conduct that the lawyer knows is criminal or fraudulent, but a lawyer may discuss the legal consequences of any proposed course of conduct with a client and may counsel or assist a client to make a good faith effort to determine the validity, scope, meaning or application of the law.

Rule 1.3 Diligence

A lawyer shall act with reasonable diligence and promptness in representing a client.

Rule 1.4 Communication

(a) A lawyer shall:

(1) promptly inform the client of any decision or circumstance with respect to which the client's informed consent, as defined in Rule 1.0(e), is required by these Rules;

(2) reasonably consult with the client about the means by which the client's objectives are to be accomplished;

(3) keep the client reasonably informed about the status of the matter;

(4) promptly comply with reasonable requests for information; and

(5) consult with the client about any relevant limitation on the lawyer's conduct when the lawyer knows that the client expects assistance not permitted by the Rules of Professional Conduct or other law.

(b) A lawyer shall explain a matter to the extent reasonably necessary to permit the client to make informed decisions regarding the representation.

Rule 1.5 Fees

(a) A lawyer shall not make an agreement for, charge, or collect an unreasonable fee or an unreasonable amount for expenses. The factors to be considered in determining the reasonableness of a fee include the following:

(1) the time and labor required, the novelty and difficulty of the questions involved, and the skill requisite to perform the legal service properly;

(2) the likelihood, if apparent to the client, that the acceptance of the particular employment will preclude other employment by the lawyer;

(3) the fee customarily charged in the locality for similar legal services;

(4) the amount involved and the results obtained;

(5) the time limitations imposed by the client or by the circumstances;

(6) the nature and length of the professional relationship with the client;

(7) the experience, reputation, and ability of the lawyer or lawyers performing the services; and

(8) whether the fee is fixed or contingent.

(b) The scope of the representation and the basis or rate of the fee and expenses for which the client will be responsible shall be communicated to the client, preferably in writing, before or within a reasonable time after commencing the representation, except when the lawyer will charge a regularly represented client on the same basis or rate. Any changes in the basis or rate of the fee or expenses shall also be communicated to the client.

(c) A fee may be contingent on the outcome of the matter for which the service is rendered, except in a matter in which a contingent fee is prohibited by paragraph (d) or other law. A contingent fee agreement shall be in a writing signed by the client and shall state the method by which the fee is to be determined, including the percentage or percentages that shall accrue to the lawyer in the event of settlement, trial or appeal; litigation and other expenses to be deducted from the recovery; and whether such expenses are to be deducted before or after the contingent fee is calculated. The agreement must clearly notify the client of any expenses for which the client will be liable whether or not the client is the prevailing party. Upon conclusion of a contingent fee matter, the lawyer shall provide the client with a written statement stating the outcome of the matter and, if there is a recovery, showing the remittance to the client and the method of its determination.

(d) A lawyer shall not enter into an arrangement for, charge, or collect:

(1) any fee in a domestic relations matter, the payment or amount of which is contingent upon the securing of a divorce or upon the amount of alimony or support, or property settlement in lieu thereof; or

(2) a contingent fee for representing a defendant in a criminal case.

(e) A division of a fee between lawyers who are not in the same firm may be made only if:

(1) the division is in proportion to the services performed by each lawyer or each lawyer assumes joint responsibility for the representation;

(2) the client agrees to the arrangement, including the share each lawyer will receive, and the agreement is confirmed in writing; and

(3) the total fee is reasonable.

Rule 1.6 Confidentiality Of Information

(a) A lawyer shall not reveal information relating to the representation of a client unless the client gives informed consent, the disclosure is impliedly authorized in order to carry out the representation or the disclosure is permitted by paragraph (b).

(b) A lawyer may reveal information relating to the representation of a client to the extent the lawyer reasonably believes necessary:

(1) to prevent reasonably certain death or substantial bodily harm;

(2) to prevent the client from committing a crime or fraud that is reasonably certain to result in substantial injury to the financial interests or property of another and in furtherance of which the client has used or is using the lawyer's services;

(3) to prevent, mitigate or rectify substantial injury to the financial interests or property of another that is reasonably certain to result or has resulted from the client's commission of a crime or fraud in furtherance of which the client has used the lawyer's services;

(4) to secure legal advice about the lawyer's compliance with these Rules;

(5) to establish a claim or defense on behalf of the lawyer in a controversy between the lawyer and the client, to establish a defense to a criminal charge or civil claim against the lawyer based upon conduct in which the client was involved, or to respond to allegations in any proceeding concerning the lawyer's representation of the client;

(6) to comply with other law or a court order; or

(7) to detect and resolve conflicts of interest arising from the lawyer's change of employment or from changes in the composition or ownership of a firm, but only if the revealed information would not compromise the attorney-client privilege or otherwise prejudice the client.

(c) A lawyer shall make reasonable efforts to prevent the inadvertent or unauthorized disclosure of, or unauthorized access to, information relating to the representation of a client.

Rule 1.7 Conflict Of Interest: Current Clients

(a) Except as provided in paragraph (b), a lawyer shall not represent a client if the representation involves a concurrent conflict of interest. A concurrent conflict of interest exists if:

(1) the representation of one client will be directly adverse to another client; or

(2) there is a significant risk that the representation of one or more clients will be materially limited by the lawyer's responsibilities to another client, a former client or a third person or by a personal interest of the lawyer.

(b) Notwithstanding the existence of a concurrent conflict of interest under paragraph (a), a lawyer may represent a client if:

(1) the lawyer reasonably believes that the lawyer will be able to provide competent and diligent representation to each affected client;

(2) the representation is not prohibited by law;

(3) the representation does not involve the assertion of a claim by one client against another client represented by the lawyer in the same litigation or other proceeding before a tribunal; and

(4) each affected client gives informed consent, confirmed in writing.

***

Rule 1.9 Duties To Former Clients

(a) A lawyer who has formerly represented a client in a matter shall not thereafter represent another person in the same or a substantially related matter in which that person's interests are materially adverse to the interests of the former client unless the former client gives informed consent, confirmed in writing.

(b) A lawyer shall not knowingly represent a person in the same or a substantially related matter in which a firm with which the lawyer formerly was associated had previously represented a client:

(1) whose interests are materially adverse to that person; and

(2) about whom the lawyer had acquired information protected by Rules 1.6 and 1.9(c) that is material to the matter;

unless the former client gives informed consent, confirmed in writing.

(c) A lawyer who has formerly represented a client in a matter or whose present or former firm has formerly represented a client in a matter shall not thereafter:

(1) use information relating to the representation to the disadvantage of the former client except as these Rules would permit or require with respect to a client, or when the information has become generally known; or

(2) reveal information relating to the representation except as these Rules would permit or require with respect to a client.

Rule 1.16 Declining Or Terminating Representation

(a) Except as stated in paragraph (c), a lawyer shall not represent a client or, where representation has commenced, shall withdraw from the representation of a client if:

(1) the representation will result in violation of the rules of professional conduct or other law;

(2) the lawyer's physical or mental condition materially impairs the lawyer's ability to represent the client; or

(3) the lawyer is discharged.

(b) Except as stated in paragraph (c), a lawyer may withdraw from representing a client if:

(1) withdrawal can be accomplished without material adverse effect on the interests of the client;

(2) the client persists in a course of action involving the lawyer's services that the lawyer reasonably believes is criminal or fraudulent;

(3) the client has used the lawyer's services to perpetrate a crime or fraud;

(4) the client insists upon taking action that the lawyer considers repugnant or with which the lawyer has a fundamental disagreement;

(5) the client fails substantially to fulfill an obligation to the lawyer regarding the lawyer's services and has been given reasonable warning that the lawyer will withdraw unless the obligation is fulfilled;

(6) the representation will result in an unreasonable financial burden on the lawyer or has been rendered unreasonably difficult by the client; or

(7) other good cause for withdrawal exists.

(c) A lawyer must comply with applicable law requiring notice to or permission of a tribunal when terminating a representation. When ordered to do so by a tribunal, a lawyer shall continue representation notwithstanding good cause for terminating the representation.

(d) Upon termination of representation, a lawyer shall take steps to the extent reasonably practicable to protect a client's interests, such as giving reasonable notice to the client, allowing time for employment of other counsel, surrendering papers and property to which the client is entitled and refunding any advance payment of fee or expense that has not been earned or incurred. The lawyer may retain papers relating to the client to the extent permitted by other law.

Advocate

Rule 3.1 Meritorious Claims And Contentions

A lawyer shall not bring or defend a proceeding, or assert or controvert an issue therein, unless there is a basis in law and fact for doing so that is not frivolous, which includes a good faith argument for an extension, modification or reversal of existing law. A lawyer for the defendant in a criminal proceeding, or the respondent in a proceeding that could result in incarceration, may nevertheless so defend the proceeding as to require that every element of the case be established.

Rule 3.3 Candor Toward The Tribunal

(a) A lawyer shall not knowingly:

(1) make a false statement of fact or law to a tribunal or fail to correct a false statement of material fact or law previously made to the tribunal by the lawyer;

(2) fail to disclose to the tribunal legal authority in the controlling jurisdiction known to the lawyer to be directly adverse to the position of the client and not disclosed by opposing counsel; or

(3) offer evidence that the lawyer knows to be false. If a lawyer, the lawyer's client, or a witness called by the lawyer, has offered material evidence and the lawyer comes to know of its falsity, the lawyer shall take reasonable remedial measures, including, if necessary, disclosure to the tribunal. A lawyer may refuse to offer evidence, other than the testimony of a defendant in a criminal matter, that the lawyer reasonably believes is false.

(b) A lawyer who represents a client in an adjudicative proceeding and who knows that a person intends to engage, is engaging or has engaged in criminal or fraudulent conduct related to the proceeding shall take reasonable remedial measures, including, if necessary, disclosure to the tribunal.

(c) The duties stated in paragraphs (a) and (b) continue to the conclusion of the proceeding, and apply even if compliance requires disclosure of information otherwise protected by Rule 1.6.

(d) In an ex parte proceeding, a lawyer shall inform the tribunal of all material facts known to the lawyer that will enable the tribunal to make an informed decision, whether or not the facts are adverse.

Rule 3.4 Fairness To Opposing Party And Counsel

A lawyer shall not:

(a) unlawfully obstruct another party's access to evidence or unlawfully alter, destroy or conceal a document or other material having potential evidentiary value. A lawyer shall not counsel or assist another person to do any such act;

(b) falsify evidence, counsel or assist a witness to testify falsely, or offer an inducement to a witness that is prohibited by law;

(c) knowingly disobey an obligation under the rules of a tribunal except for an open refusal based on an assertion that no valid obligation exists;

(d) in pretrial procedure, make a frivolous discovery request or fail to make reasonably diligent effort to comply with a legally proper discovery request by an opposing party;

(e) in trial, allude to any matter that the lawyer does not reasonably believe is relevant or that will not be supported by admissible evidence, assert personal knowledge of facts in issue except when testifying as a witness, or state a personal opinion as to the justness of a cause, the credibility of a witness, the culpability of a civil litigant or the guilt or innocence of an accused; or

(f) request a person other than a client to refrain from voluntarily giving relevant information to another party unless:

(1) the person is a relative or an employee or other agent of a client; and

(2) the lawyer reasonably believes that the person's interests will not be adversely affected by refraining from giving such information.

Transactions With Persons Other Than Clients

Rule 4.1 Truthfulness In Statements To Others

In the course of representing a client a lawyer shall not knowingly:

(a) make a false statement of material fact or law to a third person; or

(b) fail to disclose a material fact to a third person when disclosure is necessary to avoid assisting a criminal or fraudulent act by a client, unless disclosure is prohibited by Rule 1.6.

Rule 4.2 Communication With Person Represented By Counsel

In representing a client, a lawyer shall not communicate about the subject of the representation with a person the lawyer knows to be represented by another lawyer in the matter, unless the lawyer has the consent of the other lawyer or is authorized to do so by law or a court order.

Rule 4.3 Dealing With Unrepresented Person

In dealing on behalf of a client with a person who is not represented by counsel, a lawyer shall not state or imply that the lawyer is disinterested. When the lawyer knows or reasonably should know that the unrepresented person misunderstands the lawyer's role in the matter, the lawyer shall make reasonable efforts to correct the misunderstanding. The lawyer shall not give legal advice to an unrepresented person, other than the advice to secure counsel, if the lawyer knows or reasonably should know that the interests of such a person are or have a reasonable possibility of being in conflict with the interests of the client.

***

Maintaining The Integrity Of The Profession

Rule 8.3 Reporting Professional Misconduct

(a) A lawyer who knows that another lawyer has committed a violation of the Rules of Professional Conduct that raises a substantial question as to that lawyer's honesty, trustworthiness or fitness as a lawyer in other respects, shall inform the appropriate professional authority.

(b) A lawyer who knows that a judge has committed a violation of applicable rules of judicial conduct that raises a substantial question as to the judge's fitness for office shall inform the appropriate authority.

(c) This Rule does not require disclosure of information otherwise protected by Rule 1.6 or information gained by a lawyer or judge while participating in an approved lawyers assistance program.

Chapter 9

Client Communication
and Problem Solving Skills

Highlights

- Lawyers in the U.S. should have effective interpersonal skills and be excellent problem solvers.
- Client communications must be clear; the use of overly complicated language should be avoided.
- Active listening and non-verbal communication let the client know the lawyer is listening and build trust.
- Effective questioning assists the lawyer in understanding and communicating the client's story.
- Lawyers in the U.S. engage in creative problem solving, including assessing a client's problem, evaluating options, assisting the client in choosing an option, and implementing the option.
- Cultural expectations affect client relationships, communication, and problem solving; lawyers must be aware of the cultural norms of their clients.

Introduction

Lawyers practicing in the U.S. assume a number of roles, including: (1) interviewing and counseling clients, (2) negotiating with opposing counsel and parties, (3) planning transactions and drafting agreements, (4) bringing and defending claims, and (5) selecting the forums for, and participating in, dispute resolution. Each role requires the application of a variety of interpersonal skills, such as trust building, verbal and nonverbal communication, and problem solving.

The defining feature of a lawyer trained and practicing in the U.S. is the ability to analyze the law for the specific purpose of solving a client's problems. One of the advantages of the common law system is its flexibility in accommodating developing legal concepts. Nevertheless, such flexibility may result in uncertainty. American lawyers must master diagnosing a client's legal problem, identifying options for resolving the problem, and assisting the client in choosing an option.

This chapter is divided into five sections: (1) trust, (2) nonverbal communication, (3) verbal communication, (4) problem solving, and (5) multicultural awareness.

The Client

As you read this chapter, consider how you might establish a relationship and work towards problem solving with two very different clients: Mr. Ahmed Al-Shirazi and Mr. Stephen Mathews.

We first met Mr. Al-Shirazi in Chapter 3. Mr. Al-Shirazi is a young man in his 20s who immigrated to the U.S. from Iraq as a teenager. He was recently "attacked" by Jeff Jones. Mr. Jones chased him with a stick and threatened to "bash his head in." Mr. Al-Shirazi has been unable to eat, sleep, or leave his home without fear since the incident. He wants our firm to sue Mr. Jones for the mental anguish he has suffered.

We first met Mr. Mathews in Chapter 8. Mr. Mathews is a lawyer with an American law firm. He was born and raised in the U.S., by American parents, and attended the University of Michigan for undergraduate and law school. He has been charged by the attorney grievance commission for the state bar with commingling client funds and wants our firm to represent him in his disciplinary hearing.

How will you approach each client? How will their cultural differences impact your approach?

The Importance of Trust

Building Trust

Absent trust, it is unlikely clients will confide in, or listen to, their lawyers. Lawyers in the U.S. seek to foster client confidence, as well as maintain a positive working relationship. A client should have confidence in the lawyer's ability to solve legal problems. A client should also believe that the lawyer will maintain confidences, consider the client's interests paramount, and work diligently on the client's behalf. Finally, a client should feel sufficiently comfortable with the lawyer to confide sensitive information.

Encouraging Communication

Periodic communication is crucial in obtaining a client's trust and generating goodwill. Client communications in the U.S. are expected to be open and accurate. A lawyer should avoid technical legal terms. A lawyer should also remember the duty, discussed in Chapter 8, to deliver negative, as well as positive, news. A client is much more likely to develop trust in a lawyer who regularly communicates in a straightforward manner.

Active listening is equally important to building trust. The client must believe that the lawyer understands what is being communicated. Eye contact, nods, and other nonverbal signs of active listening build trust. Nonverbal and verbal communication skills are discussed below.

Providing Reassurance

Competency and empathy also build trust. A lawyer demonstrates competence to a client by accurately explaining the relevant law, discussing experiences with similar types of legal problems, and brainstorming solutions to the client's problems. A lawyer demonstrates empathy by acknowledging and accepting the client's emotions.

Maintaining Confidentiality

Finally, client confidentiality is essential to maintaining trust. Explaining confidentiality may reassure a client concerned about disclosing sensitive information. Further, as discussed in Chapter 8, disclosure of a client confidence is a breach of the rules of professional responsibility and threatens the attorney-client privilege. Lawyers should avoid discussing client problems with third parties, in public, or via electronic communications.

Nonverbal Communication

Various forms of nonverbal communication play an important role in building client relationships. Forms of nonverbal communication important to practicing law in the U.S. include: (1) spatial relationships, (2) body language, and (3) vocal characteristics such as pace, pitch, and tone.

Spatial Relationships

The appearance of a lawyer's office may impact a client's perception of professional competence. The office should be organized. Further, it should provide for several seating arrangements. A lawyer may wish to sit behind the desk, when it is imperative to establish authority. Alternatively, a lawyer may wish to sit next to a client, when it is important to convey empathy. The appropriate distance between a lawyer and a client will vary. Americans generally prefer an intermediate distance. An extended distance may be seen as negative, indicating dislike. Conversely, a lawyer who sits too close may be perceived as threatening. Americans typically prefer some degree of personal space.

Body Language

Lawyers everywhere communicate through body language. Facial expressions are the most important. In the U.S., it is crucial to maintain eye contact to signal respect and attentiveness. Avoiding eye contact is viewed negatively, indicating indifference or deceit.

Messages from body movements are more subtle than facial expressions; nevertheless, they are generally perceived in a consistent manner by Americans. Leaning the entire body forward, toward the speaker, conveys attentiveness. A backward lean implies indifference or rejection. Arms in an open position communicates acceptance. Arms closed in upon the chest suggest rejection. American posture tends to be informal, but slouching—in a standing or seated position—may be perceived as disrespectful.

Vocal Characteristics

A lawyer must be aware of speech patterns to communicate effectively. A lawyer's pace, pitch, and tone impact client perceptions. Pace—or the speed at which one speaks—is particularly important in interviewing and counseling, discussed in Chapters 10 and 11. A measured pace encourages a thoughtful discussion. A rapid pace discourages the sharing of information. Pitch is related to pace. High pitch accompanies fast pace and suggests anxiety. Low pitch accompanies slow pace and is perceived as calming. Tone includes word emphasis and voice quality. A varied tonal pattern, connoting interest and enthusiasm, is preferred. Gruff or bland patterns are negatively perceived.

Most nonverbal communication operates on a subconscious level. A lawyer's verbal communication is most effective when it is consistent with nonverbal messages.

Hidden Dynamics

Closely related to nonverbal communication skills is the skill of managing hidden dynamics. Hidden dynamics include inhibitors, facilitators, and encouragers.

Inhibitors prevent clients from sharing information with their lawyers. Clients may feel inhibited by cultural, social, age, or language differences and be reluctant to provide information that might undermine their case or be embarrassing. Clients may withhold information which they believe will lead their lawyer to evaluate them in a negative manner, prove detrimental to their case, conflict with what is perceived as appropriate client behavior, or prove to be irrelevant to their legal problem. Certain clients may also be reluctant to share information with members of different genders, races, or cultures.

Facilitators aid a client in communicating information. Facilitative techniques, such as demonstrating empathy and respect, assist clients in sharing concerns. Similar to facilitators, encouragers act to put clients at ease. Encouragers validate a client's story and reduce a client's discomfort. There are several important facilitative and encouraging techniques. The first is empathy. Empathy includes acknowledging the client's feelings. For example, using nonverbal cues such as nodding and verbal cues such as "I see." The second is recognition. Recognition motivates a client to be more open and cooperative. For example: "Thank you for giving me such important information." The third is known as "expectations" or "rewards." By conveying an expectation that the information sought is necessary and that sharing the information is in the client's best interest, a lawyer may overcome inhibitors.

Listening

The ability to listen is crucial to developing a relationship with the client, as well as in evaluating a client's legal concerns. Active, rather than passive, listening encourages the client to talk. In addition to being aware of body language and the hidden dynamics discussed above, the lawyer should consider the meaning the client is ascribing to words, as well as the cultural and legal implications raised by the words. Active listening involves minimal verbal interruptions. The lawyer then reassures the client that the story has been understood, by summarizing key points.

Verbal Communication

The use of language is important in attorney-client communications. In the U.S., there is an ongoing effort to avoid overly technical or unnecessary legal language in all communications. In addition, vocabulary is adapted to the needs, education, and experience of the client. Beyond these basic communication concerns, lawyers consider the importance of immediacy, scene setting, and effective questioning.

Immediacy

Immediate messages are generally viewed more positively; the level of immediacy in a particular communication depends on a number of factors. The first factor is the medium of the communication. Face to face communication is the most immediate, followed by telephone conversations, email, and letters. Other factors include the use of present tense, active voice, and short sentences with a subject-verb-object construction.

Effective Scene Setting and Storytelling

Words create a scene in the listener's mind. The more descriptive the words, the easier it is for the listener to empathize with the client's viewpoint. Storytelling provides a similar advantage. Persuasive stories involve compelling characters and storylines. For a lawyer, the audience includes opposing counsel and parties, the judge and jury, and the client. American lawyers "discover" the story from the facts and present it in a persuasive manner.

Effective Questioning

Lawyers in the U.S. are constantly asking questions. As discussed above, when initially interviewing clients it is important to utilize active listening skills before beginning actual questioning. In other situations, however, the lawyer may begin asking questions immediately.

Effective questioning depends on the audience, but several guidelines control. First, preparation is crucial. Second, consideration must be given to the appropriate time to ask broad versus narrow questions. A broad, or open, question invites the client to prioritize and elaborate on the information. A narrow, or closed, question elicits specific information. Third, follow-up questions generated by the client's answers tend to provide the most precise information.

When meeting with a client, lawyers will usually begin with open questions, followed by closed questions. Open questions allow a client to select the words in which to tell the story. They overcome inhibitors by allowing the client to discuss sensitive information; they promote completeness by respecting the client's thought patterns. For example: "What happened next?"

Closed questions focus on specific topics and allow the lawyer to control the flow of information. As a result, they are often more effective for obtaining complete information. Nevertheless, closed questions provide less of an opportunity for the lawyer to express empathy and other facilitators. Hence, they are generally used as a follow-up to open questions. "Yes-No" questions are the ultimate example of closed questions.

Problem Solving

Providing legal advice in the U.S. or to American clients requires a lawyer to be a creative problem solver. This goes beyond the process of applying a client's facts to a statute and reaching an "answer." Problem solving involves assessing the client's legal problems, evaluating various options for resolving the problems, assisting the client in choosing an option, and taking action on the option.

Assessment involves the client and lawyer working together to identify the legal problems. Identification of the legal issues frames the relationship between the lawyer and the client. It also involves the lawyer advising the client which problems have a potential legal solution and which do not. Evaluating options requires the lawyer to provide the client with an analysis of the advantages, costs, risks, and chances of success of each potential solution. Lawyers are also expected to provide information about fees and the time involved in implementing the solutions.

After the options are explained and evaluated, the rules of professional responsibility discussed in Chapter 8 require the client to make all controlling decisions. Clients consider both the legal and non-legal aspects of any decision. In the U.S., such factors may include business, financial, political, and personal concerns. After the client has chosen an option, it is the responsibility of the lawyer to implement it. In addition to the legal responsibilities of interviewing, counseling, negotiating, planning transactions, drafting documents, bringing and defending claims, and participating in dispute resolution, a lawyer has an obligation to keep the client informed and to regularly consult with the client on the progress made in resolving the legal issues.

Multicultural Considerations

Cultural expectations affect many aspects of client relationships, communication, and problem solving. A few of the potential areas of misunderstanding are discussed below. It is important for lawyers from all cultures to be aware of the cultural norms of their clients and the systems in which they choose to practice.

Conflict

Cultures have a broad range of attitudes toward conflict. In many cultures, public conflict is considered undesirable. Individuals in such cultures often prefer to suffer a loss, rather than bring attention to it. This is particularly true if the person responsible for the loss enjoys higher status. Conversely, in the U.S., conflict tends to be viewed as productive. It is socially acceptable to complain when something goes wrong. Hence, more matters are considered appropriate for legal resolution in the U.S. than in other countries. Further, legal disputes in the U.S. are resolved through procedures other cultures may consider overly adversarial.

Importance of Formality

In many cultures, authority figures such as lawyers are given a high degree of respect and deference. In such cultures informality, such as the use of a first name, is construed as disrespect. In the U.S., even professional relationships are informal.

Verbal and Nonverbal Communication

Many cultures are high-context. Words and body language are chosen to imply messages that are not spoken. In the U.S., a low-context culture, a relatively high proportion of what one communicates is expressed in words.

Expressions of Emotion

In many cultures, it is unacceptable to discuss emotions about personal matters except with family or friends. Discussions about feelings or overt expressions of sympathy may be offensive; empathy is expressed by changes in tone of voice or facial expression. Conversely, Americans tend to discuss their emotions frequently and spontaneously. Public displays of emotion are not uncommon.

Individualism and Collectivism

In many cultures, individuals make decisions based on what is best for their family, a group, or society collectively. In other cultures, a group reaches a consensus and decides for the individual, usually on the basis of the group's needs. In the U.S., individualism is highly valued. Individuals are not disparaged for reaching decisions based on what is in their own best interests.

Analyzing the Client's Legal Needs and Issues

Let us return to Mr. Al-Shirazi and Mr. Mathews. How will you approach each client? How will their cultural differences impact your approach?

First, remember the importance of establishing trust with the client. In both cases, it will be crucial to effective communication and problem solving. Nevertheless, your approach may vary. For instance, with Mr. Mathews it is probably best to sit behind the desk to establish authority. Conversely, it may be most effective to sit next to Mr. Al-Shirazi to communicate empathy. We know that eye contact will be important to Mr. Mathews. Perhaps a more indirect approach, indicating respect, may be effective with Mr. Al-Shirazi. In both cases, of course, you will want your posture, vocal patterns, and active listening skills to reflect interest and attentiveness.

Mr. Al-Shirazi and Mr. Mathews will undoubtedly have differing views on conflict, expressions of emotion, and the importance of formality. They will also most likely respond differently to verbal and nonverbal cues. You should be aware of these differences as you interact and attempt to establish a rapport.

With respect to problem solving, the goal is to identify and evaluate the options for resolving the client's legal problems and assist the client in choosing an option. In Chapter 8, we discussed the options available to Mr. Mathews for resolving his legal problem concerning the commingling of client funds. Mr. Al-Shirazi would have at least three options with respect to his wish to sue Mr. Jones: litigation, alternative dispute resolution, or forgoing legal process. As a practical matter, problem solving most often takes place during client counseling sessions. In Chapter 11, on client counseling, we will discuss the options of litigation, alternative dispute resolution, or forgoing legal process in the context of counseling another of our clients.

Checklists for client communications and problem solving, as well as a problem solving decision tree, are included in the sample documents below.

Sample Documents

Document 1
Problem Solving Checklist

Assess the legal problem

- Identify the nature of the problem
- Formulate questions
- Gather information
- Organize and summarize the information
- Define the desired objectives

Evaluate the options

- Use the information gathered
- Break the problem down into manageable parts
- Brainstorm and use other techniques to generate options
- Analyze the options
- Identify steps of each option necessary to achieve desired objectives

Assist the client in decision-making

- Decide on possible options for action
- Decide on any further information necessary to effectuate each option
- Decide on resources necessary to effectuate each option
- Assist the client in choosing an option

Take action to resolve the legal problem

- Implement action on the option chosen by the client
- Provide information to the client on an ongoing basis
- Meet regularly with the client to evaluate progress on resolving the problem

Note that at any stage of this process, it may be necessary to return to an earlier stage.

Document 2
Communication Checklist

Goals

- ▶ Identify the legal problem from the client's perspective
- ▶ Actively listen to the client's concerns and acknowledge the client's feelings
- ▶ Provide information and advice that address the client's goals and objectives
- ▶ Actively involve the client in the process of brainstorming and evaluating solutions
- ▶ Assist the client in making all decisions which are likely to have a substantial impact, whether legal or non-legal

Skills

Preparation

- Identify objectives
- Choose an appropriate communication format

Procedures

- Present options
- Be responsive

Psychological

- Build trust
- Deliver negative as well as positive news
- Exhibit respect

Cultural

- Understand the client's identity, culture, language, and background
- Use appropriate vocabulary
- Explain terms
- Translate complex concepts in various ways

Verbal

- Model immediacy in communications
- Utilize storytelling and scene setting techniques
- Employ effective questioning

Nonverbal

- Employ active listening
- Understand spatial relationships
- Utilize appropriate body language
- Control vocal characteristics
- Monitor hidden dynamics

Best Practices

▶ Ensure the confidentiality of oral and written communications

▶ Provide the client with sufficient explanations to permit intelligent participation in the decision making process

▶ Advise the client of all aspects of the case including potential risks, benefits, and probable outcomes

▶ Obtain informed decisions from the client

▶ Maintain ongoing communication with the client and inform the client of significant developments in the case

▶ Maintain case files that document and summarize all communications with the client

Document 3
Problem Solving Decision Tree

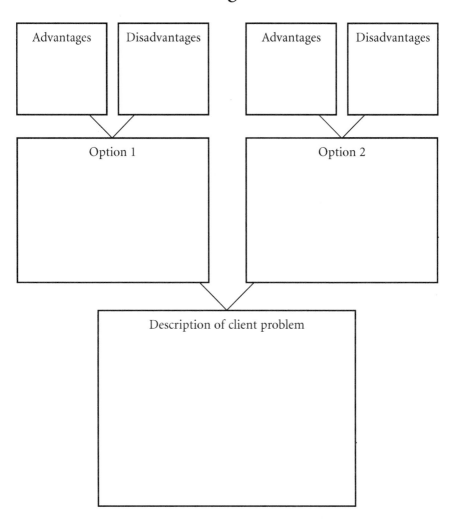

Part Five

Practice Skills: Interviewing and Counseling

Chapter 10

Client Interviewing

Highlights

- The interviewing process involves welcoming the client, obtaining a description of the problem, establishing an overview of the problem, verifying legal theories, and clarifying goals.
- In obtaining a description of the problem, the lawyer asks the client for a chronological description of events utilizing open questions.
- In establishing an overview of the problem, the lawyer utilizes closed questions to flesh out the details and explore inconsistencies in the client's story.
- In verifying legal theories, the lawyer checks the client's recollection of the facts against the legal elements.
- In clarifying goals, the lawyer and client agree on objectives for resolving the client's problem and set an agenda.

Introduction

In the U.S., a lawyer has two goals in interviewing a client. The first goal is to establish a comfortable relationship with the client. The second is to elicit the relevant facts.

Preparation prior to the interview is crucial. The interviewing process itself can be viewed as having five stages: (1) the introduction, (2) obtaining a description of the problem, (3) establishing an overview of the problem, (4) verifying the legal theories, and (5) clarifying goals and setting an agenda. In conjunction with, or immediately following the interview, counsel should prepare a written agreement regarding representation and fees and a memorandum to the file memorializing the interview.

This chapter covers initial client interviews in four sections: (1) preparation, (2) the interview, (3) written agreements regarding representation and fees, and (4) post-interview memoranda. Chapter 11 covers client counseling sessions.

The Client

Consider our firm's potential clients, Dr. Raphael Sosa and his son Candido, as you read this chapter. Dr. Sosa and his son wish to sue Javier Sanchez. Sanchez is Dr. Sosa's brother-in-law and Candido's uncle. Dr. Sosa is a 38-year-old dentist, temporarily residing in Miami, Florida, but permanently residing in Havana, Cuba. Candido is twelve years old. Javier is a 50-year-old surgeon permanently residing in Miami, Florida.

Last spring, Dr. Sosa's wife drowned while attempting to cross the Florida Straits from Cuba to the U.S. with Candido. Candido was rescued and brought to Miami. Dr. Sosa and his wife had been separated for two years. Candido lived with his mother, but visited his father regularly. In Miami, Candido was placed in the custody of his Uncle Javier.

In late July, Dr. Sosa was granted permission to come to Miami to retrieve Candido. Javier, however, refused to surrender Candido to his father for the reason that Dr. Sosa planned to return to Cuba with his son. According to Candido, Javier repeatedly told him, "Your father wants to take you back to Cuba, where the people are government slaves with no freedom. Your father is a communist who doesn't care about you. He doesn't want you to be free. Your Aunt Sara and I care about you and won't let that happen. Tell him you won't go with him. You will have a better, freer life here." After an extended hearing process, a court order was issued by the Immigration and Naturalization Service requiring Javier to surrender Candido. Candido was ultimately returned to his father.

Since summer, Candido has suffered extreme anxiety, is withdrawn, has trouble sleeping, and has lost weight. Neither medical treatment nor psychiatric counseling have eliminated these problems. Dr. Mehmet, his psychiatrist, believes that these problems were caused at least in part by Javier's statements to Candido about his father. Dr. Sosa is considering bringing a claim against Javier for Candido's mental distress.

Candido and Dr. Sosa have remained in the U.S. to seek medical and psychiatric care for Candido and to resolve various legal issues. What do you need to know to complete a client interview of Dr. Sosa and his son?

Preparation

It is important for the lawyer to prepare as much as possible before meeting the client. The lawyer, or an associate, will have spoken to the client to arrange the time and place for the first meeting. During this conversation, the client should be asked about legal concerns. Prior to the interview, the lawyer should review available information about the client, review cases, statutes, or other information about the client's legal concerns, and outline the topics that should be covered during the meeting.

Many lawyers will first search electronically for information about the client. Reviewing information about the client should prompt the lawyer to run a preliminary check for conflicts of interest with prior clients of the firm. As discussed in Chapter 8, it is a violation of the ethical rules to represent clients with conflicting interests. Conflict checks are discussed in Chapter 18.

Reviewing information about the client's legal concerns requires the lawyer to briefly research the basic elements of the transaction or the legal claim or defense. Once information has been obtained about the client's needs, the lawyer should begin to outline the legal topics to be discussed during the counseling session. The lawyer may want to outline other issues to be covered during the interview, such as confidentiality.

The lawyer should also consider the location of the meeting. Generally the meeting will take place in the lawyer's office to promote privacy and limit interruptions. Meetings may be held at the client's office, if the availability of documents is an issue. Wherever the meeting takes place, the lawyer should take care to limit attendance to preserve the attorney-client privilege discussed in Chapter 8.

The Interview

Overview of the Process

Following preparation, the lawyer is ready to interview the client. A primary goal of the interview is to form an attorney-client relationship. The nature of this relationship has several levels. First, it is personal: the lawyer and client learn more about each other and begin to develop a level of trust. Second, it is professional: the lawyer learns about the client's goals and preferred methods of accomplishing those goals. Third, it is contractual: the lawyer agrees to perform specified legal services and the client agrees to pay. A secondary goal of the interview is to learn as much as possible about the facts. There may be facts that the client has correctly perceived as relevant. There will also be facts not perceived as relevant but important, as well as facts perceived as important but not legally dispositive.

The interviewing process may be broken down into five stages. Stage one involves welcoming the client. The lawyer may also touch on the confidentiality of the discussion, discussed in Chapter 8, and the fees for legal services, discussed in Chapter 18. During stage two, the lawyer invites the client to tell his story. The lawyer will begin with open-ended questions, discussed in Chapter 9, to encourage the client to describe the problem and the preferred solution. During stage three, the lawyer will provide an overview of the problem. The lawyer will review the scenario described by the client, asking questions to establish the chronology and legally relevant facts. During stage four, the lawyer will use narrow questions, discussed in Chapter 9, to confirm those facts that will assist in forming possible legal solutions to the client's problems. During stage five, the lawyer will discuss goals and objectives, receive directions from the client, and finalize the next steps to be taken.

Beginning the Interview

It is customary for lawyers in the U.S. to spend some time getting to know the client, prior to beginning the interview. The lawyer or an assistant will meet the client at the door. As noted in Chapter 9, the seating arrangements should be conducive to an effective meeting and the lawyer's office and behavior should communicate professionalism. The client's name should be used frequently during the interview. It is customary for a lawyer to begin on a surname basis as a sign of respect. Frequent use of the client's name builds trust.

The lawyer should request the client's permission before beginning to take notes. Also, while taking notes, the lawyer must remember the importance of eye contact and active listening, discussed in Chapter 9. Effective lawyers take minimal notes while the client is telling the story and fill in the missing information as the client answers questions. Alternatively, a second lawyer may be invited to attend the interview and take notes.

It is not customary in the U.S. to record interviews or to invite non-attorneys to sit in on the interview, due to the need to protect confidentiality and the attorney-client privilege. Explaining confidentiality and the privilege at the beginning of the interview encourages the client to be more candid in describing the facts and answering questions. Lawyers also often take advantage of the beginning of the interview to discuss the firm's fee structure.

Obtaining a Description of the Problem

After putting the client at ease and explaining confidentiality and fees, the lawyer will encourage the client to describe the problem. A skilled lawyer will use open-ended questions and the active listening skills described in Chapter 9. For example, an effective beginning might be: "Tell me about the problem that brought you here today." Active listening, with minimal interruptions, assures the client that the lawyer is listening and allows the lawyer to view the problem from the client's perspective.

Most lawyers will ask the client to give a chronological description of events. The lawyer will assist the client by using neutral prompts that move the story forward without suggesting content. For example: "Please go on." Nonverbal prompts include a nod of the head and eye contact.

The primary goal of the lawyer during this stage is to learn about the facts from the client's perspective. Nevertheless, the lawyer must listen to the facts with a view towards the specific legal areas of inquiry necessary to resolve the client's problem.

Establishing an Overview of the Problem

Generally, the client will not be familiar with the law. The client may focus on subjects of little legal relevance and omit items of importance. Establishing an overview of the problem requires the lawyer to move to closed questions to organize the client's description of the facts. During this portion of the interview, it is important for the lawyer to consider not only the client's case and point of view, but also the perspective from the opposing side. The lawyer must explore inconsistencies in the client's story in order to evaluate the case.

As described in Chapter 9, closed questions ask the client to supply more detailed information. A common example of a closed question involves establishing a time line. If the client does not supply critical dates, the lawyer must ask for the information. Questions that contain a suggestion about the content, commonly known as "directive prompts," may also be used. Directive prompts should be used sparingly, however, to avoid encouraging clients to fabricate facts.

Verifying Legal Theories

The next step in the interview is to elicit facts confirming possible legal theories. The lawyer's pre-interview preparation should provide a list of the elements for each relevant theory. At this stage of the interview, the lawyer will ask questions designed to establish the validity of each element.

Recapping is a tool frequently used by lawyers in this portion of the interview. The lawyer briefly summarizes the client's recitation of the facts as refined by closed questioning. Recapping allows the client the opportunity to clear up any misunderstandings. It is also an opportunity for the lawyer to signal empathetic understanding of the client's problem. Generally, the lawyer will recap the entire narrative once the client has finished; however, if the client narrative is complex, the lawyer may recap the facts surrounding each legal topic separately.

Where a client experiences difficulty in remembering specifics, the lawyer may assist the client's memory by setting the scene, triggering detail, and providing other sources. In setting the scene, visual images are used to encourage the client to recall details about the physical setting of the event. Alternatively, a lawyer may ask the client to remember one specific detail. Finally, information from other sources may be used to refresh a client's memory. Caution should be used in reviewing private documents to refresh a client's memory, however, because in the U.S. such documents may be subject to production during discovery.

Clarifying Goals

From the initial interview through the termination of the attorney-client relationship, a lawyer must understand the client's goals. The client's lawful goals must guide the lawyer's actions.

It is the lawyer's responsibility to elicit goals from the client. A client will have immediate goals concerning the outcome of the legal problem. Sometimes the client may define the immediate goal narrowly, such as financial concerns. Other times a goal may be defined broadly, such as a desire for justice. In addition to the client's immediate goals, the client may also have overarching goals outside of the purview of the immediate case or transaction. Understanding a client's overarching goals assists a lawyer in developing a strategy for achieving immediate goals that further, or at least do not conflict with, the client's overarching goals. Understanding the client's overarching goals also assists a lawyer in building a relationship with the client.

It is the lawyer's responsibility to remember that direction must be sought frequently, not just at the client interview. Clients' goals change throughout the attorney-client relationship. As discussed in Chapter 8, the lawyer cannot follow directions that would violate the law or the rules of professional responsibility. The lawyer may also have a responsibility to alert the client if the overarching goals are inconsistent with the immediate goals or if the immediate goals are unrealistic.

At the end of the interview, the lawyer should provide the client with the next steps. The terms of the relationship should be agreed to and the next meeting should be arranged. The lawyer should inform the client about the legal work that will be done before the next meeting. It may be premature for the lawyer to give the client a complete description of the legal options; nevertheless, the lawyer may wish to provide a preliminary legal assessment of the client's problem. Finally, the common courtesies that were exhibited at the beginning of the interview should be utilized by the lawyer to close the interview.

A Note on Interviewing Transactional Clients

The nature of the interview may vary if the client's legal problem is transactional rather than litigation based. When interviewing a client about a pending transaction, lawyers start from the business deal; the terms of the deal form the "problem." Interviewing and counseling the transactional client is discussed in Chapter 14.

Agreements Regarding Representation and Fees

Prior to ending the interview, the lawyer will explain the fee structure, practical limitations of the legal representation, and the other terms of the agreement between the lawyer and the client. At the end of the interview, assuming the client chooses to retain the lawyer, the lawyer should have the client agree to an engagement letter. In certain instances, the engagement letter may be prepared in advance and executed by the client at the interview. In many situations, however, the letter cannot be adequately completed until the information from the initial interview is obtained. In these situations, the lawyer prepares a letter immediately following the interview and forwards it to the client for signature and return via overnight mail. The issue of fees and the content of engagement and non-engagement letters are discussed more fully in Chapter 18.

Post-Interview Memoranda

Following the client interview, lawyers in the U.S. compose a memo to the file. The memo will briefly summarize: (1) the identity of the client and the nature of the problem, (2) the client's stated goals, (3) the factual information provided by the client, (4) the legal information provided by the lawyer, (5) the agreed upon next steps, and (6) the lawyer's preliminary assessment of the case.

Analyzing the Client's Legal Needs and Issues

Let us return to Raphael Sosa and his son. What course will your interview take?

First, research the factual information regarding your client. It is unlikely Dr. Sosa will have a professional website in the U.S., but if you perform an internet search you may find reports about his wife's death and his legal fight to gain custody of his son. Second, consider the various types of verbal and nonverbal communication discussed in Chapter 9 that might be most effective with Dr. Sosa and his son. Third, perform preliminary research on Dr. Sosa's possible legal claims. Fourth, complete your preparation by running the conflicts check and making an interview checklist. A general interview checklist is provided in the sample documents below.

You or your assistant should greet Dr. Sosa at the door. You will want to refer to him by his surname, at least initially, and request his permission to take notes. Explain the requirements of attorney-client confidentiality, so that he is at ease in telling his story but also aware that he must be careful what he reveals to third parties.

Then encourage both Dr. Sosa and his son to "tell what happened" in their own words. Exhibit the verbal and nonverbal communication skills that build trust: nod frequently, keep your arms uncrossed, lean forward, maintain a respectful degree of eye contact, and utilize neutral prompts such as "tell me more."

After Dr. Sosa and Candido have told the story in their own words, begin to ask closed questions to obtain a chronological, step-by-step narrative of the events giving rise to the problem. For instance, you may want to question both clients to establish exactly what comments were made, when they were made, and how Candido felt about them at the time.

Your next step is to establish the validity of each of the elements of the legal claim. From your research, you know that a cause of action for mental distress exists in Florida when a person's conduct exceeds all bounds which could be tolerated by society, is calculated to cause severe emotional distress to a person of ordinary sensibilities, and causes severe emotional distress to such person. You should ask questions designed to elicit facts supporting each element; then recap, or summarize, what they have said and seek their feedback.

Further, you will need to clarify Dr. Sosa's goals. Does he wish to recover money damages only for Candido's medical and psychiatric care? Does he have punitive or other goals in mind? Has he considered how his lawsuit may affect his son?

Finally, you will need to discuss next steps and payment. It is likely you will need to do additional research on the claim of mental distress and available remedies in this case. You may also want to review Candido's medical and psychiatric bills and speak to his doctors. You should obtain Dr. Sosa's consent to this course of action and set a date for a follow up meeting. You should discuss representation and fees and advise Dr. Sosa that you will be submitting an engagement letter which he will need to sign and return.

After the meeting, you should prepare a memo to the file. A sample file memorandum summarizing the interview is included below.

Sample Documents

Document 1
Interview Checklist

Beginning the interview

- Put the client at ease and begin building a relationship
  - Maintain open body language and eye contact
  - Utilize active listening
  - Use other verbal and nonverbal cues to facilitate communication
- Explain note taking
- Discuss confidentiality
- Discuss fee structure

Obtaining a description of the problem

- Obtain a general description of the client's problems, concerns, and proposed solutions
- Utilize open ended questions
- Encourage the client to proceed chronologically
- Learn about the facts from the client's perspective

Establishing an overview of the problem

- Use closed questioning to create a chronological narrative of the events
- Ask for clarification where needed
- Discourage excessive or irrelevant detail
- Empathize with the client

Verifying legal theories

- Explore specific topics to develop legal theories
- Gather data to prove theory elements
- Use appropriate techniques to refresh memory
- Recap frequently
- Stay on task, avoid being sidetracked by the client

Clarifying goals

- Summarize important points of the meeting
- Clarify client goals
- If appropriate, provide preliminary assessment
- Establish an agenda for next steps; clarify client and lawyer responsibilities
- Arrange for signing of engagement letter
- Decide on date of next meeting

Document 2
Memorandum to the File

[Firm Stationery]

MEMORANDUM

TO: File
FROM: Associate
DATE: September __, 20__
RE: First Interview of Raphael Sosa and his son, Candido.

Attorney Work Product

At 9:00 a.m. this morning, I met with the firm's new clients: Raphael Sosa and his son, Candido. Raphael and his son wish to sue Javier Sanchez. Sanchez is Raphael's brother-in-law and Candido's uncle. Raphael is a 38-year-old dentist, temporarily residing in Miami, Florida but permanently residing in Havana, Cuba. Candido is twelve years old. Javier is a 50-year-old surgeon permanently residing in Miami, Florida. The interview was conducted in English, in which both Raphael and Candido are fluent.

Raphael came to our firm because he is very concerned about Candido. Since last summer, Candido has suffered extreme anxiety, is withdrawn and reticent around him, and has lost weight. Candido also has trouble sleeping. When he does sleep, he awakens screaming. Candido has stated, and repeated to me, that he has nightmares that his father is suffocating him. Psychiatric counseling for Candido has not eliminated these problems. A letter from Dr. Mehmet, which Raphael provided, states that as a psychiatrist he believes that these problems were caused at least in part by Javier's statements to Candido about his father.

As Raphael describes the facts, last spring on May 1, 20__, Raphael's wife was lost at sea while attempting to cross the Florida Straits from Cuba to the U.S. with Candido. Candido was rescued and brought to Miami, Florida. Raphael and his wife had been separated for two years at the time. Candido had lived with his mother, although he visited his father regularly. In Miami, Candido was placed in the custody of his Uncle Javier.

In late July, Raphael was granted permission to come to Miami to retrieve Candido. Javier refused to give up custody. After an extended hearing process, a court order was issued requiring Javier to surrender Candido to the Immigration and Naturalization Service to be returned to his father.

Prior to the issuance of the order, Javier had repeatedly ignored requests from the Immigration and Naturalization Service to surrender Candido to his father. The reason given for his refusal was that Raphael planned to return to Cuba with his son.

According to Candido, during this time Javier repeatedly told him, "Your father wants to take you back to Cuba, where the people are government slaves with no freedom. Your father is a communist who doesn't care about you. He doesn't want you to be free. Your Aunt Sara and I care about you and won't let that happen. Tell him you won't go with him. You will have a better, freer life here."

Candido was eventually returned to his father. He continues to have physical and psychiatric problems requiring professional care. They have remained in the U.S. to provide Candido with the best care and to resolve the pending legal issues.

Raphael is professional and well-spoken. Candido is fragile and appears younger than twelve. He cried throughout the interview.

Following my inquiry into the facts, I asked Raphael about his goals in bringing suit against Javier. He inquired whether he can make a valid claim against Javier for Candido's emotional distress and his psychiatric and medical expenses.

I told Raphael that, depending on the results of my research, I could represent him as representative of his minor son against Javier. I explained that one possible theory of recovery would be intentional infliction of emotional distress. I explained to Raphael that we would have to prove certain things. We would need to convince the court that Javier's conduct exceeded all bounds which could be tolerated by society, was calculated to cause severe emotional distress to a person of ordinary sensibilities, and did cause severe emotional distress to such a person. I told Raphael that these are difficult elements to prove and that we may have trouble with some of them.

We set up a meeting for next Monday. I said I would do some more research on the cases in Florida concerning intentional infliction of emotional distress. I asked Raphael to collect and bring in all of Candido's medical and psychiatric bills and I received written permission from Raphael to speak with Candido's doctors.

I also told Raphael I would be faxing him an engagement letter setting out the scope of this engagement, the firm's billing practices and hourly rates, and my estimates for each stage of this litigation. I explained that I will need a signed copy of the engagement letter returned to me before I can begin working on the case. Raphael agreed to get the engagement letter back to me before the end of the week.

Chapter 11

Client Counseling

Highlights

- After interviewing the client, the lawyer will research the problem and present findings verbally in a client counseling session and/or in writing in an advice letter.
- Before the counseling session, the lawyer should prepare a counseling plan which identifies as many options as possible to resolve the client's problems.
- At the counseling session, the lawyer should outline the options for the client, discuss the advantages and disadvantages, and seek the client's opinions.
- The lawyer must be forthcoming about the costs of the various options and should not predict the success of any one option.
- Any decision on the proper course of action belongs to the client.
- When a client needs more time to reach a decision, a deadline should be agreed upon.

Introduction

After interviewing the client and researching the problem, the lawyer will meet with the client to discuss legal options. Such counseling may also be done through a client advice letter. Chapter 10 concerns client interviewing; this chapter concerns client counseling in a face to face meeting; Chapter 12 covers client advice letters.

The role of the lawyer in a client counseling session is to equip the client with the relevant information, so that the client makes an informed decision. The rules of professional conduct discussed in Chapter 8, require that the client, rather than the lawyer, decide on the manner in which to proceed. As discussed in the section on problem solving in Chapter 9, the lawyer presents options and provides advice about the potential courses of action.

This chapter discusses client counseling in four sections: (1) preparation, (2) the client meeting, (3) counseling challenges and techniques, and (4) the post-counseling session memorandum.

The Client

In Chapter 10, you interviewed Dr. Raphael Sosa and his son Candido. You learned that Dr. Sosa wishes to sue his brother-in-law, Javier Sanchez. Dr. Sosa is a 38-year-old Cuban dentist and Candido, his twelve year old son, is suffering from mental distress. Dr. Sosa claims Candido's distress was caused by remarks made by his brother-in-law about him and his homeland of Cuba. He wishes to sue his brother-in-law for Candido's mental distress. During the interview, you advised Dr. Sosa that, subject to what you learned from further research, he may have a cause of action against Javier. It is now time to meet with him and explain his legal options. What do you need to know to complete a client counseling session?

Preparation

As with interviewing, the first step is to prepare. Each client's ability to understand the technical aspects of the law must be evaluated by the lawyer; the lawyer then translates the legal concepts into language the client will understand. The lawyer must also consider the client's goals. The lawyer should compare the goals with the results of the research and outline the advantages and disadvantages of each possible course of action.

Many lawyers create a plan, prior to the counseling session, aimed at clarifying the available options. A counseling plan begins with the client's stated objectives. It then lists the various options, based on the client interview and the lawyer's research. Lastly, it lists the advantages and disadvantages of each option. A counseling plan assists the lawyer in presenting the information to the client in a comprehensible manner.

Consideration must also be given to the manner and timing of explaining the options to the client. If the client is knowledgeable, the lawyer may wish to send a letter summarizing the results of the research and the available options prior to the meeting. Alternatively, the lawyer may wish to prepare an agenda to give to the client at the counseling session and present the options as they are discussed. An agenda generally includes headings for an update on the client's goals or any new events, a summary of the research, a description and evaluation of the options, and the client's decision and next steps.

The Counseling Session

As with the interview, the lawyer should welcome the client. If the client has not previously been provided with an advice letter, the lawyer should present him with an agenda.

Beginning the Session

The lawyer begins the meeting by explaining the decisions the client will be asked to make. The lawyer should emphasize that all of the decisions belong to the client; the lawyer's role is to explain the advantages and disadvantages of the various options. The lawyer should also restate and clarify the client's goals and confirm that neither the goals nor any relevant facts have changed.

The lawyer next provides the client with a succinct description of the law as it relates to the client's problem. The lawyer should model neutrality to prevent the client from prematurely reaching a decision. Effective problem solving most often takes place where the client and the attorney consider all options before reaching a decision.

Discussing Options

In the U.S., the best lawyers generate multiple options for clients. In generating and evaluating potential solutions, the lawyer must consider both the legal and non-legal aspects of each decision. Business and financial considerations, political considerations, personal, and emotional factors may all be important. A good lawyer also educates clients about the options and how to choose among them. As discussed in Chapter 9, the lawyer must teach the client to be an effective problem solver.

The lawyer begins this portion of the session by listing the options and asking if the client has any additions. The lawyer next inquires which option the client prefers to discuss first. If no preference is expressed, the lawyer discusses the options in the order in which they were first presented.

The lawyer next presents the advantages and disadvantages of each option and seeks additional insights from the client. The lawyer should explain why a particular option is a realistic choice and how the option fits with the client's immediate and overarching goals. In addition to educating the client, this process gives the client an opportunity to correct any misunderstandings. In the ideal situation, both lawyer and client actively brainstorm the advantages and disadvantages of the options.

Making a Decision

Ultimately the lawyer requests that the client choose an option. Where a client experiences difficulty, the lawyer may assist by paring down the list and reframing the options. Reframing may assist the client in prioritizing the options and reaching a decision.

Several ethical considerations, discussed in Chapter 8, are relevant in choosing options. First, a lawyer must remember that the client's views on the success of the option is most important. Second, a lawyer inexperienced in an option or potential course of action is obligated to confer with a more experienced colleague. Where a client asks the lawyer to make the decision, it is not improper for the lawyer to articulate an option provided all ethical obligations are met.

Conclusion: Next Steps

If the client wants more time to make a decision, the lawyer should set deadlines before the client leaves. Once a client makes a decision, the lawyer should outline the next steps and the responsibility for accomplishing them.

Challenges and Techniques

There are several challenges to counseling beyond the necessity of creating and educating the client about options. First, the lawyer must maintain the client relationship. Second, the lawyer must tailor the counseling session to the nature and timing of the legal problem.

Maintaining the Client Relationship

Communicating empathy and maintaining the client relationship is often challenging for the lawyer, who is also serving as a problem solver. Active listening, neutral body language, and objective language all further the goal of collaborative decision making. The lawyer, however, should avoid being overly optimistic when explaining the options. A client may turn to malpractice actions if the results of the decision do not match expectations.

Tailoring the Counseling Session

It is important to remember that a lawyer is likely to counsel a client at numerous times throughout the relationship and that not all client problems will be litigation based. If the counseling session is based on a transaction, the lawyer must start with the business terms, become familiar with business practice, and gain knowledge about the client's business situation. Counseling the transactional client is discussed in Chapter 14. If the problem is litigation based, the initial counseling session will revolve around whether to proceed to litigation. This involves a review of the costs and benefits of litigation, as well as other options such as negotiation and mediation. Counseling the litigation client is discussed below. Of course, in either a transactional or litigation situation, the lawyer and client will discuss strategy numerous times during the course of their relationship. As a result, the nature of the relationship and the counseling session itself continuously evolves.

Post-Counseling Memoranda

As with the client interview, lawyers in the U.S. compose a memo to the file following a counseling session. The memo briefly summarizes: (1) the identity of the client, (2) the date, time, and place of the meeting, (3) who was present, (4) what was discussed, (5) what was decided, and (6) the agreed upon next steps.

Analyzing the Client's Legal Needs and Issues

Let us return to Dr. Raphael Sosa. What course will your counseling session take?

A review of your memo to the file following your interview in Chapter 10 establishes that Dr. Sosa wishes to sue his brother-in-law, Javier Sanchez, for his son Candido's mental distress. Your review of the file memo, together with your additional research, suggests several courses of action. You prepare a counseling plan, to assist you in explaining the advantages and disadvantages of the available options to Dr. Sosa. A counseling plan for Dr. Sosa is included in the sample documents below. You then prepare an agenda to give to Dr. Sosa when he arrives.

Begin the meeting by greeting Dr. Sosa and providing the agenda. Explain to Dr. Sosa that he may have a cause of action against Javier for intentional infliction of emotional distress. Further, such a conclusion generates a number of decisions which only he, as the client, can make. Then, reaffirm your understanding of his goals: to sue Javier and to recover monies to assist in paying his son's medical and psychiatric bills.

Next, describe the applicable law. A straightforward description of the law could begin by reminding Dr. Sosa that a cause of action for intentional infliction of emotional distress exists in Florida when a person's conduct exceeds all bounds which could be tolerated by society, is calculated to cause severe emotional distress to a person of ordinary sensibilities, and causes severe emotional distress to such person. You could explain that the element relating to the severe distress caused by the conduct would most likely be satisfied here because, according to psychiatric testimony, Javier's statements contributed to Candido's emotional distress. Further, the distress could be considered severe, as evidenced by the nightmares and weight loss which followed.

Nevertheless, you should note that there are several issues on which Javier might prevail. The first is whether Javier's conduct exceeded all bounds which could be tolerated by society. Such conduct can consist of words alone, but the words must have serious meaning and be truly harmful. Deliberately false and malicious statements are generally considered actionable because they are capable of serious effect. In this case, Javier's statements could be viewed as having real meaning, especially the false statement that Dr. Sosa was an uncaring parent. Conversely, Javier could argue that this and other statements are not extreme and that many of his statements regarding Cuba are true. A related issue is whether the conduct was calculated to cause severe emotional distress to a person of ordinary sensibilities. Here, it could be argued that the comments were directed at Candido, a child who had recently suffered the loss of one parent, and they were directly intended to alienate him from his father. However, Javier could argue that he had his nephew's best interests in mind and did not intend to cause him emotional distress.

Utilize the counseling plan to briefly list, electronically or on paper, the options generated by the review of Dr. Sosa's interview and the relevant law. Such options might include: pursuing civil litigation, pursuing alternative dispute resolution, or refraining from action. Inquire if Dr. Sosa has any additions. Next, using the counseling plan, chart the advantages and disadvantages of each of the options while discussing them with Dr. Sosa.

You must ask Dr. Sosa to decide on an option. You might assist by reframing the options, but ultimately Dr. Sosa must decide. The advantages and disadvantages of the counseling plan include the probability of a monetary recovery in general terms. It may be helpful to Dr. Sosa, especially with respect to the litigation option, to estimate the chance of success in percentages. For example, you might say that his likelihood of success at trial is 60% in his favor, 40% in Javier's favor. But remember, you must give realistic advice.

Dr. Sosa may want additional time to decide on an option. If so, set a deadline and another meeting. Also, advise him of any time-sensitive issues. Finally, remember to prepare a memorandum for the file detailing what was discussed at the counseling session.

Sample Documents

Document 1
Counseling Checklist

Beginning the meeting

- Put the client at ease and begin building a relationship
  - Maintain open body language and eye contact
  - Utilize active listening
  - Use other verbal and nonverbal cues to facilitate communication
- Confirm the client's principal goals remain the same
- Provide an assessment of the law
- Provide the client with an overview of the meeting

Discussing options

- Provide specific options for the client to consider
- Explore each option individually, discussing advantages and then disadvantages
  - Be realistic, include costs and likelihood of success
  - Include consequences beyond those that are legal, such as social, ethical, and psychological consequences
- Summarize the advantages and disadvantages of each option for the client

Making a decision

- Ask the client to choose an option
- Empathize with the client

Conclusion: Next steps

- Outline the actions to be taken by the lawyer and the client to further the chosen option
  - If the client needs more time to consider an option, provide a deadline
- Arrange for the next client contact

Document 2
Counseling Plan

[Firm Stationery]

MEMORANDUM

TO: File
FROM: Associate
DATE: September __, 20__
RE: Plan for Counseling Session with Raphael Sosa.

OBJECTIVE

At our interview session on September __, 20__, Raphael Sosa expressed the desire to sue his brother-in-law—Javier Sanchez—based on statements Javier made to Raphael's son, Candido. Research indicates Raphael may bring a claim for intentional infliction of emotional distress in Florida based on Javier's statements concerning Raphael and his plan to take Candido back to Cuba. At the interview, Raphael expressed the goals of holding Javier accountable for Candido's medical and psychiatric expenses and reaffirming his relationship with Candido.

COURSES OF ACTION

Option One

Filing Civil Action

Advantages

- Positive outlook for success on the merits
- Best chance for award of significant damages, although proving damages for emotional distress may prove difficult
- Good probability for collecting money damages from Javier, who has a medical practice and significant assets

Disadvantages

- Significant money involved for attorney fees and court costs
- Significant time involved
- Exposure to the inconvenience and possible embarrassment of discovery depositions and trial

- Exposure to negative publicity
- Possible negative impact on Raphael's relationship with Candido

Option Two

Engaging in Alternative Dispute Resolution, such as Mediation or Negotiation

Advantages

- Some money involved, but less than litigation
- Some time involved, but less than litigation
- Little risk of exposure; mediation and negotiation are both private proceedings
- Allows for alternative relief, such as an apology from Javier
- Some monetary recovery is likely, but not as much as would be if successful in litigation
- Probability for collecting money damages from Javier is improved over litigation

Disadvantages

- Low probability of large recovery, mediation and negotiation both involve compromise
- May impact ability to bring later suit

Option Three

Refraining From Action

Advantages

- No monetary costs involved, other than those expended to date
- No time involved
- Allows Candido to move on with his life; may strengthen father-son relationship
- No publicity or public scrutiny

Disadvantages

- No possibility of collecting damages from Javier
- Aggravation and frustration involved in refraining from action
- Adverse effect on probability of success in civil suit, if later decide want to sue

Part Six

Writing and Practice Skills: Letter Writing and Electronic Communications

Chapter 12

Letter Writing

Highlights

- Advice to clients may be transmitted by a counseling session, a letter, or both.
- In addition to advice letters, lawyers in the U.S. often write letters regarding the status of proceedings and demand letters.
- Letters written by lawyers in the U.S. are generally formal in tone.
- Most client advice letters contain an introduction, factual summary, statement of legal conclusions and reasoning, recommendations, invitation for further discussions, and closing.
- Status letters follow a similar format; the introductory paragraph provides the context of the case, the factual and legal analysis paragraphs describe the factual and legal proceedings to date, the results and options section outlines what options are available.
- Demand letters generally include the specific action requested, support for the request, and a statement of the consequences should the reader not comply with the request.

Introduction

Chapter 11 focused on advice given during a client counseling session. This chapter focuses on several types of letters, including advice letters, frequently written by lawyers in the U.S. Chapter 13 focuses on other types of communication frequently used by lawyers, including emails.

In the U.S., lawyers are cautioned to consider any written product as potential evidence to be used in court. In addition, lawyers must consider the audience, tone, and purpose, as well as the organization and clarity of any letter. Finally, lawyers in the U.S. seek to respond to their client's concerns in an empathetic manner in order to foster the attorney-client relationship.

This chapter discusses formal letter writing in five sections: (1) audience, tone and purpose considerations relevant to all letters, (2) organization and clarity principles relevant to all letters, (3) opinion and advice letters to clients, (4) status letters to clients, and (5) demand letters to opposing counsel and parties. Letters relating to negotiations and settlement are discussed in Chapter 17.

The Client

As you read this chapter, consider our newest clients: the Palmer family. Dr. and Mrs. Robert Palmer are the parents of Julie Palmer. The Palmers have asked our firm to explore the possibility of suing Julie's ice hockey coach, Suzy Ford, for intentional infliction of emotional distress.

Julie is fifteen and a sophomore at Palm Beach Preparatory Academy in Palm Beach, Florida. She is a gifted student from an affluent family and expected to attend an Ivy League college. This summer Julie sought to improve her ice hockey skills by joining a summer league. Julie, a talented goalie, was thrilled to be selected for the Devils. The Devils play from June to August. The Florida Women's Ice Hockey Championship is held at the end of August.

Suzy has been the coach at Palm Beach Prep for eight years. She is a demanding, but successful, coach. Her summer team won the state championship last year.

Several weeks into the summer, Mrs. Palmer noticed that Julie was resisting going to practice. Upon questioning, Julie admitted that Suzy frequently criticized her in front of the team. "It's embarrassing," she told her mother.

The Palmers attended every game. Suzy did scream at the players, continuously yelling, "What the hell do you think you're doing out there!" Suzy's attitude concerned the Palmers, but they were reassured by the fact that she remained on good terms with the other parents. Many outwardly applauded

Suzy for her "tough love" approach; others praised her for always compli-
menting the team when the members played well.

By August, the Devils were tied with another team for the right to advance
to the league tournament. Suzy scheduled a practice for the eve of the final
game. Julie arrived home from practice in tears. She ran to her room and refused to come out, saying only, "Coach hates me, I can't do anything right."

When her parents arrived at the rink the next day, they asked Mr. Stock,
Julie's best friend's father, what had happened at practice. Mr. Stock told them
that Julie had played badly and Suzy "just lost it" and berated her repeatedly.
Mr. Stock could see that Julie was upset and "Suzy must have known it too,"
but "she just couldn't stop."

Despite the practice controversy, Julie kept her position as starting goalie.
Julie did not play well, allowing the other team to score three goals. Each time,
Suzy yelled, "Quit playing like a damn girl." Later, however, when Julie deflected the puck just before the buzzer rang, Suzy praised her profusely. Suzy
also berated other players during the game.

During the final period, the game was tied. The other team had pulled their
goalie to have more players on the ice. One of them unexpectedly took the
puck down the rink and slammed it into the net Julie was guarding. Suzy
snapped. She stormed onto the ice screaming that Julie had "singlehandedly lost
the game," was "worthless," and "would never play hockey again." Julie crouched
on the ice sobbing. Suzy shook her head disgustedly and walked away, saying,
"Julie is a big baby."

Julie no longer wants to go to college. She is withdrawn, spending all of her
time alone. She refuses to eat and has lost weight. Since the start of the new
school year, she has been disciplined several times. What must you consider when
writing an advice letter to the Palmers?

Audience, Tone, and Purpose

In writing letters, as with memoranda, the lawyer must know the intended
audience. Factors to be considered include the recipient's age, level of education, legal experience, and mental and emotional condition. It is important
for the lawyer to address the subject matter of the letter at the level of analysis that is appropriate for the reader. Likewise, the level of formality of the letter and the degree of empathy expressed will vary with the audience. All letters
from a lawyer, however, should be professional in tone.

Equally important as the tone and the audience is the purpose of the letter.
Many letters counsel a client about available options. An example is a client

advice letter. Letters also provide information. Examples include status and demand letters. Lastly, letters may seek to persuade, maintain relationships, or obtain direction.

Organization and Clarity

Organization of a letter generally follows a specific format. For instance, most client advice letters include a heading, salutation, introduction, factual summary, statement of legal conclusions and reasoning, recommendations, invitation for further discussions, and closing. Nevertheless, there remain many organizational decisions for the drafter. The placement of information influences the way the audience interprets the letter, just as it does in office memoranda discussed in Chapter 7.

In client advice letters, as in memoranda, introductory paragraphs set forth the issues to be considered and provide a roadmap for the reader of the information to be discussed. The introductory paragraph should also develop the client relationship. Development of a positive relationship makes the client more likely to confide in the lawyer. It also makes the client more receptive to negative information.

In addition to careful organization, it is important for the language of the letter to be suitable for the audience. The lawyer should avoid technical terms and legalese, such as "hereinafter" and "heretofore." If technical or legal terms are necessary, the lawyer must define the terms within the letter. Finally, whatever the organization, the lawyer should conclude in a manner that responds to the client's concerns in an empathetic manner.

Opinion and Advice Letters to Clients

Opinion Letters

Opinion letters express the opinion of a lawyer or firm on the legality of a client's proposed course of action. The lawyer or firm may be liable, if the client relies on the letter and is later sued. Opinion letters generally follow a strict format, established by the firm or its malpractice insurer, and require the approval of a senior lawyer.

Advice Letters

Advice letters communicate the lawyer's legal analysis to the client. Advice letters convey an objective analysis of the law and a discussion of the client's options. They may answer a specific question asked by a client or supplement or replace a client counseling session. Audience, tone, purpose, organization, and clarity are all important components of an advice letter. An American lawyer's primary goal in an advice letter to a client, however, is to answer the client's questions.

In the U.S., advice letters generally include the following sections: a heading, salutation, introduction, factual summary, statement of legal conclusions and reasoning, recommendations, next steps and an invitation for further discussions, and closing. The heading should include the lawyer's contact information, the date, and the client's full name and address. It should also include a reference or "Re" line briefly describing the matter. The salutation follows the heading and should be formal in tone. Clients are addressed by surname.

The first substantive paragraph of the letter defines and briefly answers the issues, provides a roadmap informing the reader of the document's organization, and seeks to develop a relationship with the reader by setting the tone. It is customary to frame the answers in terms of probabilities and to avoid guarantees. As discussed in Chapters 8 and 9, legal issues in the U.S. are more fluid than in other legal systems and it is difficult to predict the outcome of any problem with certainty.

Most advice letters next include a brief summary of the relevant facts. Similar to the statement of facts in an office memorandum, the facts should be conveyed in a chronological, objective manner. Objectively stating the facts offers the client an opportunity to provide additional facts or correct any assumptions the lawyer has made. The fact section should conclude with the statement that the legal advice provided is based on, and limited to, the facts stated and subject to change if other facts are disclosed.

The factual summary is followed by a discussion of the lawyer's legal conclusions and reasoning. Similar to the office memorandum, this section of the letter will be organized around the legal issues with each issue and its conclusion discussed separately. The depth of the discussion will depend on the audience. The lawyer may explain relevant cases and statutes but will generally avoid citations in the letter.

If the law is unsettled, the letter should discuss all sides of the argument. It is common for the lawyer to present the law and arguments supporting the client's position before presenting those in opposition. Lawyers should not omit opposing law or arguments; omissions may provide the client with an overly optimistic view of a legal course of action.

The lawyer's practical recommendations will follow the analysis and reasoning. As with the client counseling session, discussed in Chapter 11, the lawyer should begin by listing the client's options. After listing the options, the lawyer will discuss the advantages and disadvantages of each. Also as discussed in Chapter 11, the lawyer must remind the client that it is the client's decision on how to proceed that controls.

In providing recommendations, the lawyer should remember that written communications in the U.S. may become evidence. The reason for the recommendations must be clearly explained and the disadvantages, especially the costs, of any recommendations fully explored. If any discussions regarding the advice provided in the letter occur, the lawyer should document them in a memorandum to the file, similar to those discussed in Chapters 10 and 11.

The final substantive paragraph of the advice letter should be a summary of next steps. First, the lawyer will thank the client for the opportunity to be of service and invite the client to communicate any questions or concerns. This furthers the relationship building purpose of the letter. Second, the lawyer will advise the client of the next steps, subject to the client's approval. Lastly, the lawyer will set out any actions the client should take and any time limits on acting.

The advice letter should close in a formal manner. Common closings include "Regards," "Sincerely," or "Respectfully."

Status Letters to Clients

Status letters keep clients informed about the progress of their legal matter. As discussed in Chapter 8, lawyers in the U.S. have an ethical obligation to communicate regularly with their clients regarding any pending legal matters.

Status letters generally include the same heading, salutation, next steps and invitation for further discussions, and closing as an advice letter. The other sections differ slightly. In the first paragraph, the lawyer provides the context of the case. The lawyer should seek to further the relationship with the client as well as summarize the status of the case.

In the next paragraph, the lawyer briefly summarizes any factual developments or legal proceedings since the date of the last communication. If required, the lawyer explains the applicable law. In most cases, however, the law will have been adequately discussed in the initial advice letter.

The discussion of options will be similar to those in the advice letter, but limited in scope to the new developments. In some instances, no new options will be generated. As with the advice letter, any discussion of options should be based on probabilities rather than guarantees. As discussed in Chapter 13, status letters are often sent by email.

Demand Letters to Opposing Counsel or Party

Through a demand letter, a lawyer requests the opposing party—or their counsel—to take, or refrain from taking, certain actions. Where the opposing party has hired counsel, the demand letter must be directed to counsel. Where the opposing party does not have counsel, a lawyer drafting a demand letter should clearly identify the represented party. The recipient of the letter is more likely to act favorably on the demand if the letter provides credible support for the request. Finally, as noted in Chapter 8, the rules of professional conduct prohibit a lawyer from making any misrepresentations.

A demand letter will generally have the same heading, salutation, and closing as an advice or status letter. The introduction to the demand letter should include the purpose of the letter and the specific request to act or refrain from acting.

The request should be followed with an explanation of the facts and law that support the demand. Unlike the advice letter, the demand letter should include only the facts and law supporting the request. Also contrasting with the advice letter, the resolution of the issue should be framed narrowly in a demand letter to avoid foreclosing later strategic decisions.

After making the request and providing the factual and legal support, the lawyer should provide a completion date. The date should be reasonable and explanations given for its importance.

Lastly, the lawyer should state the consequences should the opponent fail to comply with the demand. Consequences may include proceeding to court, canceling a deal, turning over a debt to a collection agency or a variety of other activities.

Analyzing the Client's Legal Needs and Issues

Let us return to the Palmer family. Dr. and Mrs. Palmer have asked our firm to explore the possibility of suing Suzy Ford, their teenage daughter's ice-hockey coach, for intentional infliction of emotional distress. What must you consider when writing an advice letter to the Palmers?

Dr. and Mrs. Palmer are middle-aged, well-educated professionals. English is their first language and they most likely have consulted lawyers for various services related to their personal lives, such as wills and trusts. They specifically asked the question whether a lawsuit could be brought for intentional infliction of emotional distress on behalf of their minor daughter, indicating some familiarity with the cause of action. Nevertheless, the Palmers are not lawyers.

The purpose of your letter to the Palmers will be to advise them of the strength of their claim for intentional infliction of emotional distress. It should be formal and professional and may address complex issues. It need not include citations to case law.

As an advice letter, your letter will include a heading, salutation, introduction, factual summary, statement of legal conclusions and reasoning, recommendations, an invitation to further discussion, and a closing.

The introduction should specifically reference the Palmer's question regarding intentional infliction of emotional distress and provide your estimation of the probability of success. The facts related to the claim of intentional infliction of emotional distress should be stated objectively and chronologically. Include negative facts, such as the other parents' endorsements of Suzy's tactics, as well as those supporting the Palmers' case.

Given the Palmers' background, the discussion of the legal conclusions and reasoning can be detailed and complex. Note that this will vary given the client. In the Palmers' case, it is clear that their daughter is in severe emotional distress caused by Suzy Ford's behavior. The main question will be whether that behavior exceeds all bounds tolerated by society. The explanation of such behavior will require you to explain some Florida case law. As this matter will be disputed, it is important to discuss both sides of the argument. Discuss the law and facts supporting the Palmers' case first, before discussing those benefiting Suzy. Also, be careful not to overstate your case.

As with client counseling discussed in Chapter 11, the recommendations section of the letter involves listing the client's options together with the advantages and disadvantages. Options available to the Palmers include civil litigation and negotiation. Advantages and disadvantages include a comparison of the time, money, and privacy involved in each option. Close with a discussion of next steps and any associated time limits. Stress to the Palmers that they control the choice of how to proceed.

An advice letter to the Palmers and a demand letter to Suzy are reproduced in the sample documents section below.

Sample Documents

Document 1
Client Advice Letter

[Firm Stationery]

[Date]

Dr. and Mrs. Robert Palmer
Three Ocean View Drive
Palm Beach, Florida

CONFIDENTIAL ATTORNEY CLIENT COMMUNICATION

Re: Julie Palmer/Suzy Ford—Intentional Infliction of Emotional Distress

Dear Dr. and Mrs. Palmer:

It was a pleasure meeting you last week. As promised, I have researched the grounds for a suit against Suzy Ford for intentional infliction of emotional distress ("IIED") with regard to her actions towards your daughter, Julie. My research indicates that we could make a viable legal claim that Suzy Ford is responsible for Julie's emotional distress under Florida law. Unfortunately, however, the law is less than clear and we would face certain legal hurdles. Another option includes negotiation of a settlement. Each of these options has advantages and disadvantages. This letter summarizes the facts as I understand them, analyzes the laws of Florida on intentional infliction of emotional distress, and reviews the available options.

Factual Background

Please review the following factual account for accuracy. My discussion of your legal claim is based on my understanding of these facts. The analysis may change if the facts are other than stated.

Julie is fifteen and a sophomore at Palm Beach Preparatory Academy in Palm Beach, Florida. This summer Julie sought to improve her ice hockey skills by joining a summer league. Julie, a talented goalie, was thrilled to be selected for the Devils. The Devils play from June to August. The Florida Women's Ice Hockey Championship is the end of August.

Suzy has been the coach at Palm Beach Prep for eight years. She is a demanding, but successful, coach. Her summer team won the state championship last year.

Julie complained often during the practice season that Suzy criticized her in front of the team. At the close of the season, Julie's team was tied with another for the right to advance to the league tournament. Suzy scheduled a practice for the day before the final game. When Julie arrived home from the practice, she was crying. She ran to her room and refused to come out.

Suzy's behavior towards Julie concerned you as parents, but none of the other parents were upset. In fact, some outwardly applauded Suzy. The fact that Suzy remained on good terms with the other parents reassured you.

You attended the final game. Despite the practice controversy, Julie kept her position as starting goalie. Julie did not play well at first, allowing the other team to score three goals. Each time, Suzy yelled "Quit playing like a damn girl!" Later however, when Julie deflected the puck just before the buzzer rang, Suzy praised her profusely. Suzy also berated other players during the game.

During the final period, the game was tied. The other team pulled their goalie to have more players on the ice. One of them unexpectedly took the puck down the rink and slammed it into the net Julie was guarding. Suzy stormed onto the ice screaming that Julie had "singlehandedly lost the game," was "worthless," and "would never play hockey again." Julie crouched on the ice, sobbing. Suzy shook her head disgustedly and called Julie "a big baby."

To this day, Julie remains severely embarrassed. She says she no longer wants to go to college. She is withdrawn, spending all of her time alone in her room. She refuses to eat and has lost weight. Since the start of the new school year, she has been disciplined several times.

Mr. Stock is the father of Zoe Stock, Julie's best friend. During a witness interview, he stated that, if asked, he would testify that at the practice before the final game, Suzy "just lost it" and berated Julie repeatedly. He saw that Julie was upset and "Suzy must have known it too," but "she just couldn't stop." In general, Mr. Stock believes that Suzy is "a little over the top" but that this is "a good tactic to get the girls to stop acting like prima donnas and prepare for the real world." He never heard any parents object to Suzy's approach. "Good parents," in his view, "want their kids to play sports to develop discipline and succeed."

Legal Analysis

A cause of action for IIED exists in Florida, under existing case law, when a person's conduct exceeds all bounds which could be tolerated by society, is calculated to cause severe emotional distress to a person of ordinary sensibilities, and causes severe emotional distress to such person. A court would likely find that the third element relating to the severe distress caused by the conduct is satisfied here because Suzy's statements, at least in part, caused Julie's emotional distress. It is also likely the distress would be considered severe, as evidenced by the weight loss, withdrawal, and difficulties in school. It would be advisable to have medical and psychiatric testimony to support the arguments. Nevertheless, it is probable that a court would find that this element of IIED is met, based on the nature of Suzy's statements and the fact that they were made to a minor under her supervision and control.

A more difficult element to consider is whether Suzy's conduct exceeded all bounds which could be tolerated by society. Case law provides that such conduct can consist of words alone. But the words must have serious meaning and be truly abusive or harmful, not merely vulgar. Vulgarities are not actionable, in the eyes of the courts, because they are not intended to have real meaning or serious effect. On the other hand, deliberately false and malicious statements are actionable because they are assumed to be calculated to cause severe emotional distress and are capable of serious effect.

Accordingly, in one Florida case the court concluded that a store clerk's comment to a customer, "[Y]ou stink to me," was not likely to cause a person of ordinary sensibilities to suffer severe emotional distress. Thus, the customer had no right to sue for IIED. Conversely, in another Florida case, when a woman told a girl that her mother was an adulterer, the woman's conduct was actionable because the false comment was objectively likely to shame a young girl and shock her sensibilities.

In Julie's case we would argue that Suzy's statements have real meaning, especially the public statements that Julie was "worthless" and a "baby." Nevertheless, Suzy could argue that this and other statements are not as extreme as those false statements which charged immoral conduct. Further, she could say that most of what she said was true based on Julie's performance. Perhaps most damaging, Suzy could argue that none of the other parents found her comments, to Julie or their own daughters, objectionable. Indeed some, as Mr. Stock, found the statements laudable. This has the potential to severely undercut the argument that Suzy's conduct exceeded all bounds which could be tolerated by society.

A further issue is whether the conduct was calculated to cause severe emotional distress to a person of ordinary sensibilities. To meet this element, the statement must be directed at someone who is likely to experience emotional distress when she hears it. Courts will be more likely to find the defendant's comments were calculated to cause severe emotional distress where they are directed at a child who would inevitably be shocked by the remarks. Here the comments were directed at a minor, but Julie at fifteen is older than the children previously found impressionable by the courts.

Legal Recommendations

Based on the forgoing legal analysis, it is possible a jury would award you monetary relief against Suzy for her intentional infliction of emotional distress. Nevertheless, trials are costly, time-consuming, stressful, and unpredictable. As a result, you may want to consider negotiating an out of court settlement. Such a settlement would allow us to structure our own relief. For instance, it may help Julie to move on if she were to receive a written apology from Suzy. A settlement would also relieve Julie from the stress of litigation, including oral questioning from Suzy's attorney and testimony at trial. Further, a negotiated settlement would involve significantly fewer costs and fees than a trial. Finally, a settlement could likely be completed over a period of months, as opposed to the years involved in litigation. In the unlikely event we could not reach a settlement, we would still have the option to proceed to litigation.

After you have had an opportunity to consider the options and consult with Julie, please call and set up an appointment so that we may discuss your case in more detail. I am available at your convenience to assist you in making a decision that is best for all of you under the circumstances.

Sincerely,

Lawyer's Name and Signature

Document 2
Demand Letter

[Firm Stationery]

[Date]

Ms. Suzy Ford
123 Palm Beach Ave.
Palm Beach, Florida

CONFIDENTIAL

Re: Julie Palmer/Suzy Ford—Intentional Infliction of Emotional Distress

Dear Ms. Ford:

This firm represents Dr. and Mrs. Robert Palmer, in their claim against you for intentional infliction of emotional distress ("IIED") arising out of your behavior towards their daughter, Julie. As you may be aware, liability for IIED exists in Florida when a person's conduct exceeds all bounds which could be tolerated by society, is calculated to cause severe emotional distress to a person of ordinary sensibilities, and causes severe emotional distress. Reviewing the pattern of your abusive behavior towards Julie, it is clear that the elements of IIED are satisfied.

The facts that lead to this claim are unfortunate. Less than a year ago, Julie Palmer was an impressionable girl of fifteen. A student at the private college preparatory school of Palm Beach Preparatory Academy, Julie sought to improve her ice hockey skills during the summer by joining the Devils ice hockey team.

As the coach of the Devils as well as the girl's ice hockey team for Palm Beach Prep, you have an extensive background in training and mentoring young female athletes. It is well known that such girls are anxious to win the approval of their coaches and loathe to be criticized in front of their peers. Nevertheless, throughout the summer practice season you continuously, publicly, and profanely criticized Julie and her teammates. Reported remarks include: "What the hell do you think you're doing out there" and "Quit playing like a damn girl!"

Further, your treatment of Julie at the last practice before the final game sent her home in tears, unable to even communicate with her parents. A bystander reported that you "just lost it" and berated Julie repeatedly. He saw that Julie was upset and believes you "must have known it too," but he says you "just couldn't stop."

Finally, your conduct at the final game was incomprehensible. Each time Julie—as the goalie—allowed the other side to score, you screamed at her. Later, when Julie allowed a player on the opposing team to score the final goal to win the game, you reportedly stormed onto the ice screaming that Julie had "singlehandedly lost the game," was "worthless," and "would never play hockey again." Most shocking of all, as Julie, a girl of fifteen who had been entrusted to your care and supervision, crouched on the ice sobbing, her own parents heard you disgustedly call her a "big baby." All of this transpired while both teams, parents, referees, and bystanders looked on.

As a result of your behavior, Julie says she no longer wants to go to college. She is withdrawn, spending all of her time alone in her room. She refuses to eat and has lost weight. Since the start of the new school year, she has been disciplined several times.

A cause of action for IIED has existed in Florida since 1958. As noted above, IIED will be found when a person's conduct exceeds all bounds which could be tolerated by society, is calculated to cause severe emotional distress to a person of ordinary sensibilities, and causes severe emotional distress to such person.

A jury would likely find that the third element relating to the severe distress caused by the conduct is satisfied here on the basis that your statements caused Julie's emotional distress. It is also likely a jury would find the distress to be severe, as evidenced by Julie's weight loss, withdrawal, and difficulties in school. The nature of your statements, the fact that they were repeated over an extended period of time in a public arena, to a fifteen-year-old private school student entrusted to your care and guidance as an experienced member of her school faculty, could well lead a jury to conclude that your conduct was calculated to cause emotional distress and exceeded all bounds which can be tolerated by society.

In light of these instances of misconduct, a trial court may very well award the Palmers damages. Nevertheless, my clients are willing to consider settlement in order to avoid the costs, publicity, and inconveniences of litigation. The Palmers welcome a meeting with you and, if you wish, your attorney to expeditiously resolve this dispute.

Please give careful consideration of this matter. I invite you to call my office as soon as possible to arrange a meeting. If I do not hear from you by _____, 20__ at 5:00 p.m., I will pursue other legal remedies.

Sincerely,

Lawyer's Name and Signature

Chapter 13

Electronic Communications

Highlights

- Consideration should be given by a lawyer to the form of communication. Email and telephone conversations are most appropriate as quick methods of communicating routine matters.

Email Communications

- Professional communication, including email, must be respectful of the attorney-client relationship.
- Email is easily accessed by third parties and can almost always be retrieved; lawyers must be conscious of the duties surrounding confidentiality and privilege.

Telephone Communications

- Telephone communications should also be respectful of the attorney-client relationship; the tone should be formal and information should be promptly disclosed.

Electronic Communications at Meetings

- The personal use of communication devices should be kept to a minimum at client or other professional meetings; where necessary their use should be explained in advance.

Introduction

Many lawyers in the U.S. and elsewhere find that email or telephone conversations are the easiest methods of communicating with clients and opposing counsel. Nevertheless, traditional letters, discussed at Chapter 12, are often better suited for complex or confidential information. Further, for all of the reasons discussed in Chapter 8 on ethics and Chapter 9 on communication skills, face to face conversations are best for sensitive matters and for building relationships.

Email and telephone conversations are most appropriate as a quick method of communicating routine matters with clients, colleagues, and other lawyers. Nevertheless, the lawyer must be careful and, as with letters, pay attention to audience, tone, purpose, and organization.

Additionally, personal electronic devices such as cellular telephones should be used judiciously. Most U.S. partners, clients, and judges are insulted by a lawyer texting, surfing the web, or otherwise engaging with electronic devices rather than listening.

This chapter discusses electronic communications in seven sections: (1) audience, tone, and purpose considerations relevant to all emails, (2) organization and clarity principles relevant to all emails, (3) email replies and acknowledgements, (4) email ethics, (5) emails and relationship building, (6) telephonic communications, and (7) the use of electronic communication devices.

The Client

As you read this chapter, consider our clients the Palmer family, whom we met in Chapter 12. Dr. and Mrs. Palmer are the parents of Julie Palmer. They met with our firm to discuss difficulties Julie is having with her ice hockey coach, Suzy Ford. The Palmers asked our firm to explore the possibility of suing Suzy for intentional infliction of emotional distress.

In Chapter 12, we considered the issues raised in writing an advice letter to the Palmers. In what situations might it be preferable to contact the Palmers by email and what format should the email take? In what circumstances is it appropriate to contact opposing counsel or parties by email?

Email Audience, Tone, and Purpose

As with letters, discussed in Chapter 12, a lawyer's email message should reflect a tone that is appropriate for the audience, as well as the purpose of the communication. The recipient's age, level of education, legal experience, and mental and emotional condition should be considered. The level of formality and the degree of empathy expressed will vary with the audience.

Also as with letters, the purpose of the communication should be provided by the lawyer in the reference or "Re" line. Email is a quick method of communicating routine matters; the subject line should contain a brief summary of the message. The recipient of the email will appreciate knowing immediately what action is needed. The same reference should be retained when the lawyer sends further email on the same topic, provided it remains accurate.

Finally, a lawyer must remember that although more informal than a letter, an email is much more accessible. Email may be forwarded endlessly and read by virtually anyone; deleted email is almost always retrievable. As a result, the tone of an email should remain not only professional, but also positive. Negative messages are best delivered by telephone or in person, followed by a memorandum to the file memorializing the conversation.

Email Organization and Content

In the U.S., lawyers receive a large volume of email. Effective organization allows the recipient to prioritize and respond to the email appropriately. Of particular importance are addresses and reference lines, salutations, the message, and the closing.

Addresses and Reference Lines

As noted earlier, the email should contain an informative reference line. This allows for ease of filing, as well as for prioritization. In addition, the lawyer should carefully check the email address of the recipient before sending. For confidentiality and the attorney-client privilege to attach, emails must only be sent to their intended recipients. Similarly, emails should not be forwarded or sent "to all" absent careful consideration.

Salutations

A professional email should begin with a salutation. Although email is a less formal method of communication than a letter, lawyers customarily address their first email to a client or another professional using the individual's surname. Thereafter, the manner in which the recipient responds to the email will determine the degree of formality needed.

The Message

The text or message of an email should include meaningful content. Legal material should not be sent without an explanation. The best lawyers draft concise messages and, where available, include an attachment. If an attachment is not available, the lawyer will provide a brief summary of the information and conclude with the specific nature of the response needed and a deadline for responding. Finally, the immediacy of email creates special considerations with respect to dates and times. Lawyers should avoid references such as "tomorrow" and identify the time zone where relevant.

Closing

Lawyers conclude professional emails by thanking the recipient responding to the communication. As with letters, such a conclusion furthers relationship building. The lawyer will then close the email with a signature block. Also as with letters, the closing should be formal and respectful. Common closings include "Regards," "Sincerely," or "Respectfully." A signature block follows, including the lawyer's name, firm name, office telephone number, fax number, and email address. Most email correspondence generated by lawyers in the U.S. also includes a confidentiality warning, discussed below.

Email Replies and Acknowledgements

Email replies should follow the same conventions for addresses, reference lines, salutations, and closings as original emails. Lawyers in the U.S. place the answer or response to the original email in the first sentence of the email, to eliminate the necessity of "scrolling down." When responding, legal recipients must be careful not to forward confidential information as part of "the thread" of the email.

Effective lawyers make every effort to respond to clients, opposing counsel, and colleagues with an acknowledgement of their email, even if it is only sending a "thank you." Acknowledging communications strengthens relationships.

Email Ethics

Email and Legal Advice

The nature of email conditions the sender to expect an immediate response. A lawyer confronted with a client or colleague seeking legal advice should send a prompt response that the inquiry has been received and that an in-depth response will be forthcoming after the lawyer evaluates the issue. In the U.S., this generally satisfies the recipient's expectation of a prompt email response. The lawyer should then research and draft a response in the form most appropriate for the issue.

Email and Confidentiality

As discussed in Chapter 8, rules of professional conduct regarding confidentiality and attorney-client privilege often attach to a lawyer's communications with and about a client. Email communications present special concerns because they are easily misdirected, forwarded, and otherwise accessible to third parties.

Many lawyers place confidentiality warnings on email. Such warnings inform the recipient that the information is confidential and request a recipient who is not the addressee to destroy the message. Compliance with such warnings is unenforceable. Accordingly, lawyers will generally only include information in an email that they are willing to have made public.

Email and Relationship Building

As discussed in Chapter 9, communication is an important part of the attorney-client and other professional relationships. The recipient of an email message is unable to receive any verbal or body language cues to interpret the communication. More importantly, the lawyer is unable to view or hear the recipient's response to the email message. Intentions on both sides are easily misconstrued. As a result, a lawyer should follow up complex or difficult messages by telephone or personal meeting, followed by a memorandum to the file.

Telephonic Communications

As with email communications, telephone communications should be cognizant of lawyers' time and the need for efficiency. Among lawyers in the U.S., telephone conversations and messages are expected to promptly disclose the purpose of the communication, to be aware of confidentiality and privilege issues, and to be brief.

Voicemail greetings should be functional. First, greetings should convey the name and firm or corporation of the person being contacted, to confirm that the caller has reached the correct party. Second, the greeting should convey the "shortcut" for proceeding directly to the point where a message may be left. Third, the message should convey information for contacting another party, such as an administrative assistant.

Voicemail messages should be equally functional. The caller should leave a full name, firm or business name, and contact information including telephone area code. The caller should then concisely state the purpose of the call without revealing sensitive or confidential information.

Finally, as with email communications, prompt responses to voicemail messages are generally expected. Many law firms in the U.S. have a twenty-four hour response rule, irrespective of holidays and vacations. As with the email, any response requiring legal advice should be carefully considered both as to content and format, but the telephone communication should be promptly acknowledged.

Use of Electronic Communication Devices at Meetings

The general rule in the U.S. is that a lawyer attending a meeting with a colleague, client, or judge is expected to pay attention and avoid engaging with personal electronic devices. The results of violating this rule vary. Lawyers may be reprimanded by a judge, dismissed by a client, or negatively reviewed by a senior partner, among other sanctions. In those situations where it is necessary to receive or return communications electronically during a meeting, the lawyer should advise the other attendees in advance.

Analyzing the Client's Legal Needs and Issues

Let us return to the Palmer family. Dr. and Mrs. Palmer have asked our firm to explore the possibility of suing Suzy Ford, their teenage daughter's ice-hockey coach, for intentional infliction of emotional distress. In Chapter 12, we considered the issues raised in writing an advice letter to the Palmers. In what situations might it be preferable to contact the Palmers by email and what format should your email take? In what situations might it be appropriate to contact Suzy Ford or her counsel by email?

Client Communications

It is best not to send your advice letter in an email or as an email attachment. Confidential legal advice is best provided in a memorandum or formal letter, followed by a client counseling session. There are situations, however, when you will communicate with the Palmers via email. Email is an effective method of communicating routine matters. Assume the Palmers have chosen to pursue civil litigation. You filed a complaint for intentional infliction of emotional distress with the court and Suzy Ford's attorney, Tom Mohan, moved to dismiss the complaint for failure to state a claim. The court set a hearing for next month. This information may easily be transmitted by email, but certain formalities should be retained.

As with your letter to the Palmers, your email should reflect their age, education, and knowledge of legal matters. The email should also retain the formal tone of the letter. The purpose of your email should be communicated in the "Re" line. For example: Palmer v. Ford, March 15th Hearing on Motion to Dismiss the Complaint. This allows the Palmers to know what the email is about, without the necessity of opening it. It allows you, or your assistant, sufficient information to accurately file it.

Be careful to send the email to the Palmers' proper email address, to avoid waiving confidentiality. Begin the email with a formal salutation. For example: "Dear Dr. and Mrs. Palmer."

Your message should contain meaningful content. The Palmers are not lawyers and most likely have not previously been involved in a lawsuit. A message informing them of the upcoming hearing on the motion to dismiss should provide an explanation of the allegations of the motion, your response, the court's anticipated ruling, and the procedural options thereafter. It should also discuss the nature of the hearing and invite the Palmers to attend.

Close the email by thanking the Palmers. Include a formal signature block with the firm's contact information and the standard confidentiality provision.

A sample email to the Palmers is included in the sample documents below.

Opposing Counsel Communications

Also assume that you have a trial before another judge scheduled for the same week as the hearing. You do not expect the trial to actually take place that week, but want to alert opposing counsel of the potential conflict. This is also information which may easily be transmitted by email, but again the formalities discussed above should be retained. A sample email to Tom Mohan, Suzy Ford's attorney, is included in the sample documents below.

Sample Documents

Document 1
Client Email

Re: Julie Palmer/Suzy Ford: March 15th Hearing on Motion to Dismiss the Complaint

Dear Dr. and Mrs. Palmer:

Since our last meeting on _____, 20__ , Tom Mohan, Suzy Ford's attorney, has moved to dismiss our complaint for failure to state a claim. Suzy's attorney is essentially arguing that, even assuming all the facts alleged in our complaint are true, the law does not provide a remedy for Suzy's actions. We will respond with a discussion of the law on intentional infliction of emotional distress as applied to this case, similar to the analysis provided in our demand letter to Suzy.

The hearing before the judge on the motion will take place at 9:00 a.m. on March 15, 20__. It will involve oral argument by opposing counsel and myself on the motion. The judge may make his decision at the hearing or he may wait and issue a written opinion. It is not necessary for you to attend, but you are more than welcome to join me if you wish.

Assuming the motion is denied, Suzy must file an answer to our complaint. We will then begin the process of discovery, which we discussed at our last meeting. In the unlikely event the motion is granted, the case would be dismissed. However, it is highly probable that the judge would allow us to amend and refile the complaint.

I am attaching an electronic copy of the motion and the court's notice regarding the hearing. Please do not hesitate to contact me for more detailed information concerning the motion or the progress of your case. Please contact my office before March 15th if you wish to attend the hearing. Otherwise, I will contact you on March 16th.

Thank you for allowing our firm to represent you in this matter. We will continue to apply best efforts on your behalf and report to you as your case continues.

Sincerely,

Lawyer Name
Firm Name
Telephone and Fax Number
Email

This electronic message and all contents and attachments contain information from _____, which may be privileged, confidential or otherwise protected from disclosure. The information is intended to be for the addressee only. If you are not the addressee, then any disclosure, copy, distribution or use of this message, or its contents or any of its attachments, is prohibited. If you have received this electronic message in error, please notify us immediately and destroy the original message and all copies.

Document 2
Opposing Counsel Email

Re: Julie Palmer/Suzy Ford: March 15th Hearing on Motion to Dismiss the Complaint

Dear Tom:

I received your Motion to Dismiss in the *Palmer v. Ford* matter and the notice of hearing for March 15th. I have notified my clients of the hearing, but I wanted to let you know I am also scheduled for trial before Judge Woods that week so I may have to request an adjournment. I hope this won't create any difficulties for you. I will give you a call as soon as I know more about Judge Woods's trial docket.

Thanks for your anticipated cooperation. It is much appreciated.

Sincerely,

Lawyer Name
Firm Name
Telephone Number
Email

This electronic message and all contents and attachments contain information from _____, Esq. which may be privileged, confidential or otherwise protected from disclosure. The information is intended to be for the addressee only. If you are not the addressee, then any disclosure, copy, distribution or use of this message, or its contents or any of its attachments, is prohibited. If you have received this electronic message in error, please notify us immediately and destroy the original message and all copies.

Part Seven

Writing Skills: Transactional Drafting

Chapter 14

Introduction to Contract Drafting

Highlights

- In the U.S., lawyers who draft contracts and other non-litigation documents are often referred to as transactional lawyers.
- A transactional lawyer may provide a number of services for the client, including negotiating the deal, reviewing supporting documents, drafting the contract memorializing the agreement, and administering post-closing tasks.
- The process of drafting a contract generally begins with determining the client's objectives.
- Once the client's objectives are determined, the lawyer must consider the legal and factual context of the document.
- Few documents are created from "scratch"; lawyers make liberal use of form books, sample documents, and checklists.
- Although each contract should be tailored to fit the requirements of the unique transaction involved, most contracts in the U.S. have a similar structure.

Introduction

Chapters 14 and 15 concern transactional drafting. Many lawyers specialize in either litigation or transactional work, while others perform both. A lawyer is held to the same high level of competency by the professional rules of responsibility discussed in Chapter 8 irrespective of specialization.

The transactional lawyer generally becomes involved with the client when the transaction begins; the nature of the involvement depends on the client's needs. In any given transaction, a lawyer may provide a number of services. These include negotiating the deal, reviewing documents, drafting the contract, and handling post-closing tasks. The transactional lawyer seeks to accomplish the client's goals by producing a written agreement to govern the parties' ongoing relationship. This requires conceptualizing the relationship: who is required to do what, when they must do it, where they must do it, and how they must do it.

This chapter has four sections: (1) legal and ethical considerations in drafting contracts, (2) the drafting process for contracts, (3) the use of forms and checklists, and (4) the use of term sheets and letters of intent. Contract organization and core contract provisions are discussed in Chapter 15.

The Client

As you read this chapter, consider a long-time firm client: Vogel Pharmaceuticals, in Phoenix, Arizona. Vogel is a corporation that develops and produces prescription medications that treat a number of physical ailments, including high cholesterol. One of Vogel's most successful products is "Ultrastatin." Ultrastatin has been the most popular prescription medication on the market for treating high cholesterol for the last five years.

Larry Eckerman is the Chief Executive Officer of Vogel. Eckerman and the Vogel board of directors have become increasingly aware of the popularity of herbal remedies. Eckerman and the board believe they could greatly increase their profits by selling herbal products. Unfortunately, they have never developed such a product and lack the expertise to do so. They recently began searching for a newly developed herbal remedy to offer to their customers and were delighted to discover "WonderDRug."

WonderDRug is produced by Best Health, Inc. Best Health is a corporation in Dallas, Texas that manufactures herbal remedies. In addition to manufacturing herbal remedies, Best Health is a large contributor to political causes related to universal health care. It is specifically interested in health care coverage for natural health aids. It has a lot of support in Hollywood; "star" endorsements greatly enhance its sales. Over time, Best Health's primary mission has become the promotion of universal U.S. health care coverage for natural health aids. Best Health is always interested in introducing new herbal products into the marketplace. Many of these substances come out of the Amazon jungle.

Anna Maria Sing is a 42-year-old doctor and research scientist at Best Health. On a recent trip to Brazil and the Amazon jungle, Dr. Sing discovered a remedy for treating high cholesterol. Extracted from the bark of an indigenous tree, the Kapok, the remedy has one side effect: it may impair male virility. Dr. Sing gave the product the name of "WonderDRug."

Best Health was excited by the prospect of producing WonderDRug as a treatment for high cholesterol, but it had several concerns about selling it directly to consumers. Most notably, WonderDRug's virility impairing side effect is very unpopular with Best Health's Hollywood supporters. Several prominent Hollywood stars have gone so far as to threaten to publicly withdraw their support of Best Health's other products, should it sell WonderDRug. Best Health decided to produce WonderDRug, but to sell the product to other companies for resale to consumers.

Eckerman is not at all concerned about being popular in Hollywood. He has convinced the board of directors it could greatly increase Vogel's profits by selling WonderDRug as a non-prescription alternative, and possible gateway drug, to Ultrastatin.

In July, Eckerman met with Annick Anders, Chief Executive Officer of Best Health, to discuss WonderDRug. The parties agreed that Best Health will sell WonderDRug to Vogel at the following prices: $85 per case of WonderDRug (12 cans as a flavored liquid); $50 per box of WonderDRug as a flavored powdered mix; and $45 per bottle of WonderDRug tablets. Other issues discussed included exclusivity and certain warranties and representations.

Eckerman was concerned that, because WonderDRug requires the bark of the Kapok tree found only in the Amazon, Best Health might not be able to supply a sufficient amount of the product to keep up with the demand. He wanted to enter into an exclusive agreement with Best Health, so that Vogel had access to all of the WonderDRug Best Health could produce. Anders, however, was concerned that Vogel might not actively promote WonderDRug because it competes to some degree with Ultrastatin. She wanted to be able to sell the product to other buyers, should any express interest. Ultimately, the parties agreed to an exclusive arrangement for a period of one year.

Additionally, Best Health wanted Vogel to warrant and represent that, although it will be marketing the drug as an alternative to Ultrastatin for the treatment of high cholesterol, it will disclose the virility impairing effects. Vogel, on the other hand, wanted Best Health to warrant and represent that WonderDRug does effectively treat high cholesterol and that it has no known side effects other than impaired male virility. Both parties think they can make this deal work.

Eckerman has come to our firm on behalf of Vogel to negotiate and draft a contract memorializing the deal. What must you consider before drafting a contract for Vogel? How will you approach the drafting process?

Legal and Ethical Considerations in Contract Drafting

The basic legal requirements for a contract are relatively simple. The contract must have: (1) parties capable of contracting, (2) the agreement of such parties to contract, (3) a lawful object of the contract, and (4) sufficient consideration. There are, however, a number of federal, state, and local laws that impact contract drafting. As a result, the lawyer must be prepared to draft a contract that fully protects the client.

In addition, foreign lawyers should be aware that courts in the U.S. strictly adhere to the parol evidence rule when interpreting contracts governed by U.S. law. In general, the parol evidence rules provides that, where there is a written contract or agreement, that agreement will be enforced by a U.S. court as written. This concept is inconsistent with the United Nations Convention on Contracts for the International Sale of Goods and many jurisdictions.

Finally, the rules of professional responsibility, discussed in Chapter 8, apply to contract drafting as well as other legal services. The rules require lawyers to be competent and to apply the diligence and skill reasonably necessary for the performance of services. Any lawyer who lacks sufficient experience and training to act competently should consult with another lawyer before accepting the representation.

The Drafting Process

The procedure for drafting a contract varies depending on the needs of the client and the length and nature of the contract. Longer, more specialized contracts will generally be drafted by a team of lawyers with different specialties. Shorter, simpler contracts may be drafted by one lawyer.

Contracts also take varying forms. Many lawyers will use a master form, with blanks for specific information, with a series of different parties. Examples of such contracts include leases, insurance agreements, and consumer sales agreements. Complex contracts, such as those involving mergers and acquisitions, will involve numerous drafts and reviews by a number of experts to ensure that the contract complies with current industry practice and the most recent changes in the law. Regardless of the form of the contract, however, the process can be broken down into several steps.

Interviewing the Client

One of the most important tasks of the lawyer as transactional drafter is determining the client's objectives. The lawyer must understand the purpose of the document and the difficulties it is intended to prevent or resolve.

Chapters 9 and 10 discuss communication and interviewing techniques. The questions asked in the initial interview will be crucial to the drafting process. These should include the client's perception of the reason for the need for the contract, the client's understanding of each party's interests and concerns, and the duration of the contract. The lawyer should follow these general questions with those aimed at obtaining a specific understanding of the final content: who, what, when, where, why, and how. The lawyer's goal is to understand the client's business and any terms the parties have agreed upon, as well as to appreciate what further information will be required.

Counseling the Client

Chapter 11 discusses counseling techniques. Generally, the lawyer's role is to obtain, rather than evaluate, the client's objectives for the contract. Several exceptions exist, however: (1) a lawyer may not draft a document that facilitates fraud or other illegal conduct, (2) a lawyer has an obligation to discuss the legal impact of proposed contract objectives with the client, and (3) a lawyer should warn a client of objectives that are inconsistent with other stated goals.

Additionally, the lawyer should be aware of and counsel the client on any cultural differences between the parties or the jurisdictions involved. Of particular concern are methods of negotiation, discussed in Chapter 17, and prevalent business practices.

Finally, the transactional lawyer must carefully counsel the client regarding potential conflicts. In the U.S., the corporation is considered a legal entity having its own legal interests independent of its primary stakeholders and executives. Should differences arise, the lawyer and the individual client may find themselves in a conflicts situation. It is best to discuss the situation in advance and clarify it in an engagement letter, discussed in Chapter 18.

Identifying the Audience

The client is the primary audience for the contract. Nevertheless, the lawyer should recognize that a variety of individuals will utilize the document. The other parties to the transaction are an important audience, as they will be responsible for implementing the contract provisions. In addition, third parties may have an interest in the documents. These include banks and other financial institutions lending money to the parties. Finally, in the event a dispute arises, mediators, arbitrators, and judges may be interpreting the contract. In the U.S., a lawyer should be conscious of the court as the potential final audience of any agreement and draft documents that reflect the parties' agreement, while protecting the client's interests.

Considering the Context

In order to effectively draft transactional documents, the lawyer must evaluate the facts, research the law and similar contracts, and determine the substance of the contract. The factual context will vary for each contract. The lawyer must understand the parties' agreed terms and be familiar with their prior practices, as well as the practices of their trade. It is important to understand the business aspects of the deal in order to identify open issues in the agreement. Much of this information will be obtained during the client interview, discussed above. Other lawyers, practice manuals, and articles may offer checklists, discussed below.

The legal context will also vary. The lawyer must research the governing law in order to advise the client during the drafting process. In the U.S., contract law is generally a matter of state law. Nevertheless, a number of activities are required or prohibited by federal law. An attorney must research which laws control the client's individual factual situation.

In addition, the lawyer must accommodate any other contracts the client may have on a related issue. Each new contract must interact effectively with a client's existing contracts. Eventually, the lawyer will have sufficient information to begin drafting the document.

Developing Organization

In order to produce a document in the most efficient manner, most lawyers start with a model form or another contract from a similar transaction as a starting point for organizing a contract. The use of forms is discussed below.

Most contracts follow a standard organizational format. Within this framework, the lawyer has discretion in organizing contract substance. Such organization includes: (1) dividing the subject matter of the contract into sub-categories, (2) classifying each provision in the proper subcategory, and (3) logically arranging the order in which the subcategories are presented. The order may follow a chronological sequence or be based on the importance of the subcategory. Contract organization is discussed in Chapter 15.

Drafting Language

The substance of a contract is discussed in Chapter 15. From a language perspective, the lawyer is concerned with ambiguity, style and usage, definitions, terms of legal consequence, and format.

Ambiguity is to be avoided. It exists where a provision has inconsistent meanings. Three types of ambiguity are commonly seen in contracts. A semantic ambiguity exists when a word is capable of conflicting meanings. A syntactic ambiguity exists when conflicting meanings result from punctuation or the relationship between words in a sentence. A contextual ambiguity exists as a result of conflicting provisions.

The rules of style and usage in contract drafting require the drafter to achieve clarity and brevity. Simple words and phrases promote clarity. Meaningless legal language, repetition, and unnecessarily complicated language should be avoided.

The use of definitions in contracts is discussed more fully in Chapter 15. Choosing words that express the parties' intent is important, but the meaning of a word may be lost in a complicated sentence. Transactional lawyers strive to use short sentences consisting of subject, verb, and object.

Terms creating legal consequences are also discussed in Chapter 15. In general, in transactional drafting in the U.S., different English words create different legal relationships. The most common of these words are "may" and "shall."

Finally, the physical arrangement of a contract is important. White space, numbered lists, tabbing, indentation, and headings all assist in creating an effective document.

Reviewing the Document

Every contract must be carefully reviewed before it is submitted to the client. The lawyer should ensure that the document includes all provisions required by the law and requested by the client. Deficiencies in structure and style must be revised, typographical errors corrected, and the revised document proofread. The most minor error may impact the rights and obligations of the client.

Obtaining the Views of Other Parties

At various times in the drafting process, the lawyer may wish to circulate the contract and receive the feedback of the other parties to the transaction. Such feedback reduces time and expense by avoiding the drafting of unacceptable terms. It may also serve to build a relationship among the parties. Nevertheless, given the rules of professional responsibility, the lawyer should seek client approval before engaging in such discussions.

Post-Execution Monitoring

A lawyer is responsible for a contract as long as it has operative effect. Revisions to the document may be necessitated by changes in the law or the client's circumstances.

The Use of Forms and Checklists

Forms

As noted earlier, lawyers in the U.S. often review form contracts before beginning to draft. Such forms may be found online and in the library. Additionally, many law offices maintain form banks. Form contracts are available on most topics; many commercially prepared forms also include discussions of the applicable law. Use of a form in practice is not considered plagiarism.

Most clients will assume that a lawyer has reviewed several forms before beginning to draft. Consulting forms saves a lawyer time and a client money. It also assists a lawyer in recognizing important provisions and effective language for expressing rights and obligations.

Nevertheless, a lawyer must approach forms cautiously. Every transaction is unique; no provision should be adopted without revisions to reflect the individual client's needs. Over time, a lawyer creates a personal bank of forms as a resource. Such forms are invaluable as they reflect the thinking of the lawyer on similar transactions. Every form should be accompanied by an individually drafted checklist, discussed below.

Checklists

After determining the facts and the law and reviewing forms, most lawyers make a checklist of agreed terms and other points relating to the transaction. Form checklists are available online and in the library. The best starting point, however, is a checklist created by the lawyer for a similar transaction. As with form contracts, the lawyer should use the model checklist only as a guide.

The checklist should answer the questions of who, what, where, when, how, and why as well as include the agreed upon terms. It should also include the factual information obtained from the client during interview and counseling sessions and the legal information assembled during the research process. The checklist ensures that the lawyer includes all necessary provisions. It also assists the lawyer in organizing the contract and determining which provisions should be grouped together and the order in which they should appear.

The Use of Term Sheets and Letters of Intent

Term Sheets

In many transactions, the lawyer will begin drafting the contract after completing the checklist. In others, the lawyer may prepare a term sheet to be circulated among the parties. A term sheet is an outline of the proposed contract. It facilitates negotiation of, and agreement to, the contract by allowing all of the parties the opportunity to respond to essential terms early in the process.

Letters of Intent

A related, but different, document from the term sheet is the letter of intent. The letter of intent is signed by all of the parties and signifies that they have "agreed to agree." Letters of intent are most common in transactions where one of the parties is seeking to obtain financing or government approval. In many legal systems, a letter of intent is unenforceable as a contract. In the U.S., although letters of intent were traditionally not binding under common law, recent cases have held the breaching party liable. The determining factor appears to be whether there is an indication of an intent to be bound coupled with a specific obligation. As a result, lawyers must weigh the benefits of entering into a letter of intent with the potential downside of incurring undesired obligations.

Analyzing the Client's Legal Needs and Issues

Let us return to Larry Eckerman and Vogel Pharmaceuticals. Vogel, the producer of a number of prescription medications, is interested in purchasing WonderDRug, an herbal remedy for high cholesterol with virility impairing side effects, from Best Health. How will you approach the contract drafting process?

First, begin by interviewing Eckerman to determine Vogel's objectives, the general outline of the deal, and the details negotiated by Eckerman and Anders. You will learn that the parties have agreed that Best Health will sell Wonder-DRug to Vogel at the following prices: (1) $85 per case of WonderDRug, (2) $50 per box of WonderDRug, and (3) $45 per bottle of WonderDRug tablets. Further, Best Health will provide WonderDRug to Vogel exclusively for one year. Finally, Best Health will warrant and represent that WonderDRug does effectively treat high cholesterol and that it has no known side effects other than impaired virility. Vogel will warrant and represent that it will disclose the potential virility impairing effects of WonderDRug in males.

As part of the initial interview or a later counseling session, confirm that the Vogel and the Best Health boards of directors have approved the transaction. You or a partner may also want to raise with Eckerman the potential difficulties involved with a pharmaceutical company moving into sales of herbal remedies as well as the risks accompanying the side effects.

Second, carefully review all state and federal laws. For example, as a contract for the sale of goods, your contract will be governed by Article 2 of the Uniform Commercial Code. Article 2 is deferential to the contractual arrangements of private parties; it is considered a "default" law providing stand-in rules only where the essential terms of the contract have not been decided by the parties, but you will want to become familiar with the terms of Article 2 before drafting.

Third, confirm that Vogel does not have any other contracts with Best Health. Review any potentially related contracts by Vogel with third parties.

Fourth, once you have an understanding of the facts and the law, consult sample forms of contracts for the sale of goods. The sample contracts will help you in drafting checklists to ensure that you do not forget any key provisions and assist you with the organization of the contract, both discussed in Chapter 15. A sample contract checklist is included in the sample documents below.

Fifth, after consulting with your colleagues and client, you may wish to prepare a term sheet to be circulated to the parties to facilitate agreement with the essential terms early in the drafting process. A proposed term sheet for the Vogel-Best Health contract is also included in the sample documents below.

Sample Documents

Document 1
Contract Checklist

Title

- Identifies the nature of the contract, without being overly detailed
- All caps, centered, bold print

Introduction

- Identifies the parties
  - Identifies individuals using complete names and defined term names that will be used throughout the document
  - Identifies corporations and other entities using exact names as they appear in organization documents and defined term names that will be used throughout the document
- Identifies the nature of the transaction
- Provides a date

Background

- Includes facts explaining the nature and purpose of the agreement
- States the intentions of the parties
- Should not include covenants or other substantive provisions

Definitions

- Defines terms which are used outside of their normal meaning
- Should not include covenants or other substantive provisions
- Once defined a term should only be used in its defined sense in the document and should be capitalized or bolded

Consideration

- Provides a short statement of consideration or agreement
- Avoids legalese
- Examples: "In consideration of the mutual promises set forth in this Agreement, the parties agree as follows:" or "Accordingly, the parties agree as follows:"

Core Provisions

- Term of the contract and possibility and procedures for renewal
- Covenants or promises: establish rights and duties
- Conditions: trigger, excuse or modify rights and duties

- Representations and warranties: statements of fact made by one party and relied on by the others
- Waivers and releases: extinguish rights and duties
- Events of default, procedures for declaring default, remedies to redress default

General Provisions

- Choice of Law
- Choice of Forum
- Alternative Dispute Resolution
- Modification
- Integration
- Severability
- Waiver
- Merger
- Survivability
- Assignment
- Delegation
- Force Majeure
- Notices

Language of Agreement

- Evidences the parties' agreement to the terms of the contract
- Includes date referenced in the introductory section
- Example: "The parties agree to the terms of this Agreement entered into on the date first referenced above."

Signature Blocks

- Individual names are typed above or below signature line
- Organization names are typed above signature line containing "by," with the person's name and title typed below the signature line

Document 2
Checklist for Letter of Intent

Non-binding Provisions of a Letter of Intent

- Provides that the letter of intent is not binding
- Identifies the parties
- Identifies the subject matter of the transaction
- Identifies the payment price or compensation terms
- Provides for a method of payment
- Identifies the definitive agreement(s) that are contemplated
- Identifies the primary material terms to be included in the agreement(s)
  - Examples include conditions to be filled before the transaction is consummated, such as financing, non-customary representations and warranties, non-customary covenants, and indemnification terms
  - In the U.S. it is customary to avoid setting forth all of the material terms in order to avoid unintentionally creating a binding letter of intent

Binding Provisions of a Letter of Intent

- Describes the due diligence each party will be permitted to conduct
- Provides for termination rights under the letter of intent
- Provides for exclusivity in dealing during the term of the letter of intent
- Provides for the confidentiality of information disclosed
- Identifies those provisions of the letter of intent intended to be legally binding
  - Examples include the provisions controlling due diligence, the parties' obligations to deal exclusively with one another, the respective rights relating to termination, and any terms that may have been agreed to by the parties
- Provides an explicit expiration date and time for the letter of intent

Document 3
Term Sheet

Preamble

This Term Sheet summarizes the proposed terms and conditions under which Vogel Pharmaceuticals, Inc. ("Vogel") will purchase liquid, powder, and tablet forms of the herbal remedy WonderDRug from Best Health, Inc. ("Best Health"). The Confidentiality provision of this Term Sheet shall be a binding obligation irrespective of whether the transaction is consummated. No other legally binding obligations will be created until a definitive agreement is executed. This Term Sheet shall be governed in all respects by the laws of Arizona.

Closing Date

As soon as practicable following Best Health's acceptance of this Term Sheet.

Purchase of Goods

Best Health will agree to sell exclusively to Vogel, and Vogel will agree to buy exclusively from Best Health, all WonderDRug products produced by Best Health for a period of one year beginning on _____ 20__ and ending on _____, 20__.

Purchase Price

- $85.00 per case (12 cans) of liquid WonderDRug;
- $50.00 per box of powdered WonderDRug;
- $45.00 per bottle of tablets of WonderDRug.

Payment Terms

Vogel will agree to pay Best Health within thirty days after receipt by Vogel of Best Health's invoice, via electronic transfer.

Exclusivity

Best Health will agree not to sell, give away, or deliver WonderDRug to any entity or individual other than Vogel for a period of one year.

Warranties

- Best Health will agree to warrant and represent that the WonderDRug is a non-prescription product which treats high cholesterol and that WonderDRug has no known side effects other than the possibility of impaired male virility.

• Vogel will agree to warrant and represent that it will market Wonder-DRug, as a non-prescription alternative to its pharmaceutical product Ultrastatin, for the treatment of high cholesterol and that it will disclose that WonderDRug may impair male virility.

Confidentiality

The terms and conditions of this Term Sheet shall be held confidential by the parties.

Expiration

This term sheet expires in ten working days, on _____, 20 __, if not accepted by Best Health.

Executed this _____ day of _____, 20___.

VOGEL PHARMACEUTICALS, INC.   BEST HEALTH, INC.

By: _____   By: _____

Its: _____   Its: _____

Chapter 15

Drafting the Contract

Highlights

- In the U.S., an enforceable contract does not require any particular structure; a letter, or many other types of documents, may be found to constitute a contract.
- Generally, however, lawyers include the following sections: title, introduction, recitals, definitions, transitional clause, the body of the contract, general provisions, concluding statement, and signature block.
- The transitional clause precedes the body of the contract and provides the "words of agreement" signifying the exchange of promises as consideration for the contract.
- The body of the contract contains the core substantive contract provisions. Common provisions include deliverables, covenants, conditions, representations and warranties, guarantees and indemnities, waivers and releases, termination, events of default, and remedies.
- General provisions include matters not covered elsewhere in the contract, such as choice of law, choice of forum, notice, force majeure, assignment and delegation, successors and assigns, integration or merger, amendments and modification, and severability.

Introduction

No particular structure is required to form a contract in the U.S. Generally, however, a contract has an introductory section, a main body, and an end. The introductory section includes a title, a date, the identity of the parties, and a brief description of the nature of the contract. It then provides background information in the form of recitals, followed by the definitions. The main body of the contract includes the rights and obligations of the parties together with other core contract terms. Finally, the contract ends with a concluding statement, signature blocks, and any attachments.

General contract drafting principles were discussed in Chapter 14. This chapter focuses on the actual drafting of the contract. It has two sections: (1) contract organization, and (2) core substantive contract provisions.

The Client

In Chapter 14, you worked with a long-time firm client, Vogel Pharmaceuticals. Vogel, the producer of a number of prescription medications, is interested in purchasing WonderDRug, an herbal remedy for high cholesterol, from Best Health. In Chapter 14, you considered how to approach the contract drafting process and what forms or aids you might use in preparing a sales contract for Vogel. Review the client facts from Chapter 14, as well as the sample documents. As you read this chapter, consider how you will organize the contract for Vogel and what core substantive provisions you will include.

Contract Organization

Organization of the Contract

Most contracts contain the following parts: title, introduction, recitals, definitions, transitional clause, the body of the contract containing the core substantive terms, general provisions, concluding statement, and signature block.

Complex Contracts

A complex contract may include a title page and a table of contents. The title page and table of contents precede the introductory statement of the contract. The title page states the title of the contract; it may also include the names of the parties. The table of contents assists the reader in locating specific provisions.

The Title

If the contract does not have a title page, the title is centered at the top of the first page. It generally appears in bolded, capitalized text. The text should identify the substantive nature of the contract in a manner which distinguishes it from the other documents in the electronic files.

Introduction

The first paragraph below the title is known as the introductory statement or simply the introduction. It includes the type of contract as reflected in its title, the names of the parties, and the date of the contract.

In the U.S., the date referenced is assumed to be the date when the contract is signed. It is also assumed to be the date the contract becomes operative, known as the "effective date." If the date of signing is not the effective date, the effective date should be specifically provided for within the substantive terms of the contract.

The parties should be identified by their full legal names. It is also common to include their citizenship or place of residence. Addresses are generally not included in the introduction, but rather in the notice provision discussed below. After the party has been identified, it is common to provide for a shortened name or the party's legal position in the contract. This term should then be used consistently within the contract.

Recitals

Recitals, also known as background provisions, are factual statements that describe the reason for the contract. Recitals may address the parties' backgrounds, their relationship to each other, their motives for entering into the contract, or any other relevant facts. Recitals are often referenced by a court to resolve disputes relating to the interpretation of ambiguous contract terms. Recitals are not enforceable provisions of the contract, however, and should not include specific provisions providing for the rights and duties of the parties. All agreed terms should appear in the body of the contract.

Definitions

Definitions provide a defined term for proper names, complex concepts, or words that have a meaning specific to the contract. A definitions section is not required and, where used, may appear in a variety of positions in a contract. Traditionally, the definitions section follows the recitals and appears before the substantive provisions of the contract. Where the recitals include terms requiring definition, however, the definitions section may precede the recitals. Further, depending on the nature of the contract, definitions may appear at the beginning of the substantive contract terms or at the end of the contract. Regardless of where the definitions are placed, the words defined should be capitalized and placed in alphabetical order. Thereafter, the words are capitalized throughout the contract and used only in their defined sense. Where a provision in the contract refers to the contract itself, the defined term "Agreement" is used to refer to the contract.

Finally, as with recitals, definitions are not enforceable provisions of the contract. All agreed terms should appear in the body of the contract.

Transitional Clause

A transitional clause, also known as the "words of agreement" or "words of consideration," follows the definitions and precedes the body of the contract. As noted in Chapter 14, consideration is necessary for each party to be bound to perform under the contract. The transitional clause is a simple statement. For example: "The parties agree as follows." Such language signifies the exchange of promises as consideration for the contract and alerts the reader that all of the provisions that follow are enforceable. In contemporary drafting in the U.S., lawyers avoid convoluted words of agreement containing phrases such as "wherefore," "hereafter," and other legalese.

Core Substantive Provisions

The main body of the contract includes all of the agreed upon substantive provisions of the transaction. The general content of the substantive provisions—deliverables, covenants, conditions, representations and warranties, guarantees and indemnities, releases, termination, default and remedies—are discussed later in this chapter. The provisions should be organized chronologically, or in another logical framework dictated by the transaction, and divided into sections and subsections.

Dispute Resolution Provisions

Litigation can be time-consuming and expensive. As a result, many parties include dispute resolution sections in their contracts, either in the core provisions section or the miscellaneous provisions section. The content of alternative dispute resolution provisions is discussed in Chapter 16.

Miscellaneous Provisions

Miscellaneous provisions, also known as "boilerplate" or "general" provisions, follow the core provisions of the contract. Miscellaneous provisions relate to the administration and enforcement of the contract, including provisions on choice of law, choice of forum, notice, and similar matters.

Although referred to as boilerplate, the miscellaneous provisions are as important as the core provisions. The lawyer must carefully consider the language of each provision and its impact on the other sections of the contract and the client's interests. The following miscellaneous provisions are found in many contracts.

Choice of Law

The choice of law provision designates which law will govern the interpretation and enforcement of the contract. In the U.S., this is generally the law of the state of one of the parties, as private contractual relations are governed by state law. Specific federal laws are referenced, as applicable. If a foreign treaty may affect the contract, the parties must consider the best governing law for the contract and designate their preference in the choice of law provision.

Choice of Forum

The choice of forum provision designates where, and by whom, disputes arising under the contract will be resolved. The country of any of the parties may be chosen as the forum. In the U.S., the contract must identify a specific state. Alternative dispute resolution forums, such as arbitration, may also be chosen.

Choice of Language

The choice of language provision designates the language used to interpret the contract in the event of disputes. The choice of language provision also requires the controlling language to be used in all communications and documents related to the contract.

Notice

Most contracts require that the parties provide each other with notice in specified circumstances. This provision describes to whom the notice must be sent, where, and by what method.

Force Majeure

The force majeure provision will excuse delay, or discharge the duty of performance, in the event of natural disasters, labor disputes, changes in government policies or laws, or similar events. Each force majeure provision must be drafted to reflect the applicable law and the parties' intentions. In the U.S., for instance, the Uniform Commercial Code will allow default where performance becomes "commercially impracticable." Lawyers drafting international contracts may wish to specifically adopt or reject this provision.

Assignment and Delegation

An assignment provision permits or restricts the parties from assigning their respective rights under the contract to a third party. A delegation provision permits or restricts the parties from delegating their respective obligations under the contract to a third party. In the U.S., both provisions are commonly grouped in the same section.

As with force majeure provisions, assignment and delegation provisions must be drafted to reflect the applicable law and the intentions of the parties. In the U.S., for instance, the Uniform Commercial Code renders anti-assignment clauses unenforceable in certain cases relating to the assignment of rights to payment. Similarly, a general prohibition against assigning rights may not be effective against an involuntary assignment arising by operation of law as in a bankruptcy. To be effective under U.S. law, the assignment provision must identify the prohibited involuntary assignment.

Successors and Assigns

The successors and assigns provision is closely related to the assignment and delegation provision. The provision binds a transferring party's successor and assigns to the terms of the contract and requires the non-transferring party to perform its obligations to the assignee. The successors and assigns provision is increasingly omitted as duplicative in U.S. contracts.

Integration or Merger

The integration or merger provision provides that the executed contract constitutes the entire agreement between the parties and supersedes all previous negotiations and agreements. In the U.S., this provision evidences the parties' intent to invoke the parol evidence rule discussed in Chapter 14.

Amendments, Modification, and Waiver

Amendment, modification, and waiver provisions provide that the contract may not be amended, modified, or waived unless agreed to in a signed writing. Such provisions are consistent with the parol evidence rule discussed in Chapter 14. Nevertheless, certain courts in the U.S. have allowed parties to amend or waive provisions by their conduct or by oral agreement. The lawyer's choice of governing law may therefore determine the effectiveness of these provisions.

Severability

The severability provision provides that in the event any part of the contract becomes unenforceable, the remaining provisions will continue in full force and effect. Lawyers should carefully consider the intent of the parties in drafting this provision. The parties may wish to terminate the contract if a core provision is rendered unenforceable.

Concluding Statement

The concluding statement signals the end of the substantive provisions of the contract and transitions to the signature block. As with the transitional clause, the concluding statement should be simple and avoid legalese. For example: "Agreed to and executed on the date stated in the introduction."

Signature Blocks

The contract must be signed to be enforceable. The format of the signature blocks is determined by whether the party is an individual or a business or governmental entity. For an individual, the full name of the person identified in the introduction appears under or above the signature line. For business and governmental entities in the U.S., the entity's legal name is inserted as a heading above the signature line. The word "by" precedes the signature line to signify that the individual signing is acting as an agent for the entity. The name and title of the individual appears under the signature line.

In the U.S., not all contracts require signatures to be witnessed and notarized. Where required, notaries verify only that the individuals signing the documents have proper identification.

Attachments

Any exhibits, schedules, or other items referred to in the contract must be attached at the end of the contract.

Core Substantive Contract Provisions

The main body of the contract contains the core substantive provisions of the contract. This section should contain all of the promises that the parties have made, be logically organized, and use headings and subheadings. The necessary core provisions will vary with the nature of the transaction. Following are common core contract provisions.

Deliverables

Deliverables, also known as action statements or items, establish the principal exchange between the parties. In the U.S., a contract for the sale of goods governed by the Uniform Commercial Code would include a description of the items to be sold, the seller's agreement to sell and the buyer's agreement to buy the items, the purchase price, and the time, place, and methods for delivery and payment.

Covenants

Covenants create the rights and duties of the parties under the contract. A duty is a legally enforceable obligation to do or refrain from doing certain things. The nonperformance of a contractual duty makes the breaching party liable in damages to the other party or, alternatively, subject to a decree of specific performance. It may also excuse the other party's performance, temporarily or permanently. The words "shall" or "shall not" are generally used to create a duty.

A possessor of rights is the party to whom the duty is owed. The right entitles that party to enforce the duty. The words "is entitled to" are used to create a right to do or refrain from doing something.

A privilege creates a discretionary authority to act. A privilege differs from a right in that the other party has no corresponding duty. The word "may" is used to create a privilege.

Conditions

Conditions trigger, excuse, or modify rights and duties. A party has a right to rely on the covenants of the other side and is relieved of its duty to fulfill those covenants if the other party fails to perform. Performance under a contract may also be conditioned on truth of the representations and warranties, discussed below, of the opposing party. Non-satisfaction of a condition means that the legal consequence does not come to fruition.

Representations and Warranties

Representations and warranties record statements of fact made by one party and relied on by the other. A party may only make representations and warranties regarding subjects under its control. A representation is a statement of presently existing fact that is intended to induce reliance and action by the other party; it does not concern future events. A statement regarding a future event over which the party has control is framed as a covenant. A statement regarding a future event over which the party does not have control is framed as a condition.

A warranty is a statement made concerning facts or representations where the warrantor promises to ensure that the facts are as stated and will remain so throughout the term of the contract. A breached or incorrect warranty may result in an action for damages. Representations and warranties should be drafted in the present or past tense.

Guarantees and Indemnities

A guarantor is one who promises that, if another party does not perform a duty, the guarantor will. A guaranty provision requires the signer to perform a third party's obligations. Indemnities involve a contractual obligation where one party, the indemnitor, engages to hold another, the indemnitee, harmless from losses to third parties. A common indemnity provision covers any losses from a breach or inaccuracy of a representation or warranty.

Waiver and Release

Waiver and release are closely related concepts. Waiver involves the intentional, voluntary relinquishment of a known right. Release involves the discharge or abandonment of a right of action. A provision waiving a right, claim, or privilege constitutes a forfeiture of those rights. A provision releasing a right, claim, or privilege constitutes a cancellation of the ability to assert those rights.

Termination

Termination provisions provide for the termination of the contract. They may include language describing when and how the contract will terminate, as well as the notice required for termination.

Events of Default and Remedies

An event of default is an occurrence that gives the non-defaulting party the right to seek remedies such as termination of the contract or damages. The default and remedies section of a contract generally begins with a listing of what events will constitute "events of default." Common events of default include failure to perform an obligation, particularly failure to pay monies when due, or breach or inaccuracy of a representation or warranty.

The provisions that establish a default are generally followed by provisions that specify: remedies, whether those remedies are automatic or elective on the part of the non-defaulting party, how the election of remedies is to be made, and whether the remedies are mutually exclusive or cumulative. Events of default under one contract may constitute an event of default under another contract; this is known as a "cross-default."

Analyzing the Client's Legal Needs and Issues

Let us return to Vogel and its contract for the sale of the herbal remedy WonderDRug. How will you organize the contract and what core substantive provisions will you include?

Your contract for the purchase of WonderDRug should include an introduction, recitals, definitions, transitional clause, core substantive provisions, general terms, concluding statement, and signature blocks.

Draft the introductory section to identify the corporate parties to the contract by name and legal position. For example: "Vogel Pharmaceuticals, Inc. (Buyer) and Best Health, Inc. (Supplier)." Draft the recitals to contain background information about the parties and any other information about their intent that might be useful to the court in the event the contract requires interpretation. For example: "Buyer is a pharmaceutical company that develops and produces medications; Supplier manufactures and promotes the use of homeopathic and herbal remedies." Define and capitalize those terms that do not have a plain dictionary meaning. For example: "Product means Wonder-DRug in its liquid, powder, or capsule form."

Draft a simple transitional clause of consideration to follow the definitions. For example: "In consideration of the mutual promises below, the parties agree as follows."

Draft the substantive provisions so that it is clear which party has the legal obligation to perform. Set forth enough detail so that the parties can easily determine their rights and obligations. You must include price, quantity, delivery, and the term or length of the agreement. Remember as to quantity, that Best Health has agreed to supply to Vogel and Vogel has agreed to buy all of the WonderDRug that is produced during the term of the contract. This may be considered an output agreement under the Uniform Commercial Code. The Uniform Commercial Code provides that the quantity term in an output contract means such actual output as may occur in good faith. This meaning will be automatically included in your contract, unless you provide otherwise. For each legal obligation, draft a corresponding provision regarding the remedy in the event of a breach. Also, include provisions permitting the parties to terminate the agreement.

Finally, draft those miscellaneous or general provisions that are needed in this specific transaction. Always include choice of forum, choice of law, and notice. Follow the miscellaneous terms with simple language of agreement. For example: "Each of the parties has caused this Agreement to be executed by an authorized representative as of the date first written above." Close the contract with signature blocks.

A Supply and Purchase Agreement for the Vogel-Best Health transaction is included in the sample documents below.

Sample Documents

Document 1
Supply and Purchase Agreement

This Supply and Purchase Agreement, ("Agreement") is entered into this __ day of _____, 20__, between Vogel Pharmaceuticals, Inc., ("Buyer"), having its principal place of business in Phoenix, Arizona and Best Health, Inc., ("Supplier"), having its principal place of business in Dallas, Texas.

RECITALS

1. Buyer is the developer, producer, and seller of prescription medications including Ultrastatin, the most popular prescription medication on the market for treating high cholesterol for the last five years.
2. Supplier is the manufacturer and seller of herbal remedies, including WonderDRug.
3. WonderDRug, extracted from the bark of the Kapok tree, is a newly discovered natural remedy for the treatment of high cholesterol.
4. Buyer and Supplier desire to enter into an exclusive supply and purchase agreement where Buyer shall purchase and Supplier shall sell all WonderDRug produced for a period of one year.

DEFINITIONS

1. "Forms of the Product" means the liquid, powder, and tablet forms of WonderDRug.
2. "Product(s)" means WonderDRug extracted from the bark of the Kapok tree found in the Amazon.
3. "Term" means the duration of this Agreement from _____, 20__ to _____, 20__.

In consideration of the mutual promises set forth below, Buyer and Supplier agree:

TERMS AND CONDITIONS

1. *Term.* This Agreement is for an initial term of one year, commencing on _____, 20__ and terminating on _____, 20__. This Agreement may only be renewed by mutual written agreement by the Buyer and Supplier.

2. *Description—Sale of Goods.* Buyer shall purchase exclusively from Supplier and Supplier shall sell exclusively to Buyer all Forms of the Product produced by Supplier during the Term of this Agreement.

3. *Price.* Buyer shall pay the following prices to Supplier:
    a. $85.00 per case (12 cans) of liquid Product;
    b. $50.00 per box of powdered Product;
    c. $45.00 per bottle of tablets of Product.

4. *Purchase Order.* Buyer shall submit purchase orders, on the first day of each month, for the entirety of Supplier's stock of the Product, providing: (i) what percentage, which must add up to 100%, of the available Product that shall be produced in each of the agreed upon forms: liquid, powdered, and tablet, and (ii) the expected delivery date.

5. *Acknowledgment.* Supplier shall confirm the purchase order with an acknowledgment within 7 days of receiving the purchase order, and shall provide: (i) a report containing the amount of Product available for production that month, (ii) the quantities that correspond to Buyer's percentage breakdown of each Form of the Product Buyer will receive, (iii) confirmation of the delivery date, and (iv) an invoice with the total purchase price for that month.

6. *Delivery and Shipments*
    a. *Delivery.* Supplier shall deliver the Product in accordance with the date requested in the purchase order and confirmed in the acknowledgement to Buyer at Buyer's warehouse:
        12345 First Street
        Phoenix, Arizona
    b. *Partial Shipment.* No partial shipment shall be accepted by Buyer unless authorized by the Buyer or in connection with properly executed notice of force majeure.
    c. *Shipment Costs.* The Products shall be shipped free on board ("F.O.B.") Supplier's facility.
    d. *Shipment Method.* Supplier shall arrange for shipment of Product by contacting Buyer and shall use Buyer's carrier of choice. It shall be Buyer's responsibility to file any claims for loss with the common carrier.
    e. *Right of Inspection.* Buyer shall have the right to inspect the goods at the time and place of delivery.
    f. *Procedure as to Rejected Goods.* Within 24 hours of delivery, Buyer shall provide notice to Supplier of rejection of any Product. Such notice shall specify in detail the basis of Buyer's rejection. Any rejected Product shall be returned at Supplier's expense. Supplier shall have the option of replacing the rejected Product or crediting Buyer's account.

7. *Payment Terms.* Payments shall be made to Supplier within Thirty (30) days after receipt by Buyer of Supplier's invoice by electronic transfer to:
    Bank of Texas
    Account # 12345678
    Routing # 012345678

8. *Title.* Title to the goods shall remain with the Supplier until Buyer receives possession of the Products.

9. *Risk of Loss.* Risk of loss of the Product shall pass to the Buyer upon delivery F.O.B. Supplier's facility.

10. *Exclusivity.* Supplier covenants that it shall exclusively sell all Forms of the Product to Buyer during the Term of this Agreement. Supplier further covenants that it will not sell, give away, or deliver to any other person, firm, or entity the Product or any Form of the Product, without the prior consent of the Buyer.

11. *Buyer's Warranties.*
    a. Buyer warrants and represents that it will market the Product as a non-prescription alternative to Ultrastatin for the treatment of high cholesterol.
    b. Buyer warrants and represents that it will disclose that the Product may impair male virility.

12. *Supplier's Warranties.*
    a. Supplier warrants and represents that the Product treats high cholesterol.
    b. Supplier warrants and represents that the Product has no known side effects other than impaired male virility.

13. *Additional Warranties.* These warranties are in addition to all other warranties, express or implied, provided by Arizona law.

14. *Confidentiality.* The terms and conditions of this Agreement shall be held in confidence by the parties. This provision shall survive the termination of this Agreement.

15. *Events of Default by Supplier.* Supplier shall be deemed to be in default under this Agreement if:
    a. The scheduled performance dates shall be exceeded by more than thirty (30) days; or

     b. Supplier defaults in the performance of any material obligation or covenant under this Agreement and does not substantially cure such default or breach within thirty (30) days after Supplier's receipt of written notice from Buyer; or

     c. Any material representation or warranty made by Supplier is breached and remains uncured after thirty (30) days following Supplier's receipt of written notice from Buyer.

16. *Buyer's Remedies in the Event of Supplier's Default.* If any event of default occurs and is not cured within the applicable period, Buyer, at its sole option, may employ any remedy then available to it, including, but not limited to, the following:

     a. Proceed by appropriate court action to enforce performance by Supplier of the applicable covenants and obligations of this Agreement and to recover damages for the breach thereof; or

     b. Terminate this Agreement upon thirty (30) days' prior written notice; or

     c. Pursue any other rights or remedies available to Buyer under the laws of the State of Arizona.

17. *Events of Default by Buyer.* Buyer shall be deemed to be in default under this Agreement if:

     a. There is a default by Buyer in payment (except in the case of a bona fide dispute); or

     b. Buyer defaults in the performance of any material obligation or covenant under this Agreement and does not substantially cure such default or breach within thirty (30) days after Buyer's receipt of written notice from Supplier; or

     c. Any material representation or warranty made by Buyer is breached and remains uncured after thirty (30) days following Buyer's receipt of written notice from Supplier.

18. *Supplier's Remedies in the Event of Buyer's Default.* If any event of default occurs and is not cured within the applicable period, Supplier, at its sole option, may employ any remedy then available to it, including, but not limited to, the following:

     a. Withhold performance until all such defaults have been cured; or

     b. Terminate this Agreement upon thirty (30) days' prior written notice; or

     c. Proceed by appropriate court action to enforce performance by Buyer of the applicable covenants and obligations of this Agreement and to recover damages for the breach thereof; or

d. Pursue any other rights and remedies available to Supplier under the laws of the State of Arizona.

GENERAL PROVISIONS

1. *Forum.* The parties consent to the exclusive jurisdiction of the state and federal courts located in Arizona for the determination of all issues related to this Agreement.

2. *Choice of Law.* This Agreement shall be governed by the laws of the state of Arizona without regard to the conflict of laws principles.

3. *Merger/Integration.* This Agreement is intended by the parties as a final expression of their purchase and sale arrangement and is intended also as a complete and exclusive statement of the terms of their agreement.

4. *Modification.* The terms of this Agreement may not be modified except upon written consent of the parties.

5. *Severability.* Any portion of this Agreement which is held to be invalid or unenforceable by a court of competent jurisdiction shall be ineffective only to the extent of the prohibition without invalidating the remaining provisions of this Agreement.

6. *Waiver.* No right or claim arising out of a breach of this Agreement can be discharged in whole or in part by a waiver or renunciation of the right or claim unless the waiver or renunciation is supported by consideration and is in writing signed by the aggrieved party.

7. *Assignment and Delegation.* No right or interest in this Agreement shall be assigned by either Buyer or Supplier without the written permission of the other party. No delegation of any obligation owed, or of the performance of any obligation, by either party shall be made without the written permission of the other party.

8. *Force Majeure.* Neither party shall be considered in default or be liable for any failure to perform or delay in performing any provision of this Agreement for any reason beyond its control, including: an act of God, fire, explosions, hostilities or war (declared or undeclared), striking or work stoppage involving either party's employees or governmental restrictions. The party declaring force majeure will provide prompt notice in writing of the commencement of the condition, the nature of the situation, and the termination of the condition. The declaring party shall use every reasonable means to resume full performance of this Agreement as promptly as possible.

9. *Notice.* All notices or other communications required or permitted under the terms of this Agreement shall be made in writing and shall be deemed given: (i) upon hand delivery, (ii) upon receipt and written response from the other party by email, (iii) by commercial overnight courier with written verification of receipt, or (iv) three (3) business days after deposit of same in the Certified Mail, Return Receipt Requested, first class postage and registration fees prepaid and correctly addressed to the parties at their respective addresses. Notice shall be effective upon receipt.

    a. Notice to Seller shall be addressed to:

        Best Health, Inc.
        Attn: Chief Executive Officer
        12345 First Street, Suite 1000
        Dallas, Texas

    b. Notice to Buyer shall be addressed to:

        Vogel Pharmaceuticals
        Attn: Chief Executive Officer
        121 Executive Drive
        Phoenix, Arizona

The Parties agree to the terms of this Agreement, as of the date first referenced above.

BEST HEALTH, INC.   VOGEL PHARMACEUTICALS, INC.

_____   _____
By: Annick Anders   By: Larry Eckerman
Its: Chief Executive Officer   Its: Chief Executive Officer

Part Eight

Practice Skills:
Alternative Dispute Resolution
and Negotiation and Settlement

Chapter 16

Alternative Dispute Resolution

Highlights

- Alternative Dispute Resolution, or "ADR," is the resolution of disputes without trial. The most common forms of ADR are arbitration, mediation, early neutral evaluation, mini-trials, and summary jury trials.
- Arbitration is the most structured form of ADR; in arbitration, the parties present their positions to neutral fact-finders who issue a decision.
- Mediation involves the resolution of disputes through cooperation and problem solving; the parties work with a neutral third party who acts as a facilitator.
- Early neutral evaluation, or case evaluation, involves the evaluation of a case by neutral lawyers.
- A mini-trial process may be used to privately resolve commercial disputes; the parties make summary presentations of their best case to a neutral advisor.
- In a summary jury trial, the parties present a summary of their evidence to a mock jury.

Introduction

The resolution of disputes without trial, known as alternative dispute resolution or "ADR," is one of the fastest growing trends in the U.S. legal system. There are many reasons for ADR's popularity. Litigation in court is costly and time consuming. In addition, most proceedings are open to the public. ADR leads to faster resolutions, fewer costs, and greater privacy. The most popular ADR methods are arbitration and mediation. Additional ADR mechanisms include early neutral evaluation, mini-trials, and summary jury trials.

Counsel and clients considering ADR have several factors to weigh prior to selecting a particular dispute resolution system. First, is the need for a quick resolution of the dispute. Second, are the costs of the various dispute mechanisms and the financial resources of the parties. Third, is the necessity for a formal exchange of information. Fourth, is the required expertise of the decision maker. Fifth, is the necessity for a binding and enforceable decision. Sixth, is the desire of the parties for privacy.

This chapter provides an overview of the types of ADR popular in the U.S. It has eight sections: (1) arbitration, (2) mediation, (3) mediation-arbitration, (4) early neutral evaluation, (5) mini-trial, (6) summary jury trial, (7) common ADR contract provisions, and (8) multicultural considerations. Negotiation, a related process in which the parties resolve disputes by reconciling conflicting positions, is discussed in Chapter 17.

The Client

In Chapters 14 and 15, you worked with our client Vogel Pharmaceuticals to draft a sales contract involving the purchase of WonderDRug—developed by Dr. Sing to manage high cholesterol—by Vogel from Best Health. Eckerman, Chief Executive Officer of Vogel, reports that the purchase and the relationship with Best Health are proceeding well, thanks to your insightful drafting. Vogel, however, has a new legal issue involving an employment dispute.

As you read this chapter, consider Vogel's new legal issue. The facts of the dispute, as reported by Eckerman, are as follows.

As a result of the high sales volume generated by WonderDRug, Vogel decided to form an herbal remedy division. None of the existing Vogel executives had the skills to lead the division, so Eckerman began looking for outside talent. During his search, Eckerman continuously encountered the reputation of Dr. Anna Maria Sing.

Dr. Sing holds a law degree, as well as a medical degree, and frequently contributes articles to social media sites on the importance of herbal remedies. Of course, she is also the developer of WonderDRug. Eckerman became convinced that Dr. Sing was the perfect person to serve as vice president of sales and development for Vogel's new herbal remedy division. He tracked her down in the Amazon, working on a new drug for Best Health to reduce blood pressure, and asked her to come to Phoenix to meet the Vogel board of directors and discuss the position.

After working fifteen long years at Best Health, many of them in the jungle, Dr. Sing confided in Eckerman that she was ready for a change. She flew to Phoenix to meet the members of the Vogel board of directors and accepted the position, executing an employment contract. Pursuant to the terms of the employment contract, Dr. Sing agreed to accept a starting salary of $350,000 with Vogel and terminate her relationship with Best Health. She also agreed to a covenant not to compete, precluding her from competing in any way with Vogel for a period of one year, should the Vogel-Sing employment relationship be terminated. Lastly, she agreed to a confidentiality provision limiting the use of Vogel's confidential and proprietary information during the term of her employment and for one year thereafter.

Unfortunately, almost immediately upon commencement of Dr. Sing's employment relationship with Vogel, things began to sour. According to Eckerman, Dr. Sing proved incapable of appreciating the shareholder expectations at a pharmaceutical firm such as Vogel. Every project she proposed was too costly or in conflict with Vogel's existing pharmaceutical products.

When she subsequently met with Eckerman to tell him that she wanted to resign from Vogel, he was neither surprised nor disappointed. However, when she revealed she wanted to return to Best Health and the jungle to continue her work on an herbal cure for high blood pressure, Eckerman became furious. He immediately told her that her proposed employment with Best Health would violate the non-compete provision in her employment contract. The non-compete provision, drafted by a young attorney in the employment section of our firm, states: "If this agreement is terminated by Employee for any reason, Employee must not become employed, for a period of one year after termination, with any competitor of Vogel in the pharmaceutical industry." As Eckerman tells it, however, Dr. Sing was unimpressed. She responded that "Best Health isn't in the pharmaceutical business" and "I can hardly compete from the Amazon," and left the room.

Vogel has a number of ongoing lawsuits over its pharmaceutical products at the moment and does not particularly wish to become involved in employment litigation with Dr. Sing. What alternative methods of dispute resolution might you suggest?

Arbitration

Arbitration is the most common and the most structured form of alternative dispute resolution. In arbitration, the parties present their respective positions to a neutral fact-finder, or a panel of fact-finders, whom then issue a decision. There is neither a judge nor a jury. The arbitrator may be a lawyer or an expert in the subject matter of the dispute.

Parties usually agree in advance by contract to arbitrate a dispute. There is no prohibition, however, from entering into an agreement to arbitrate after a dispute arises. Arbitration proceedings operate under rules administered by an arbitration organization, such as the American Arbitration Association.

The organization appoints the arbitrator and administers the proceedings. Arbitrations begin by a claimant filing a written arbitration claim with the arbitration organization and serving it on a respondent. The respondent answers and may counterclaim.

The pre-trial and trial procedures discussed in Chapter 2 are not required. The arbitrator is bound by neither procedural nor substantive law in making his decision. Accordingly, unless the parties otherwise agree, the rules of evidence, the rules of procedure, and stare decisis are inapplicable to arbitration proceedings.

Although arbitration proceedings are less formal than judicial proceedings, the process is more rigorous than other methods of ADR. The parties or their counsel submit written reports to the arbitrator. They also engage in oral argument before the arbitrator in a hearing, and may prepare exhibits and call witnesses. Following the hearing, the arbitrator issues a written arbitration award.

The arbitrator's award is generally binding. Courts may validate or invalidate agreements to arbitrate and they may confirm or vacate an arbitrator's decision. Courts rarely, however, review the merits of an arbitrator's decision. The exception is the limited number of disputes that state and federal courts require to go to arbitration. The decision of an arbitrator in such cases is not binding.

A binding arbitration award is effective as a judgment; arbitration awards are legally enforceable in all 50 states and the federal courts. A non-binding award is only advisory. Any party may refuse to accept the decision and have the dispute resolved by the courts.

Mediation

Mediation—similar to the process of conciliation, popular outside of the U.S.—involves parties resolving their disputes with the assistance of a mediator. The mediator facilitates a settlement in a private setting. Participants include the parties, their lawyers or representatives, and the impartial mediator.

Parties may mediate voluntarily by agreement, entered into either before or after a dispute arises, or as mandated by a court. Mediation differs from litigation and arbitration in that a resolution reached through mediation is never binding. The parties may, however, enter into a binding contract memorializing the mediation agreement.

In preparation for mediation, the parties identify their interests and evaluate their positions, determining in advance a range of acceptable resolutions. The parties also study and evaluate the other side's positions. In addition, many mediators require the parties or their counsel to submit a mediation statement in advance of the mediation session. The mediation statement summarizes the case from the party's perspective and provides a set of goals for the mediation.

The process of mediation begins with each party providing an opening statement to the mediator summarizing the facts of the dispute and the party's contentions. Following the opening statements, the parties engage in an exchange of information and views. Sometimes such sessions occur with the mediator alone, other times the exchanges occur in "joint" sessions with all of the parties present.

Certain mediators view their role as exclusively facilitative; they do not pressure the parties to accept a resolution. Rather, through active listening, they assist the parties in generating their own solutions. Other mediators may define the issues for the parties, evaluate the value of the case, and endorse specific resolutions. Mediators generally have the power to clarify what the parties want, focus their needs and interests, aid in the exchange of information, and suggest alternative ways to reach agreement.

Resolutions reached through mediation are not binding. Nevertheless, the mediator, the parties, or counsel may draft a mediation agreement which is signed by the parties. Such agreements are enforceable contracts.

Mediation-Arbitration

Mediation-Arbitration is a process that provides the parties with an opportunity to mediate a case before submitting it to binding arbitration. In some mediation-arbitrations, the mediator drafts an advisory opinion, suggesting how the case might be resolved if it were arbitrated. In other cases, the mediator also acts as the arbitrator.

Early Neutral Evaluation

Early Neutral Evaluation, also known as case evaluation, is most effective when used early in the dispute resolution process to resolve complex, civil issues. It involves a neutral, or a panel of neutrals, who obtain information from the parties and their attorneys and evaluate the case. The recommendations of the neutral may narrow the issues to be resolved and may suggest a dispute resolution method or combination of methods for later use. Often, the neutral acts as the subsequent mediator or arbitrator.

Mini-Trial

The mini-trial process is private and is most often used to resolve commercial disputes. The lawyers make summary presentations of their best case before a neutral advisor. The advisor may question the attorneys regarding the strengths and weaknesses of their case without regard to the rules of evidence, before rendering a decision. The advisor's decision is nonbinding. Nevertheless, it is often highly persuasive, as representatives of the business clients involved typically attend mini-trial proceedings to evaluate the value of the case.

Summary Jury Trial

In a summary jury trial, the lawyers present a summary of their evidence and arguments to a mock jury. The jurors may be selected from a jury pool or may be obtained from a jury consulting organization. The jury, after hearing the evidence and presentation, deliberates and returns a recommended verdict. The advisory verdict provides counsel and their clients with a basis to predict what the actual jury would do after a complex trial. The lawyers may question the mock jurors to learn their rationales.

Contracts Providing for ADR

As discussed in Chapters 14 and 15, the purpose of a commercial contract is to enable the parties to engage in business in a predictable manner. Where a dispute arises, both sides benefit from resolving it quickly with a minimum investment of time and money. Accordingly, many commercial contracts contain some form of a dispute resolution clause.

Arbitration

Contract provisions providing for arbitration generally share several common elements. First, such provisions identify whether the requirement to arbitrate applies to all disputes arising under the contract or is limited to certain types of disputes. Second, they identify whether a single arbitrator will preside or whether there will be a panel. Third, they identify the procedure for choosing the arbitrator or arbitrators. Fourth, they identify whether the process of the arbitration will be submitted to an arbitration organization and, if so, which arbitration organization. Fifth, they identify the location of the arbitration and the law to be applied to substantive issues. Sixth, they identify the allocation of the costs associated with arbitration.

Mediation

Contract provisions providing for mediation also generally share several common elements. First, such provisions provide a definition of mediation, as its meaning may vary. Second, they establish a procedure for selecting a mediator. Third, they establish a time period in which to complete mediation and refrain from resorting to another process. Fourth, they identify whether the process of mediation is subject to specific procedural rules. Fifth, they identify the allocation of costs associated with mediation.

In addition to the common characteristics of contract provisions providing for mediation noted above, many contracts also provide that any information exchanged or offers made during mediation cannot be used in subsequent arbitrations or litigation should the mediation prove unsuccessful. Such confidentiality provisions aid the parties in resolving the dispute by encouraging them to more freely exchange information.

Multicultural Considerations

Many U.S. lawyers prefer arbitration to transnational litigation because arbitration allows the parties flexibility and more control over the process. Further, arbitration awards are often more likely to be enforced than judgments made in foreign courts. Organizations commonly utilized for international arbitrations include the American Arbitration Association, the International Arbitration Association, the International Chamber of Commerce, the International Center for Settlement of Investment Disputes, the Center for Public Resources, the World Intellectual Property Organization, and the Commercial Arbitration and Mediation Center of the Americas.

For drafting purposes, the International Chamber of Commerce provides a simple arbitration clause to the effect that all disputes "arising in connection with the present contract shall be finally settled under the rules of Conciliation and Arbitration of the International Chamber of Commerce by one or more arbitrators appointed in accordance with the Rules." However, many lawyers in the U.S. also regularly provide for choice of law, choice of forum, choice and qualifications of arbitrators, and the language to be used in the arbitration proceedings.

Analyzing the Client's Legal Needs and Issues

Let us now return to Vogel's newest legal problem involving the termination of Dr. Sing's employment and non-compete agreement. Vogel does not wish to become involved in employment litigation with Dr. Sing. What alternative methods of dispute resolution might you recommend?

The primary options for Vogel are arbitration or mediation. Early neutral evaluation, mini-trial, and summary jury trial would be premature as you have not yet commenced litigation.

Arbitration

Arbitration is a common method of resolving employment litigation disputes. However, a mandatory arbitration provision is generally included in the employment agreement. The associate in our firm who drafted Dr. Sing's employment agreement neglected to include an arbitration provision. Accordingly, Vogel cannot force Dr. Sing to enter into arbitration, she must do so voluntarily. Arbitration is less costly and time consuming than litigation. It also has the advantage of resulting in a binding, enforceable judgment. However, it does not allow the parties to fashion their own business solution to the dispute. Sample contract arbitration clauses are included in the sample documents below.

Mediation

Mediation will allow Vogel and Dr. Sing to fashion their own resolution, with the assistance of a trained facilitator. Again, our firm could have included a mandatory mediation clause in the employment and non-compete agreement executed by Dr. Sing. As our associate neglected to do so, however, Vogel cannot force Dr. Sing to mediate. Sample contract mediation clauses are included in the sample documents below.

Assume Eckerman prefers mediation and is able to convince Dr. Sing to voluntarily participate. The first step is to agree on and hire a mediator. It is not necessary to hire a lawyer as a mediator, but Vogel wishes to engage a lawyer experienced in employment law for this case. You check with the local bar association and receive three recommendations. Together with counsel for Dr. Sing, Hillary Day, you agree on lawyer Laura Keashly. Ms. Keashly requests both parties to sign an agreement, agreeing to equal responsibility for her fees.

After hiring the mediator, you must prepare. Ms. Keashly has requested a mediation summary prior to the mediation session. The mediation summary provides an overview of the dispute from Vogel's point of view and suggests goals for the mediation. You meet with Eckerman to discuss Vogel's position, Dr. Sing's position, and to determine a range of acceptable solutions. A Mediation Summary for Vogel is included in the sample documents.

You attend the mediation session accompanied by Eckerman. Also present are Dr. Sing, her attorney, and Ms. Keashly. At the mediation session, you give an opening statement summarizing the facts of the dispute and Vogel's contentions. Eckerman insists that the only possible resolution is for Dr. Sing to forgo working for Best Health until the expiration of the non-compete clause. Hillary Day explains Dr. Sing's position that the non-compete provision is not enforceable.

Both sides engage in an exchange of information and views. Ms. Keashly, as mediator, listens and asks questions, but does not render a decision. It is up to the parties to reach a compromise solution. In the event a resolution is reached, you should prepare a writing memorializing the agreement and have it executed by Eckerman and Dr. Sing.

Sample Documents

Document 1
Arbitration Clauses

Checklist of Possible Contract Provisions Covering Arbitration

1. Require the parties to complete arbitration before resorting to litigation.
2. Establish the scope of arbitration.
3. Provide for the name of a particular arbitration service provider and the application of its rules or provide for a method of selecting the provider or the individual arbitrator(s).
4. Provide for the location of the arbitration.
5. Provide for costs of arbitration and payment of attorneys' fees.
6. Provide sanctions for failure to participate.
7. Provide for confidentiality.
8. Consider providing for the rights and remedies available to non-breaching parties in the event a party breaches the terms of the arbitration.
9. Cultural considerations: Provide for arbitrators familiar with the cultures, languages, and laws of the parties' respective countries.

Sample Arbitration Clauses

Simple arbitration clause

Arbitration. All claims and disputes arising under or relating to this Agreement are to be settled by binding arbitration in the state of [provide name of the same state as governing law]. Judgment on the award rendered by the arbitrators may be entered in any court having jurisdiction.

Arbitration clause with additional conditions and obligations

Arbitration. All claims or disputes arising under or relating to this Agreement are to be settled by binding arbitration in the state of [provide name of the same state as governing law]. The arbitration shall be conducted by [provide name of arbitration service provider, such as American Arbitration Association] on a confidential basis under its Commercial Arbitration Rules. The number of arbitrators shall be [one or three] and any arbitrator shall be experienced in [provide industry or other relevant required experience]. Any arbitration hearing requiring the parties' physical presence shall be held in [city and state]. The parties will share equally in the costs of arbitration, provided however, that in the event of a breach of the terms of arbitration the non-breaching party shall be entitled to payment of all costs and attorneys' fees associated with the arbitration in addition to any other damages. The award of the arbitrator(s) shall be in writing and may be entered in any court having jurisdiction.

Document 2
Mediation Clauses

Checklist of Possible Contract Provisions Covering Mediation

1. Require the parties to complete the mediation before resorting to arbitration or litigation.
2. Establish the scope of mediation.
3. Provide for the duration of mediation.
4. Provide for location of mediation.
5. Provide for the name of a particular mediation service provider and the application of its rules or provide for a method of selecting the provider or the individual mediator.
6. Provide for costs of mediation and payment of attorneys' fees.
7. Provide sanctions for failure to participate.
8. Provide for confidentiality.
9. Cross-cultural considerations:
    a. Provide a definition of mediation
    b. Provide for a mediator familiar with the cultures, languages, and laws of the parties' respective countries.

Sample Mediation Clauses

Simple mediation clause
Mediation. All claims and disputes arising under or relating to this Agreement shall be referred to mediation before, and as a condition precedent to, the initiation of an adjudicative proceeding including arbitration. The mediation shall be held in [city and state] and shall be conducted by and in accordance with the rules of [provide name of a mediation service provider such as the American Arbitration Association].

Mediation clause with additional conditions and obligations
Mediation. All claims and disputes arising under or relating to this Agreement shall be referred to mediation before, and as a condition precedent to, the initiation of an adjudicative proceeding including arbitration. The mediation shall be held in [city and state] and shall be conducted by and in accordance with the rules of [provide name of a mediation service provider such as the American Arbitration Association]. If during mediation, a party makes a written offer of compromise which is not accepted and the refusing party fails to obtain a more favorable judgment or award, then the offering party shall be entitled to payment of all costs and attorneys' fees associated with the mediation

from the refusing party. If a settlement is reached during mediation it shall be reduced to writing and shall be binding upon the parties, their executors, administrators, successors, and assigns.

Document 3
Vogel Pharmaceuticals, Inc.'s
Mediation Summary

Mediator: _____

Mediation Date: _____

Introduction

Vogel Pharmaceuticals, Inc. ("Vogel") is a corporation which develops and produces prescription medications and has recently begun an herbal remedy division. Vogel entered into an employment contract with Dr. Anna Maria Sing. Dr. Sing accepted the position of Vice President of Sales and Development for Vogel's new herbal remedy division. As part of the agreement, Dr. Sing agreed to a covenant not to compete precluding her from competing in any way with Vogel for a period of one year, should the Vogel-Sing employment relationship be terminated. Dr. Sing recently resigned from Vogel and re-joined her former employer, Best Health, Inc. ("Best Health") in violation of the non-compete agreement. The employment contract is governed by the laws of Arizona, a state which recognizes the validity of non-compete agreements. Vogel seeks to enforce the non-compete.

Procedural background

For a variety of reasons, the parties prefer to resolve their dispute privately. As a result, no civil litigation has been commenced.

Factual background

Vogel, of Phoenix, Arizona, has a long history of developing and manufacturing prescription medications that treat a number of physical ailments, including high cholesterol. One of Vogel's most successful products is "Ultrastatin", the most popular prescription medication on the market for treating high cholesterol for the last five years.

Anna Maria Sing is a 42 year old doctor and research scientist. While employed at Best Health, a corporation in Dallas, Texas, that manufactures herbal remedies, Dr. Sing discovered an herbal remedy in the Amazon for treating high cholesterol. Dr. Sing gave the product the name of "WonderDRug".

In 20___, Vogel decided to enter the herbal remedies market and executed an exclusive contract with Best Health to purchase WonderDRug in liquid, powder, and capsule form for sale to consumers. As a result of the high sales volume generated by WonderDRug, Vogel formed an herbal remedy division. Vogel recruited Dr. Sing to serve as Vice President of Sales and Development for the new division.

Dr. Sing accepted the position, according to the following terms: (1) she agreed to accept a starting salary of $350,000 with Vogel and terminate her relationship with Best Health, (2) she agreed to a covenant not to compete, precluding her from competing in any way with Vogel for a period of one year, should the Vogel-Sing employment relationship terminate, and (3) she agreed to a confidentiality provision limiting the use of Vogel's confidential and proprietary information during the term of her employment and for one year thereafter.

Unfortunately, almost immediately upon commencement of Dr. Sing's employment with Vogel, things began to sour. On October 30, 20__, Dr. Sing provided written notification to Vogel of her immediate resignation. She returned to Best Health to develop an herbal cure for high blood pressure.

Vogel informed Dr. Sing that her employment with Best Health violates the non-compete provision in her employment contract. The non-compete provision, states: "If this agreement is terminated by Employee for any reason, Employee must not become employed, for a period of one year after termination, with any competitor of Vogel in the pharmaceutical industry."

Claims and Defenses

Vogel has a claim for breach of contract against Dr. Sing for violating the non-compete clause of her contract. Specifically, within one year of her employment with Vogel, Dr. Sing has become employed with Best Health, a competitor.

Dr. Sing asserts that the non-compete clause is unenforceable.

Contested Legal Issue

Vogel and Dr. Sing disagree on whether the non-compete clause is enforceable under Arizona law.

Arizona courts will enforce non-compete agreements that have a legitimate business purpose, where the employee received benefit for the agreement, the agreement is reasonable in time and scope, and the agreement does not violate public policy. *Valley Med. Specialists v. Farber*, 982 P.2d 1277, 1283 (Ariz. 1999); *American Credit Bureau v. Carter*, 462 P.2d 838, 840 (Ariz. Ct. Ap. 1969).

Legitimate Business Purpose

Dr. Sing is a scientist and the former Vice President of Vogel's herbal remedies division. Vogel had a good business reason for asking her to sign the non-compete agreement: protection of their trademarks and customer information.

Benefit to the Employee

Dr. Sing received a benefit for signing the non-compete. The employment agreement containing the non-compete was presented to her prior to her acceptance of employment with Vogel and she was awarded her position as Vice President of Sales and Development at an annual salary of $350,000 in exchange for executing the agreement.

Public Policy

No public policy exists which would prevent the enforcement of the non-compete. It does not eliminate Dr. Sing's ability to work or constitute an undue financial burden.

Reasonable Scope

The only significant area of dispute can be on the reasonableness of the time and scope of the non-compete agreement. There is no magic number or definition of what is reasonable. Rather, the courts look to the facts and circumstances to determine reasonability.

The non-compete between Vogel and Dr. Sing is one year long. Non-competes ranging from six months to one year are generally considered reasonable in Arizona to protect the business interests of the employer.

Scope includes the geographic area and the type of work prohibited by the non-compete. Dr. Sing asserts that excluding the complete pharmaceutical industry is unreasonable. However, the courts have found that the geographic scope may be as broad as necessary. A national scope is necessary to protect Vogel's business interests.

Dr. Sing also asserts that the language in the non-compete agreement prohibiting her from employment in the pharmaceutical industry cannot be enforced with respect to her employment with Best Health as a provider of herbal remedies. Dr. Sing relies on the Dietary Health Supplement Act of 1994, wherein herbal products are considered dietary supplements not regulated by the FDA. Vogel believes that it could convince a jury that within the context of the Vogel-Sing employment agreement the use of the term "pharmaceutical industry" implies the inclusion of the herbal remedies industry at least to the extent it produces products in competition with the pharmaceutical industry.

Relief Sought

Vogel seeks to enforce the terms of the bargained for agreement and require Dr. Sing to cease her employment with Best Health for a period of one year.

Nevertheless, in appreciation of the mediation process and the defenses raised by Dr. Sing, Vogel is willing to consider an alternative resolution of this matter allowing Dr. Sing to continue her employment with Best Health provided that Dr. Sing forego any severance compensation she would otherwise be due from Vogel and that she release any and all claims against Vogel arising out of her employment.

Thank you for your assistance in our efforts to resolve these matters. We look forward to working with you at the mediation.

Dated: Respectfully submitted,

                                                _____
                                                Counsel's Name and ID Number
                                                Law Firm Name
                                                Law Firm Address
                                                Law Firm Telephone Number
                                                Attorneys for Vogel
                                                Pharmaceuticals, Inc.

Chapter 17

Negotiation and Settlement

Highlights

- Ninety percent of the legal matters dealt with by lawyers in the U.S. are estimated to involve negotiation.
- Negotiation may be divided into two categories: transactional and dispute resolution.
- Preparation for negotiation includes an assessment of the interests, rights, and power of both sides, as well as obtaining negotiation authority from the client.
- A lawyer's approach to negotiations may be adversarial, problem solving, or a combination of the two.
- In an adversarial approach, the goal is to maximize the client's gains and minimize the client's losses.
- In a problem solving approach, the goal is to find solutions that will integrate and increase the resources of both sides so that a mutually agreeable solution is reached.

Introduction

Lawyers are regularly involved in negotiations; in fact, as much as ninety percent of the legal matters dealt with by lawyers in the U.S. are estimated to involve the negotiation process. Negotiations may be divided into two categories: transactional and dispute resolution. In transactional negotiations, the parties strive to voluntarily agree to terms that will govern their relationship. Buying and selling goods is an example of the type of facts giving rise to a transactional negotiation. In dispute resolution negotiations, the parties attempt to resolve their conflict through means other than litigation. The primary example is a settlement discussion in a lawsuit. The goal of a negotiator, whether the negotiation is transactional or dispute oriented, is to communicate persuasively with the other side to satisfy the client's objectives and resolve the matter.

A lawyer has four potential roles in negotiations: evaluator, advisor, negotiator, and drafter. As an evaluator, a lawyer provides perspective on a client's problem. As an advisor, a lawyer counsels clients on their options during the negotiation process. As a negotiator, a lawyer is the exclusive communicator with the other party or its lawyer. As a drafter, a lawyer reduces the agreement to writing.

This chapter discusses negotiation as it is commonly practiced in the U.S. It has eight sections: (1) approaches to negotiation, (2) context in negotiation, (3) preparation, (4) negotiation strategies, (5) negotiation styles, (6) the negotiation, (7) negotiation communications, and (8) multicultural considerations.

The Client

In Chapters 14 and 15, you worked with Vogel Pharmaceuticals to prepare for and draft a sales contract involving the purchase of WonderDRug by Vogel from Best Health. In Chapter 16, you advised Vogel on the best way to avoid litigation over an employment dispute with Dr. Sing by employing alternative methods of dispute resolution. As you read this chapter, consider what skills you would use to negotiate a settlement of the employment dispute with Dr. Sing if your attempts at alternative methods of dispute resolution are unsuccessful.

Approaches

There are two primary approaches to negotiation: adversarial and problem solving. Most negotiations involve both approaches. An adversarial approach focuses on the distribution of limited resources. Adversarial negotiators select "bottom lines" at which they will walk away from the bargaining table. This type of negotiation is also known as "zero-sum" bargaining.

In contrast, the problem solving approach emphasizes the integration of resources. Each side is seen as bringing value to the deal that creates benefits for both parties; such negotiations are known as "win-win" negotiations. Problem solving negotiators identify a Best Alternative To a Negotiated Agreement, or "BATNA," as a standard against which any proposed agreement should be measured. To develop a BATNA, a negotiator predicts the best thing the negotiator would be able to do if an agreement is not reached.

Context

Every negotiation involves three factors: interests, rights and power. Interests in the context of negotiation are defined as the parties' needs, desires, or concerns. Examples of interests are resolving the matter promptly, maximizing financial position, or maintaining long-term relationships. Rights are defined as independent standards demonstrating the legitimacy of a party's position. Rights may be based on case law, statutes, regulations, contracts, or accepted standards of behavior. Power is defined as the ability to coerce. A party may coerce by threatening to act, such as publicizing the nature of the dispute, or by refusing to act, such as withholding benefits.

Preparation

Negotiation preparation includes an assessment of the interests, rights, and power of both sides. It also involves obtaining negotiation authority from the client.

Interests

Assessing the parties' interests involves: (1) identifying the needs, desires, and concerns of each party, (2) prioritizing the client's interests, and (3) predicting the other party's priorities. Common interests include: financial interests, performance interests, psychological needs, reputational interests, and relationship interests. As noted in Chapter 10, when interviewing it is important to learn of a client's interests by beginning with open ended questions.

After identifying the client's interests, the lawyer must identify the interests of the opposing party. The other party and its lawyer are not the only source for identifying interests. Additional information may be obtained from other lawyers or third parties, news sources, and the internet.

Lastly, the lawyer must prioritize the interests of the client and the other party. To get an adequate assessment of the interests of both parties, a lawyer will generally work with the client to determine the client's two or three most important interests, then brainstorm the priorities of the other party.

Rights and Power

Assessing the parties' rights requires examining the manner in which legal or other objective standards affect the parties' strengths and weaknesses. Assessing the relative power of the parties involves exploring how non-legal factors affect their strengths and weaknesses. Power differentials can have a significant impact on the bargaining process. The primary sources of power in negotiations are economic, social, psychological, political, and knowledge based.

Negotiation Strategies

Client Authority

After having assessed the interests, rights, and power of the parties, the lawyer is ready to develop a negotiation strategy. As noted in Chapter 8, under the rules of professional responsibility, the client retains the ultimate authority on how to resolve a matter. As a result, the client must be consulted throughout the process.

Determining a Client's BATNA

The first step in developing a negotiation strategy is to identify a client's BATNA or "walkaway alternative." To determine a client's BATNA, a lawyer must review assessments of the parties' interests, rights, and power and generate options by identifying the possible alternatives to a settlement. From the interest assessment, the lawyer should consider the alternatives that the client can undertake outside of a relationship with the other party. Next, the lawyer should identify the rights the client could assert. Finally, the lawyer should consider alternative ways that the client could exercise power. After identify-

ing possible alternatives to negotiation, the lawyer and the client should evaluate them to determine one or two BATNAs.

Determining the Opposing Party's BATNA

After identifying the client's BATNA, the lawyer must try to predict the
other side's BATNA. The lawyer will begin the process by reviewing the assessment of the other party's interests, rights, and power and brainstorming
the other side's alternatives to negotiation with the client. Then, the lawyer
will weigh these options against the hypothesized priority interest to identify
the one or two that would best accomplish the other side's goals. By comparing BATNAs, the lawyer obtains a sense of the probability of reaching an
agreement.

Selecting an Approach

After determining each side's BATNA, the lawyer must determine whether
the approach to the negotiation will be adversarial or problem solving. In an
adversarial negotiation, the goal is to maximize gains and minimize losses. To
accomplish this goal, a lawyer will engage in an exchange of offers and counter
offers with the other side until either impasse or agreement is reached. Evaluating interests, rights, and power in terms of the parties' respective bargaining
ranges assists a lawyer in developing arguments, threats, and appeals to convince the other side to make concessions. In order to elicit concessions from
the other side, a lawyer must demonstrate that the offer is better than its BATNA.

Conversely, where a lawyer chooses to take a problem solving approach, the
goal is to find solutions that will increase the available resources to reach a negotiated agreement. The lawyer and the client will consider the priorities of
each party's interests and explore any possible solutions suggested by their priorities. Unlike the adversarial approach, the lawyer will try to broaden the
number of options for settlement. The lawyer attempts to "create value" by
considering the differences between the parties, the noncompetitive similarities between the parties, and ways of expanding resources.

Information Bargaining

Information bargaining is important in both adversarial and problem solving negotiations. A negotiation involves not only an exchange of offers or brainstorming of possible solutions, but also attempts by each party to learn more

information from the other. With this information, each party can readjust its concession strategy in adversarial bargaining or its brainstorming approach in problem-solving negotiation. In strategizing an approach for information bargaining a lawyer should consider: (1) information needed from the other party to assist in understanding their bargaining stance, (2) information to be disclosed voluntarily to the other party to facilitate strategy, and (3) information to be concealed from the other party because it might weaken strategy if disclosed.

The Agenda

After deciding on an approach to the negotiations and considering information issues, the lawyer must create an issues agenda. Sequencing of issues should facilitate the overall plan developed for the negotiation. Initial consideration of minor issues is effective to establish a cooperative relationship with the other party, but may delay the inevitable negotiation over the major issues. Beginning the negotiation by bargaining over a major issue assists a lawyer in evaluating the realistic possibility of reaching a settlement. In adversarial bargaining, this approach may lead to "logrolling" or trading off of concessions. In problem solving negotiation, it can assist in mutual brainstorming of solutions.

Venue

In determining the location for a negotiation, lawyers consider the overall strategy and the impact, if any, of the venue. Most lawyers prefer the advantage of their own office, as it gives them a certain amount of control. Nevertheless, as with interviewing and counseling discussed in Chapters 10 and 11, holding the negotiation at a neutral location or where documents and witnesses are located may have certain advantages. Furthermore, as discussed in Chapter 13, telephonic or electronic devices should be limited to short exchanges of information when negotiating. A face-to-face meeting is always preferred.

Timing

As part of the strategic planning, a lawyer should consider how to handle external deadlines and examine the advantages of different timing agendas. Lawyers using an adversarial approach often wait until the eve of trial or other deadline to pressure a less powerful opponent into a deal.

In addition, lawyers must consider whether they wish to make an offer with an internal deadline. Deadlines may hinder the development of a cooperative atmosphere and may harm any long-term relationship with the other side.

Further, a lawyer's credibility may be damaged if the internal deadline is discovered to be a "bluff."

Negotiation Styles

In addition to selecting a strategy for negotiation, a lawyer must select a style. Style is the manner in which a lawyer communicates: word choice, tone of voice, body language, eye contact, and other methods of verbal and nonverbal communication discussed in Chapter 9. Two categories of negotiating style are combative and cordial. A combative style is forceful. A cordial style is friendly. There is a broad continuum between these two styles. Further, in any given negotiation, a lawyer might switch from one style to another depending on the style of the opposing counsel.

A lawyer using an adversarial approach representing a client unwilling to make concessions may select a combative style. Conversely, a lawyer using a problem solving strategy with a client anxious to maintain good relations with an opponent may select a cordial approach.

The Negotiation

The Adversarial Approach

With the adversarial approach, the goal is to maximize the client's gains and minimize the client's losses. The lawyer must communicate offers and concessions in a way that persuades the other party to agree on terms most favorable to the client.

The Initial Offer

Many U.S. lawyers believe it is a sign of weakness to be the first party to make an offer. However, research indicates that there is no correlation between who makes the first offer and the eventual outcome of the negotiations. An advantage to making the first offer is that it allows the lawyer to evaluate the other party's reaction and adjust concession strategy accordingly. The main disadvantage occurs if the lawyer has not prepared sufficiently to know what the object of the negotiation is worth. In such situations, the lawyer making the offer is often too generous leading to a smaller return for the client. As a result, a lawyer should make the first offer only in those circumstances where the worth of the subject of the negotiation is known. A good initial offer is generally aimed further, but not too much further, than the best terms on which the lawyer thinks the other side might settle.

A common problem occurring in initial offers involves "Boulwarism." Boulwarism involves a lawyer making only one offer and informing the other side that no other terms will be accepted. Boulwarism will be successful only where the lawyer has enough information to be reasonably certain that the offer is better than the other side's BATNA and is able to convince the other side that this is true and that no further concessions will be made. A lawyer who attempts Boulwarism and fails must either make a concession, losing credibility, or stick to the initial offer and face rejection.

Finally, effective communication of the initial offer is crucial to its success. The lawyer must convince the other side that the bottom line is high, even where the client has not set a bottom line. The key to such a presentation is credibility. The factors that most affect the credibility of initial offers are specificity, justification, and consequence. Specific facts are more credible than conclusions; by presenting specific offers and demands in negotiation, a lawyer demonstrates the client's commitment to a position. Justification requires clearly communicated rationales. The logic of justification persuades the other side that the existing offer is better than its BATNA. A lawyer develops justifications from assessments of interests, rights, and power. Consequence requires that the offer communicate the results that emanate from rejection. A lawyer's statement of consequences is credible only where the other side knows that the lawyer will follow through. A strong commitment to an offer can be demonstrated by an explicit description of the consequences of its rejection. Pursuit of a BATNA is the most common consequence provided during negotiations.

Subsequent Demands and Concessions

The opposing side will generally respond to an initial offer with a counteroffer, forcing the lawyer making the initial offer to determine how to follow through with the strategy. Often, the lawyer will increase demands. The law of professional responsibility does not prohibit such a tactic; however, it may result in the loss of credibility and damage to the relationship. Once a lawyer has justified and committed to an initial offer, it is difficult to augment it. Such a tactic is usually warranted only where significant, previously unknown information is discovered.

As a result of subsequent demands, both sides may make concessions. In planning for an adversarial negotiation, a lawyer must identify various concession points between the initial offer and bottom line. The lawyer should not, however, automatically make a concession upon receiving a counteroffer.

The goal in adversarial bargaining is to maximize the client's gain. One of the ways of achieving this goal is to impress the other side that the client's bottom line is high. Research demonstrates that small, well-timed concessions pay off with better outcomes. Large concessions, or a series of concessions without comparable concessions from the other side, yield less favorable results.

Furthermore, concessions may be required in certain circumstances. Concessions are often needed to: (1) prevent deadlocks, (2) persuade the other side to make concessions, (3) maintain a good working relationship with the other side, and (4) accommodate a deadline.

The Problem Solving Approach

The Initial Offer

The biggest challenge for the problem solving negotiator is to bring the other side into the problem solving process. The lawyer's initial offer under this approach is an invitation to brainstorm. For this invitation to be effective, the lawyer must: (1) communicate a desire to take a problem solving approach in the negotiation, (2) identify the interests of the client and of the other side, (3) present a range of solutions that address these interests, and (4) open the door to joint exploration of other options.

In many negotiations, after a lawyer makes an initial offer of a proposed solution, the other side's lawyer will answer with an adversarial response. The lawyer making the initial offer must then convince the other side that a problem solving approach will satisfy their interests better than adversarial bargaining. The lawyer must reframe the discussion and focus on interests, responding to the other side's rigid positions with open ended, problem solving questions.

Exploring Solutions

After both sides agree to consider options addressing interests rather than demands, the lawyers must develop alternative solutions and fine tune them to reach a deal. Several methods aid in facilitating this process. First, both sides must remain focused on the parties' interests. The parties should make their interests explicit and counsel should concentrate on developing solutions to meet these needs. Second, the lawyers should engage in brainstorming which separates the creation of the options from the evaluation of their merits. Third, the lawyers should consider creating conditional solutions to meet unsatisfied needs, rather than arguing over whether a contingency will occur. Fourth, both lawyers should strive to engage in incorporation, including elements of the other party's proposal into the modification of their own client's proposal.

Negotiation and Settlement Letters

A settlement letter to opposing counsel will generally have the same heading, salutation and closing as the advice, status, and demand letters discussed in Chapter 12. Most settlement letters to opposing counsel also contain an introduction, factual and legal support section, and a conclusion. The introduction to a settlement letter: (1) identifies the lawyer and the client, (2) states, or confirms, the offer of settlement, and (3) confirms that the letter is the subject of confidential settlement negotiations and cannot be used as evidence. The support section sets forth the facts and law which support the case. If the lawyer can successfully argue that the facts or law relied on by opposing counsel will not prevail, such arguments are also included. The conclusion of the letter reconfirms the offer and, if not yet accepted, imposes a time limit on its availability and consequences for rejection.

Lawyers also frequently correspond with clients during or following negotiations. The purpose of such correspondence is to advise the client of the status or outcome of the negotiations, to outline the options, and to seek the client's input. Similar to advice letters, discussed in Chapter 12, settlement letters to clients include a heading, salutation, introduction describing the purpose and background of the negotiations, factual summary of the negotiations, statement of legal conclusions and reasoning related to the negotiations, recommendations, invitation for further discussions, and closing.

Multicultural Considerations

As discussed in Chapter 9, communication differs widely across cultures. Differences in communication styles may adversely affect negotiation if they are not acknowledged. Factors which should be acknowledged in cross cultural negotiations include: (1) perceptions of time, (2) perceptions of social status, (3) context, (4) location, and (5) language.

Time

Time in the U.S. is generally inflexible; meetings and telephone conferences are expected to begin on time. Lateness is considered rude. This is different, of course, from many other cultures where time may be more flexible.

Social Status

Bargaining power in the U.S. does not follow age, race, or gender lines, nor is it limited to one individual. Team bargaining where every member of the team has power over certain issues relevant to their expertise is common. Similarly, it is not considered inappropriate to bargain with someone of a different race, age, or gender.

Context

In the U.S., participants in a negotiation rely on what is said. As discussed in Chapter 9, the U.S. is a low context culture. This is significantly different from high context cultures in which the participants to a negotiation rely primarily on how a statement is made.

Location and Language

In the U.S., bargaining primarily occurs in the conference room with all participants present. Negotiations taking place with certain participants in private settings is much less prevalent than in other cultures. Furthermore, language, as well as nonverbal communication, is informal. In some cultures it might be viewed as abrasive.

Analyzing the Client's Legal Needs and Issues

Let us now return to Vogel and its employment dispute with Dr. Sing. Vogel and Dr. Sing were unable to reach agreement during mediation. Eckerman is getting pressure from the board of directors to settle this matter and instructs you to proceed to negotiation. Dr. Sing has returned to the Amazon, but authorizes her lawyer—Hillary Day—to negotiate on her behalf. How will you proceed to negotiate an agreement and obtain Eckerman's approval?

Negotiation and Settlement

Preparing for negotiation requires you to decide on a negotiation approach and identify the interests, rights, and powers of the parties. You decide on a problem solving approach.

You realize that Dr. Sing's primary interest is to continue her work in the jungle developing herbal remedies for Best Health. Vogel's primary interest is to terminate Dr. Sing's employment quickly and cheaply, without jeopardizing any of their pharmaceutical brands currently on the market or in development. Vogel also needs to reserve its rights to any discoveries Dr. Sing may have made during her employment which could be used to enhance those brands. With respect to rights and power, Arizona law controlling this contract requires non-compete provisions to be limited in scope. The term of one year is likely to satisfy the requirement. However, it is questionable whether the courts will interpret excluding Dr. Sing from the "pharmaceutical" industry as narrow in scope. Furthermore, the language of the non-compete agreement prohibiting Dr. Sing from employment in the pharmaceutical industry may not be interpreted by a court to prohibit her employment with Best Health.

After considering interests, rights, and power, you consult with Eckerman on a BATNA. Vogel's only BATNA is to bring litigation against Dr. Sing to enforce the non-compete agreement. You also create an issues agenda, deciding to make your first issue for discussion the appropriate scope of Dr. Sing's work for Best Health. Beginning the negotiation by bargaining over a major issue should assist you in evaluating the realistic possibility of reaching a settlement.

Hillary Day agrees to your office as the venue for the negotiation. You adjust your verbal and nonverbal communication style to reflect the problem solving approach. You begin by inviting Hillary to brainstorm a range of solutions to the Vogel-Sing employment dilemma. Ultimately, an agreement is reached.

A sample settlement agreement for the Vogel-Sing employment issue is included in the sample documents below.

The Settlement Letter

Having reached agreement in principle, you must now obtain Vogel's approval. You draft a letter to Eckerman advising him of the outcome of the negotiations, outlining the reasoning behind the outcome, and seeking his approval.

A sample client letter outlining the settlement agreement is included in the sample documents below.

Sample Documents

Document 1
Settlement Agreement and Release

This Settlement Agreement and Release ("Agreement") is entered into this ___ day of _____, 20__, between Vogel Pharmaceuticals, Inc. ("Employer"), having its principal place of business in Phoenix, Arizona and Dr. Anna Maria Sing ("Employee"), an individual residing in Phoenix, Arizona.

BACKGROUND

1. Employer develops and produces prescription medications and herbal remedies.
2. Employee has been employed by Employer since _____, 20__ as Vice President of Sales and Development for Employer's Herbal Remedy Division.
3. Employee executed an Employment Agreement providing for the terms and conditions of her employment, including provisions on non-competition, confidentiality, and severance.
4. Employee has provided written notification to Employer of her intention to terminate her employment with Employer.
5. Employee has accepted a position with her previous employer, Best Health, Inc. ("Best Health"), to research and develop herbal remedies.
6. Employer has notified Employee that her acceptance of employment with Best Health is a violation of Employee's non-compete clause contained in her Employment Agreement with Employer.
7. Employer and Employee agree that it would be in their best interests to sever the employment relationship.
8. Employer and Employee desire to enter into this Agreement in order to resolve and release any and all complaints or disputes related to Employee's employment or separation of employment from Employer.

DEFINITIONS

1. "Confidential Information" means all information of a technical or business nature, such as know-how, trade secrets, business plans, data, processes, techniques, customer information, inventions, discoveries, formulae, patterns, and devices that are owned by Employer.
2. "Effective Date" means _____, 20__.
3. "Employment Agreement" means the employment agreement between Employer and Employee dated _____, 20__.

In consideration of the mutual promises set forth below, Employer and Employee agree:

TERMS AND CONDITIONS

1. **Separation of Employment.** Employee's employment with Employer shall terminate on the Effective Date.
2. **Employee's Release and Discharge of Employer.** In consideration of Employer's agreement to modify the non-compete clause in the Employment Agreement, provided in paragraph 3 below, Employee completely releases and discharges the Employer from any and all past, present, or future claims, demands, obligations, causes of action, rights, damages, expenses and compensation, including the severance payment provided for in paragraph __ of the Employment Agreement, which the Employee now has or may hereafter accrue or acquire as a result of her employment with Employer.
3. **Consideration: Modification of Non-Compete as to Best Health.** In consideration of the release set forth in paragraph 2 above, Employer agrees that Employee may become employed by Best Health, subject to the following terms:
    a. *Limited Scope of Employment.* Employee may only participate in the research and development and sale of herbal remedies that are not in competition with the herbal remedies that Employee assisted in researching and developing while employed by Employer.
    b. *Development of Pharmaceutical Products by Employee Prohibited.* Employee may not, for a period of one year after the Effective Date, engage in the research, development, or sale of any pharmaceutical product.
    c. *Sales of Pharmaceutical Products and Herbal Remedies Prohibited.* Employee may not, for a period of one year after the Effective Date, be involved in the sale of any pharmaceutical products or herbal remedies to any former, current, or future customer of Employer.
4. **Covenant Not to Compete.** Except as provided in paragraph 3 limited to Best Health, Employee may not, for a period of one year after the Effective Date, become employed with any competitor of Vogel in the pharmaceutical industry.
5. **Confidential Information.** Employee acknowledges and agrees that all information of a technical or business nature, such as know-how, trade secrets, business plans, data, processes, techniques, customer information, inventions, discoveries, formulae, patterns and devices acquired by Em-

ployee in the course of her employment with Employer is Confidential Information and exclusive to Employer.

   a. *Limits on Communication.* Employee agrees that Confidential Information, whether in written, verbal, or electronic form, shall not be disclosed to anyone outside the employment of Employer without Employer's consent in a signed writing. This limit on communication regarding Confidential Information survives for a period of one year after the Effective Date, irrespective of the termination of this Agreement.

   b. *Return of Documents upon Termination.* Within two (2) days of the Effective Date, Employee shall return and hand deliver to Employer any originals or copies of any books, papers, price lists, customer contacts, bids, customer lists, supplier lists, files, notebooks or any other documents containing any Confidential Information. Employee acknowledges and agrees that all such documents and information are Employer's exclusive property.

6. **Employer's Remedy for Breach**. If Employee breaches paragraphs 3, 4, or 5 of this Agreement, Employer shall be entitled, in addition to all other remedies it may have, to immediate injunctive relief.

7. **Reemployment**. Employee waives all rights to reinstatement as an employee of Employer, its subsidiaries and affiliated companies, and agrees that she will not knowingly seek employment in the future with Employer, its subsidiaries or affiliated companies.

8. **Mutual Non-admission**. Employer and Employee agree that nothing in this Agreement shall be construed as an admission by either of them of any wrongdoing or violation of any applicable law.

9. **References**. Employer agrees that all reference checks relating to Employee will be answered in a neutral manner.

10. **Non-disparagement**. Employee agrees that she will not make any disparaging comments or statements concerning Employer, its employees, its products, or its operations.

GENERAL PROVISIONS

1. **Choice of Law**. This Agreement shall be governed by the laws of the state of Arizona.

2. **Choice of Forum and Arbitration**. All claims or disputes arising under or relating to this Agreement are to be settled by binding arbitration in the state of Arizona. The arbitration shall be conducted by the American Ar-

bitration Association on a confidential basis under its Arbitration Rules. Judgment on the award rendered by the arbitrators may be entered in any court of competent jurisdiction.

3. **Merger/Integration.** This Agreement supersedes all prior and contemporaneous agreements, oral or written, of the parties regarding Employee's employment with Employer.

4. **Modification.** The terms of this Agreement may not be modified except upon written consent of the parties.

5. **Severability.** Any portion of this Agreement which is held to be invalid or unenforceable by a court of jurisdiction shall be ineffective only to the extent of the prohibition without invalidating the remaining provisions of this Agreement.

6. **Successors in Interest.** This Agreement shall be binding upon and inure to the benefit of the executors, administrators, personal representatives, heirs, successors and assigns of the Employer and the Employee.

7. **Voluntary Release.** Employee acknowledges that this Agreement was entered into freely and voluntarily.

8. **Consultation with Attorney.** Employee understands and agrees that she has been advised to consult with her attorney before executing the Agreement.

9. **Notice.** All notices required under the terms of this Agreement shall be made in writing and shall be deemed given upon hand delivery or by commercial overnight courier with written verification of receipt.

    a. If to Employer: Chief Executive Officer of Vogel Pharmaceuticals, 121 Executive Drive, Phoenix, Arizona.

    b. If to Employee: Dr. Anna Maria Sing, 416 Palmer St. Phoenix, Arizona.

Notice shall be effective upon receipt.

The Parties agree to the terms of this Agreement, on the date first referenced above.

Vogel Pharmaceuticals, Inc.

_____   _____
By: Lawrence Eckerman   Dr. Anna Maria Sing
Its: Chief Executive Officer

Document 2
Client Letter Outlining Settlement
and Release Agreement

[Firm Stationery]

[Date]

Mr. Lawrence Eckerman
Chief Executive Officer
Vogel Pharmaceuticals, Inc.
121 Executive Drive
Phoenix, Arizona

CONFIDENTIAL ATTORNEY CLIENT COMMUNICATION

Re: Vogel / Dr. Anna Maria Sing—Separation Agreement and Release

Dear Mr. Eckerman:

At your request, I have negotiated and drafted a Settlement Agreement and Release on Vogel's behalf to resolve the employment dispute with Vogel's former Vice President of Sales and Development for the herbal remedy division, Dr. Anna Maria Sing. It is my understanding that Vogel Pharmaceuticals and Dr. Sing believe it is in their best interests to avoid litigation over the non-compete violation by Dr. Sing and to sever the employment relationship. I understand that Vogel wishes to preserve its interests in the non-compete and confidentiality covenants to the degree possible and that Dr. Sing wishes to accept a position with her former employer, Best Health. As such, I believe that the settlement agreement represents the primary interests of both parties and is a fair compromise on the issues of release of claims, confidentiality, severance, and competition.

Factual Background

My analysis and conclusion are based on the facts set forth below. Please review them carefully and inform me of any changes, corrections, or additions you deem necessary, as such considerations may affect my legal opinion. Also, please note that this analysis is limited to the breach by Dr. Sing of the non-compete clause of her original employment agreement with Vogel.

In 20__ , Vogel entered into an employment contract with Dr. Sing. Vogel sought a Vice President of Sales and Development with a proven track record in developing herbal remedies for its new herbal remedy division, to complement its well established pharmaceutical product line. Dr. Sing, then a research scientist with Best Health, sought an opportunity to use her law as well as her medical degree, to gain valuable business experience, and to substantially increase her income. Under the terms of the employment agreement, Dr. Sing's compensation package included an annual salary of $350,000, in addition to benefits customarily paid to executives of Vogel including a generous severance package. The employment agreement also included a non-compete clause prohibiting Dr. Sing from becoming employed with any competitor of Vogel in the pharmaceutical industry and a confidentiality clause prohibiting Dr. Sing from disclosing confidential information.

Shortly after signing the employment agreement, Dr. Sing's relationship with Vogel began to sour. On October 30, 20__, Dr. Sing provided written notice to Vogel of her resignation and her intent to return to Best Health to research and develop an herbal cure for high blood pressure. Vogel immediately informed Dr. Sing that her employment with Best Health violates the non-compete provision in her employment contract. The non-compete provision states: "If this agreement is terminated by either party for any reason, Employee must not become employed for a period of one year after termination, with any competitor of Vogel in the pharmaceutical industry." Dr. Sing has responded that Best Health is not a competitor in the pharmaceutical industry and the non-compete provision of the contract is unenforceable.

Legal Analysis

Arizona courts will enforce non-compete agreements that have a legitimate business purpose, where the employee received benefit for the agreement, the agreement is reasonable in time and scope, and the agreement does not violate public policy.

The only area of dispute is on the reasonableness of the time and the scope of the non-compete agreement. The non-compete between Vogel and Dr. Sing is one year long. Non-competes ranging from six months to one year are generally considered reasonable in Arizona to protect the business interests of the employer. Accordingly, the courts would most likely find the time reasonable.

It is questionable, however, whether the courts will interpret a provision excluding Dr. Sing from the entire pharmaceutical industry as limited in scope.

A review of case law suggests a substantial risk that Vogel may lose this argument if the case proceeds to litigation.

Further, the language of the non-compete provision prohibiting Dr. Sing from employment in the pharmaceutical industry may not apply to her employment with Best Health. Research indicates that Best Health only engages in the sale of herbal remedies. The U.S. government does not consider herbal products to be pharmaceutical products. According to the Dietary Supplement Health and Education Act of 1994, herbal products are considered dietary supplements and are not regulated by the FDA. As a result, it would be necessary to convince the courts and a jury that, as used in the employment agreement, the term "pharmaceutical industry" implies the inclusion of the herbal remedies industry. This is possible, but by no means guaranteed.

The Settlement Agreement and Release

Given the uncertainties involved in convincing the courts to enforce the non-compete provision of the employment agreement, settlement is an attractive option. The enclosed Settlement Agreement and Release allows Dr. Sing to resume employment with Best Health without violating the non-compete provided that, for a period of one year, Dr. Sing does not engage in: (1) the research, development, or sale of any herbal remedy that is in direct competition with any herbal remedy she worked on at Vogel, (2) the research, development, or sale of any pharmaceutical product, and (3) the sale of any pharmaceutical or herbal remedies product to any former, current, or future customer of Vogel.

Additionally, by executing the Settlement Agreement and Release Dr. Sing agrees to the original confidentiality clause of the employment agreement and is prevented from divulging proprietary information related to Vogel and its business practices. In the event of a breach of the non-compete or the confidentiality covenants of the Settlement Agreement and Release, Vogel is entitled to immediate injunctive relief as well as damages.

In exchange for Vogel's modification of the non-compete to allow Dr. Sing to return to Best Health, Dr. Sing completely releases and forever discharges Vogel from any and all past, present, or future claims, including the generous severance payment provided in the employment agreement. She also waives all rights to reinstatement or reemployment and agrees not to disparage Vogel, its employees, or its products.

Conclusion

In summary, given the uncertainties involved in pursuing legal enforcement of the non-compete covenant of the employment agreement, entering into a settlement has many advantages. The Settlement Agreement and Release eliminates the expense and inconvenience of protracted litigation and provide protection for Vogel should Dr. Sing disclose confidential information or engage in competition in the pharmaceutical industry or with competitors other than Best Health. Additionally, the agreement insulates Vogel from unknown claims which may arise from Dr. Sing's employment and releases the company from any financial obligations associated with her previously agreed upon severance.

Please contact me after you have had an opportunity to review the Settlement Agreement and Release, so that we may discuss it in more detail. As always, it is a pleasure working with you.

Sincerely,

Lawyer's Name and Signature

Part Nine

Practice Skills:
Law Firm and Courtroom
Culture and Practice

Chapter 18

Law Firm Culture and Practice

Highlights

Legal Practice

- In the U.S., a law school graduate generally must pass an exam and obtain a state law license before practicing law; the license allows a lawyer to practice in all areas of law, within the state granting the license.

Law Firm Culture

- Most lawyers work in private law firms.
- Law firms in the U.S. have certain expectations on professional demeanor, the quality of work product, managing workflow and clients, and avoiding liability.

Recording Time and Billing Clients

- Lawyers in private practice track and record their time; tracking time requires a detailed description of the tasks performed.
- The most common billing arrangements are hourly and contingent fee.
- The terms of all fee arrangements should be memorialized in writing.

Introduction

Most lawyers in the U.S. work in private law firms. Law firms vary in size. The greatest number of lawyers practice in small firms. Nevertheless, more than 250 firms have over 170 lawyers. Most law firms in the U.S. share expectations on lawyer performance including professional demeanor, the quality of work product, managing workflow and clients, and avoiding liability.

In addition, recording time, billing clients, and memorializing representation and fee agreements are an inherent part of private practice. Protocols exist for recording time and billing clients, as well as for preparing engagement and non-engagement letters or agreements.

This chapter focuses on law firm culture and practice. It has five sections: (1) legal practice, (2) law firm culture, (3) recording time, (4) billing clients, and (5) drafting representation and fee agreements. Chapter 19 focuses on courtroom culture and practice.

The Associate

As you read this chapter, consider yourself as a new associate at an American law firm. What do you need to know about law firm practice in the U.S. to succeed?

Legal Practice

Admission to Practice

All of the state judicial systems require a lawyer to obtain a license before practicing law. As a general rule, in order to obtain a license, the lawyer must graduate from law school, pass a bar exam, and satisfy certain character requirements. The state supreme court regulates the legal profession within the state, often with the assistance of a state bar organization. A law license allows a lawyer to practice in all areas of law, but only in the state in which the license was issued. A license to practice in a state's courts does not automatically allow a lawyer to practice in federal court. Rather, the lawyer must apply to be certified in each federal district in which the lawyer wishes to practice. Certification for federal practice does not require an additional bar exam.

Types of Practice

In the U.S., most lawyers are engaged in private practice at law firms. Other areas of practice include in-house or corporate counsel, government service, and public interest work. All lawyers share the same basic "tool kit," irrespective of the type of practice in which they engage.

Law Firm Practice

Law firms in the U.S. vary in size. Most lawyers practice at firms with two or three lawyers. Nevertheless, more than 250 firms have over 170 lawyers and the largest American-based law firm has over 3,500 lawyers.

Large firms generally specialize in corporate practice. Lawyers work primarily on matters involving general business transactions, corporate structure, corporate finance, mergers and acquisitions, tax law, antitrust law, real estate law, litigation, banking law, labor law, and intellectual property.

Large law firms employ many different types of non-lawyer staff. These include secretaries, also known as administrative assistants, paralegals, clerks, and others. Lawyers are generally partners or associates. A lawyer begins as an associate and must be elected to partnership.

Most firms have a lower level of "non-equity partners" with an upper level of "equity partners." Equity partners—also known as capital partners, shareholders, or members—own voting shares of a firm. They acquire such shares via a capital contribution or "buy-in" which may require payment of thousands of dollars. They control management of the firm as well as associate and non-equity partner compensation. Their own compensation is determined by the firm's profits each year. Their primary responsibilities are firm management and client development.

Non-equity partners do not own voting shares. Non-equity partnership is often an interim point between associate and equity partner. Many firms require a lawyer to spend several years as a non-equity partner before being considered for advancement. Most firms do not publicly distinguish between equity and non-equity partners. Judges, clients, and other third parties may be unaware of a partner's status.

The most junior lawyers in a firm are known as associates. Associates may be divided between junior and senior associates, based on the years of service to the firm. Associates receive a salary. Their primary responsibilities involve performing client work. The path by which an associate may become a partner varies, but usually the decision is made by the associate's twelfth year of practice within the firm. Associates who do not make partner may leave the firm or may become non-equity partners.

In addition to partners and associates, firms will occasionally have contract attorneys, senior attorneys, of counsel, and special counsel. These are generally titles recognizing that the lawyer, although practicing longer than a junior associate, is not "on track" to become a partner.

Small and medium size firms are organized similarly to large firms, with a mix of partners and associates. Some small to medium firms may be "boutique" firms specializing in particular types of law. Generally, however, as the size of the firm increases there is greater specialization among the lawyers. Smaller firms tend to handle matters related to criminal law, family law, wills and trusts, personal injury litigation, and consumer disputes.

In-House Counsel

Lawyers employed at a business to provide legal services are known as "in-house" or "corporate" counsel. The lawyer in charge of the legal department of a corporation is known as the "general counsel." In-house counsel give legal advice, draft documents, negotiate, and supervise "outside counsel."

Government Service

The Department of Justice is the legal department of the federal government. The head of the Department of Justice is the U.S. Attorney General. The legal powers of the Attorney General are implemented by local U.S. Attorneys. In other federal government offices, lawyers perform specialized legal duties. Large employers of lawyers include the Environmental Protection Agency, the Federal Trade Commission, the Internal Revenue Service, and the Securities and Exchange Commission.

Each of the fifty states also has a legal department headed by an Attorney General. The Attorney General and staff represent the state in all civil matters and give advice to officials, legislators, and agencies of the state. Government lawyers are salaried; their practice is governed by rules restricting outside employment.

Government lawyers are responsible for prosecuting public offenses. Federal crimes are prosecuted by the U.S. Attorney General. State crimes are prosecuted by State Attorneys General and local prosecutors, generally known as "district attorneys." Government lawyers, known as "legal defenders," may also provide the defense for indigent individuals accused of crimes.

Public Interest Work

Public interest practice generally refers to lawyers working for non-profit firms and agencies. The goal of public interest law is to provide representation to those individuals otherwise underserved by the legal profession.

Law Firm Culture

Expectations on Professional Demeanor

Lawyers are expected to maintain a professional demeanor at all times. Dress at most law firms in the U.S. remains traditional. Men wear suits and blazers with dress shirts and ties during most of the work week. Women adopt a similar style, wearing suit coats or blazers with skirts or dress pants.

Lawyers are also expected to be respectful to court personnel, firm personnel, colleagues, witnesses, experts, and clients at all times. A lawyer's success will be enhanced by the cooperation of the judge's court clerk or a non-lawyer staff member at a lawyer's firm. Similarly, lawyers are expected to exhibit professional behavior in "public," including when interacting with social media.

Expectations on Work Product

Associates are expected to perform all assignments in a timely manner, as well as to ask for and willingly accept feedback. Work product, even where requested in "draft" form, must be free of typographical and grammatical errors and have proper citations. All information, including the spelling of names, should be independently verified. All citations, quotations, page, and section numbers should be double-checked. Spellcheck and similar software programs should not be relied on exclusively.

The importance of producing an error-free work product cannot be overemphasized. Colleagues, clients, or judges finding errors in a lawyer's work product tend to question the lawyer's work ethic. Nevertheless, as important as it is to produce an error-free work product, the time spent must be commensurate with the amount of money the client is willing to pay. An associate is expected to ascertain the amount of time the supervising lawyer expects to have devoted to the project and to advise the supervising lawyer when such time turns out to be significantly greater than anticipated.

Managing Workflow

New associates in the U.S. are responsible for managing their own workflow. Most lawyers adopt a calendaring system to prioritize work on a daily basis. Associates are expected to proactively determine the specific deadlines for an assignment from the supervising lawyer when accepting work and to check in regularly to ensure that they are "on track" with the assignment. They are also expected to set a personal deadline to complete the work before it is actually due, so that it may be properly reviewed.

Managing Time Expectations

Closely related to the subject of managing workflow is the issue of managing time expectations. Many firms do not have set working hours for attorneys. Partners may spend significant amounts of time away from the office entertaining and "developing" clients; associates are often told they may work any hours as long as the work is accomplished and they meet the firm's billable hour requirements. This apparent scheduling flexibility, however, often conflicts with partners' actual expectations regarding associate time spent in the office. Further, many firms publish minimum billable hours requirements which are misleadingly low if an associate expects to advance at the firm.

Associates are advised to independently ascertain the actual criteria on which they will be reviewed with respect to in-office time and billable hours, by observing more senior associates at the firm. In general, actual billable hour requirements in the U.S. range from 1800 to 2500 billable hours per year. It is worth noting that to accumulate eight billable hours per day, the average associate must work nine or ten hours. The process of recording hours and billing time is discussed in more detail below.

Managing Clients

Lawyers in the U.S. are expected to communicate regularly with their clients. American clients can be demanding in their expectations regarding responses to telephone messages and emails. Many firms have a twenty-four hour requirement for such responses. As noted in Chapter 13, this does not require the lawyer to give immediate legal advice but does require acknowledging the client's request. Legal advice, when it is provided, should be practical and specifically answer the client's inquiry; theoretical answers are frowned upon.

Documenting Projects to Avoid Liability and Managing Mistakes

It is not uncommon for clients to sue lawyers in the U.S. As a result, associates are expected to keep files recording the work performed. Items generally included in such files include a description of the assignment, the date it was received, all deadlines, a copy of the work product and the date it was provided, and any action taken as a result of the assignment.

Mistakes should be dealt with immediately. The lawyer should first check the file, determine how the mistake occurred, and consider available solutions. Second, the lawyer should consult with the supervising lawyer, the partner responsible for maintaining the client relationship, and the partner responsible for risk management. Third, the client should be notified.

Law Firm Compensation

Law firms generally pay lawyers by tiers or levels. In larger firms, equity partners comprise the top level, non-equity partners the second level, senior associates the third level, and junior associates the fourth or bottom level. The salary structure is intended to reflect billing rates, revenue, and value to the firm.

At many firms, lawyers participate in an annual review process related to an evaluation of performance and a determination of compensation. The process usually involves a self-review from the individual lawyer, as well as reviews from supervising lawyers. The reviews are compiled and reviewed with firm management and discussed with the individual lawyer.

First-year associates at American law firms of more than 700 lawyers— especially in larger cities—may receive annual salary offers of up to $160,000. Salaries at firms of 250 to 700 lawyers are generally in the $125,000 to $145,000 range, depending on the size of the firm and the size of the geographic market.

Multicultural Considerations and the Role of Mentors

Associates from diverse backgrounds working at American law firms in the U.S. or abroad are often advised to seek out a mentor at the firm. The role of mentor is to ensure the associate obtains preferred work assignments, is included in client meetings and client development opportunities, and receives fair compensation. Many larger firms have begun formal mentoring programs for foreign lawyers.

Recording Time

Lawyers in private practice are required to track and record their time in increments ranging from six to 15 minutes. Lawyers record their time daily, filling out electronic time sheets that are ultimately converted to invoices. Tracking time requires a detailed description of the tasks performed for the client, as well as the time spent. In describing the services performed, the associate's goal is to assist clients in understanding the value of the services in resolving their legal problems.

Lawyers billing American clients should choose their words carefully. The first step is to check with the billing attorney to determine if the client has any specific billing protocols. Where no protocols exist, the format for time entries is: (1) an action verb, such as "conferencing," "researching," "drafting," or "reviewing"; (2) the object of the verb, for instance: "researching Florida law,"; (3) the word "regarding" followed by the nature of the work performed, for instance: "researching Florida law regarding the intentional infliction of emotional distress." The language used should describe professional activity performed. Lawyers "draft," "review," and "revise," rather than write, type, or read. Letters, email, and texts are generally referred to as "correspondence."

Billing Clients

In the U.S., lawyers in private practice send clients invoices for their services on a monthly, or less frequently a quarterly, basis. The invoices contain a detailed description of the different tasks performed for the client, which lawyer performed the task, the lawyer's billing rate, and an indication of how long each individual task required.

Billing arrangements generally follow five models: (1) hourly or time-based billing, (2) contingent fees, (3) fixed fees, (4) asset based fees, and (5) value based billing. As discussed in Chapter 8, the ethical rules require that fees be "reasonable." The billing arrangement and fees charged are generally established by contractual agreement between the lawyer and client.

Hourly Billing

Hourly billing is the most prevalent, particularly at large firms. The hourly fee is based on the time the lawyer spends on the client's work. The rate will differ for the status and experience of the lawyer. If two or more lawyers are assigned to the case, the client may be billed at different rates depending on who performed the work.

Contingent Fees

The contingent fee is based on the outcome of the legal matter. The client pays the lawyer a portion of the total recovery as a fee. If the lawyer fails to recover on behalf of the client, the lawyer does not receive a fee. Lawyers generally request one-third of the recovery as a contingent fee, but the percentage may vary based on the lawyer's experience and the type of case.

Fixed Fees, Asset Based Fees, and Value Based Billing

In fixed fee billing, the client pays an agreed upon fee regardless of the length of time the matter takes or its outcome. Asset based fees are determined by the amount of the assets managed in the matter; such fees are often utilized for financial services. Value based billing occurs where the fee is negotiated based upon the value of the matter to the client.

Hybrid Fees

A combination of these fee structures may occur. For instance, a portion of the fee may be figured on an hourly fee while another portion is based on a fixed or a contingency fee.

Costs

Firms generally charge clients for the costs involved with handling their legal matters. Such costs include electronic research fees, filing fees, process serving, photocopying, printing, telephone calls, expert witnesses, and travel expenses.

Representation and Fee Agreements

Representation and fee agreements should be discussed with the client at the end of the initial interview. Assuming agreement on the terms of representation and fees, the lawyer then conducts a conflict check. If no conflicts exist, or if existing conflicts are resolved, the terms of the agreement are memorialized in a writing signed by the client.

Conflict Checks

Conflict checks involve circulation of the basic client and matter information to all lawyers in a firm. It is the recipient's responsibility to promptly review the information and report any potential conflicts of interest with other matters or other clients. The purpose of the conflicts check is to ensure that the firm is competent to handle the matter and representation would not cause any conflicts. In the event of a conflict, a waiver may often be sought from the client. If the conflict cannot be waived, or the client is unwilling to do so, the firm must decline representation. The professional responsibility aspects of conflicts are discussed in Chapter 8.

Engagement Letters

Where no conflict exists or has been waived, the parties enter into an engagement agreement. Most, but not all, engagements are letter agreements. The engagement letter should: (1) express appreciation for the opportunity to assist the client, (2) clarify the terms of representation, including who the client is, what work the firm has agreed to do for the client, the fee or rate to be charged, the payment of fees and costs and any other billing arrangements, (3) reserve the right to withdraw discussed in Chapter 8, and (4) provide for any other contractual terms related to the relationship between the client and the lawyer. If a conflict has been identified and waived, the engagement letter should also contain information confirming the waiver. Engagement letters are prepared by the lawyer, with a signature block for the client acknowledging agreement to the terms.

Non-Engagement Letters

Where unresolved conflicts exist or there is disagreement about fees or representation, the lawyer should issue a non-engagement letter. A non-engagement letter should: (1) decline representation, (2) advise the client of the duty to seek other counsel, (3) provide options for seeking legal assistance, and (4) identify any risks associated with delay and time sensitive matters. Where the reason for declining representation involves a conflict of interest, the conflict should be identified. The lawyer should obtain a signed copy of the non-engagement letter from the person seeking advice; it is not unusual for U.S. courts to find an attorney-client relationship was formed even where representation is eventually declined.

Analyzing the Role of the Associate

Let us return to you, as a new associate, working for an American firm. What do you need to know about law firm practice in the U.S. to succeed? In Chapter 3, we met our clients Plymouth Rock High School and its Principal William Diehl. We followed our clients through a lawsuit to understand how civil litigation works. But what happened internally at our law firm after the first meeting with the clients?

Assume that it is your first day at work. Mr. Semple, a senior partner at our firm, has just met with Principal Diehl. Mr. Semple calls and asks you to come to his office immediately to discuss the client meeting. You are relieved you dressed professionally for your first day. You bring a legal pad and pen with you, knowing that Mr. Semple will expect you to take notes and prepare a memorandum recording the client facts and other matters covered in the meeting. You know that the audience for such a memorandum will generally be lawyers in the law firm who might become involved in the case. The purpose of the memorandum is to record and analyze the information and consider legal strategy.

Mr. Semple will expect you to actively participate in the meeting, asking questions where necessary to prepare such a memorandum. He will also expect you to ask him for background legal information and recommendations on law review articles, cases, and sample documents to educate yourself about the law and drafting criteria. Once involved in an initial meeting and the preparation of the first memorandum, you should expect to be assigned to the matter for its duration.

For your first assignment, Mr. Semple requests that you prepare the initial memorandum for the file describing the meeting. He also asks you to prepare an office memorandum on the First Amendment rights of students in public high schools. In an apparent afterthought, he yells, "And try your hand at drafting an engagement letter. I want to move on this, just send it in draft form."

Despite the fact that Mr. Semple has asked for a draft, you know the importance of producing a flawless work product. You also realize, however, that Mr. Semple expects to receive the engagement letter as well as the two memoranda in a timely manner. As soon as you emerge from the meeting, another lawyer stops you in the hall and tells you she wants you to "get up to speed" on a new case (you have no idea what it is). You have been at work an hour and already you are overwhelmed.

You begin managing your workflow by asking both partners for specific deadlines on the assignments. You calendar both of these assignments on the firm's electronic calendaring system, as well as set a personal deadline on your own calendar so that they are completed at least a day in advance. You realize that these assignments will require you to spend at least ten hours in the office every work day for the next several weeks.

You request your administrative assistant to set up files recording the assignments, the dates they were received, and the deadlines. You will later record the date the work product was provided to the partners, a copy of the work product, any related documents, and any client action taken. Once having set up the files, you begin work on the assignments. Both matters are being billed to the clients on an hourly basis. The firm requires you to track your time in six-minute increments. You keep track of your time by keeping personal notes throughout the day. At the end of the day you record your actual time in the firm's electronic billing system.

Time entries as they would appear on a client invoice and an engagement letter are included in the sample documents below.

Sample Documents

Document 1
Engagement Letter

[Firm Stationery]

[Date]

Mr. William Diehl
Plymouth Rock High School
123 Main Street
Plymouth, MI

Re: Representation of Defendants in *Thomas v. Plymouth Rock High School, et. al.*, Civil Action No. 00-CV-4567 in the Eastern District of Michigan.

Dear Mr. Diehl:

I enjoyed meeting with you about the prospect of our firm representing you, as principal of Plymouth Rock High School (PRHS), in the lawsuit filed by PRHS student Michael Thomas. I appreciate your confidence in our abilities and this opportunity to serve you.

This engagement letter states the terms of our agreement to represent you. Please read the letter carefully and let me know if you have any questions. If you are in agreement with the terms of the letter, please sign it and return it to my attention. Because we will not begin representing you until we have received the signed engagement letter, we ask that you return the letter as soon as possible but in any event no later than next Monday.

Scope of services

Our firm will represent you in *Thomas v. Plymouth Rock High School, et. al.*, Civil Action No. 00-CV-4567 in the Eastern District of Michigan, and in any appeal arising from this case. This engagement letter covers only these matters. Separate arrangements must be made for any other matters on which you may wish to have representation.

Firm obligations

Our firm will inform you of all developments, consult with you on all significant decisions including any settlement offers, and protect confidential information provided by you under the attorney-client privilege. Furthermore, we will not represent any party with adverse interests to you in this case or in any other case on this issue. Finally, should you notify us that you wish to terminate our representation of your interests in this case, we will cooperate in transferring the representation to new counsel.

Client obligations

You agree to provide our firm with complete and accurate information needed to defend this case. Further, you agree to pay all invoices for services rendered in this case within 30 days of receipt.

Fees

You agree to pay our firm for its representation in this case on an hourly basis. Time will be recorded in increments of 1/10th of an hour. Invoices will be sent monthly. Current rates for legal personnel assigned to work on this matter are:

_____, partner $400 per hour

_____, senior associate $250 per hour

_____, associate $150 per hour

The quoted rates are subject to change on 30 days' written notice. If you decline to pay the increased rates, our firm will have the right to withdraw as counsel.

We will staff the case as efficiently as possible. The legal personnel assigned to your case may confer among themselves about the case and attend meetings, court hearings, or other proceedings together and each person will charge for the time expended.

Costs and other charges

Our firm will incur various costs and expenses in performing legal services related to your case. You agree to reimburse the firm for all costs, disbursements, and expenses in addition to all hourly fees. The costs and expenses include service of process charges, filing fees, telephone charges, messenger and other delivery fees, postage, photocopying and other reproduction costs, computerized legal research expenses, travel costs including parking, mileage, transportation, meals and hotel costs, investigation expenses, consultants' fees, expert witness, professional mediator, arbitrator and/or special master fees and similar items. We will detail these expenses on the monthly invoices.

Termination and withdrawal

You may terminate your relationship with our firm at any time. In the event you notify us of termination, we agree to promptly withdraw as counsel. You agree that our firm shall be entitled to payment for services rendered and costs incurred through the effective date of any termination.

Our firm may withdraw with your consent or for good cause. Good cause includes your failure to abide by the terms of this agreement or any fact or circumstance that would render our continuing representation unlawful or unethical.

If this letter accurately states our agreement, please sign and return it to me as soon as possible but in any event not later than Monday of next week.

I look forward to working with you.

Sincerely,

Lawyer's Name and Signature
For: [the Firm's name]

Agreed:

_____

Principal William Diehl
Plymouth Rock High School
Date:

Document 2
Invoice

[Firm Stationery]

Client Name   Date
Client Address   File:
                                         Matter:

FEES

DATE	*DESCRIPTION*	*ATTORNEY*	*TIME*	*RATE*	*TOTAL*
__	Initial meeting with client regarding representation in federal lawsuit by student for violations of free speech rights	_____	___	$_____	$_____
__	Preparation of letter regarding engagement				
__	Researching federal law regarding freedom of speech in public high schools				
__	Telephone conference with client regarding Answer				
__	Drafting Answer				
__	Correspondence to client regarding filing and service of Answer				

                    FEES: $

Costs Advanced

DATE	DESCRIPTION	ATTORNEY	TOTAL
__	Electronic research charges	_____	$_____
__	Photocopy charges		
__	Delivery charges regarding filing and serving Answer		

	COSTS:	$ _____

TOTAL DUE AND OWING: $

Chapter 19

Courtroom Culture and Practice

Highlights

- Almost any lawyer in the U.S. is eligible to become a judge.
- Federal judges are nominated by the President and approved by Congress.
- State judges are appointed by the governor or elected by vote of the state legislature, the general population, or some combination of the two.
- Trial court judges preside at the trial and consider various pre-trial and post-trial motions.
- The role of appellate courts is to address trial court errors on the law and contribute to the interpretation and development of legal doctrine.

Introduction

Courtroom culture and practice varies widely from state to state, from the state to the federal system, and from one level of court to the next. As discussed in Chapter 3, there are 51 judicial systems in the U.S., including the federal system and each of the 50 states. In addition, each of the 51 court systems consists of trial and appellate divisions.

An important aspect of exercising the legal skills of an American lawyer lies in recognizing the culture and practice of a particular judicial audience and the individual judges' needs and expectations. Even a lawyer who does not expect to litigate needs such an appreciation to engage in client interviewing and counseling, preparing memoranda, drafting correspondence and contracts, and participating in alternative dispute resolution.

This chapter has five sections: (1) training and experience of judges, (2) other court personnel, (3) differences in trial and appellate court practice, (4) differences in state and federal court practice, and (5) judicial diversity.

The Associate

As you read this chapter, continue to consider yourself a new associate in an American law firm. What do you need to know about judicial culture and practice in the U.S. to succeed?

Training and Experience of Judges

Background

Federal and state court judges in the U.S. are lawyers admitted to practice in at least one state. Almost any lawyer is eligible to become a judge; there are no additional requirements beyond graduating from law school, passing the bar examination, and obtaining a license to practice law. Most judges practice law for at least several years before being elected or appointed to the bench, but practice is not required.

Judges in the U.S. may start their judicial career at any level in the state or federal judiciary. Unlike judges in many other countries, they need not start at the "bottom" and work their way up to positions on higher courts.

Appointment versus Election

Federal judges are nominated by the President and approved by the Senate. State judges are appointed by the governor or elected by vote of the state legislature, the general population, or some combination of the two. Federal trial and appellate judges are appointed for life. Lifetime appointment removes the need for engagement in political activity. State judges are most often appointed or elected for a set term of years. Those judges elected or appointed for set terms must run for re-election.

Federal Judgeships

Congress authorizes a set number of judgeships, for each court level. It currently authorizes 9 positions for the Supreme Court, 179 court of appeal judgeships, and 678 district court judgeships. It is rare that all judgeships are filled at any one time; judges die, become incapacitated, or retire resulting in vacancies until others are appointed.

Federal Supreme Court justices and appellate and district court judges serve "during good behavior"; they retain their positions unless Congress decides to remove them for wrongdoing through a process of impeachment and conviction. Congress has used this process only a few times. As a practical matter, almost all federal judges hold office for as long as they wish.

Other Court Personnel

Magistrates

In the U.S., the term "magistrate" may refer generally to any type of judge. However, within the federal and state systems, there are specific positions designated as "magistrate judges." A magistrate judge is typically a judicial official under the supervision of a judge. Federal magistrate judges serve eight year terms, and may be reappointed indefinitely. They are appointed by the federal judges of the applicable district and may hold hearings on all non-dispositive motions and those dispositive motions to which the parties consent. Many state trial courts have magistrates with similar responsibilities.

Judge's Staff

The staff in a judge's office, also known as "chambers," are the judge's law clerks and the judicial assistant or secretary. Federal court and most state appellate court law clerks tend to be recent law school graduates. They are appointed for periods of one to two years, although some judges have career law clerks. The duties vary from judge to judge, but generally include conducting legal research, preparing memoranda (including bench memos, which appellate judges use during oral argument), and preparing draft orders and opinions. Many state trial court judges lack a budget for full time law school graduates as law clerks; they make use of law school students on a part-time basis.

The judicial assistant manages the chambers. The judicial assistant is usually responsible for organizing the judge's calendar, coordinating judicial committee activities, and maintaining office records and files.

Clerk of the Court

Each court has a clerk of the court, appointed to work with the chief judge in overseeing the court's administration and managing the movement of cases through the court. The clerk of the court has an office staff responsible for various duties including screening pleadings and other documents submitted to the court to ensure that they comply with legal requirements and court rules, managing the process by which potential jurors are identified and summoned, developing and implementing a records management system, monitoring the construction of court space and alterations, maintaining a liaison with all branches of the court and related government agencies, and providing non-confidential information to the media.

The Courtroom Deputy Clerk

The courtroom deputy clerk administers oaths to witnesses and interpreters, attends to records and exhibits, prepares criminal judgments and verdict forms, and assists with calendaring of courtroom proceedings. The courtroom calendar is known as "the docket." The courtroom deputy is employed by the office of the clerk of court.

Court Reporter

The court reporter makes and keeps a record, known as a "transcript," of all court proceedings. Federal judges each have their own court reporter, assigned to their chambers. The process of assigning court reporters varies from state to state.

Staff Attorneys

All federal, and some state, courts of appeal maintain a staff attorneys' office. Staff attorneys' duties vary, but generally they prepare memoranda of law for the judges on issues raised in motions and appeals. They may also assist the court with jurisdictional issues. As opposed to the law clerk, who is hired by and works with one judge, staff attorneys are part of the central staff of a court of appeals. They may do work for a number of judges.

Circuit Mediators

Each of the thirteen federal courts of appeal maintains a mediation program. These programs operate under a variety of names and most employ "circuit mediators," also known as "conference attorneys" or "settlement counsel." Circuit mediators, similar to staff attorneys, are part of the central staff of a court.

Differences in Trial and Appellate Court Practice

Practice in Trial Courts

As discussed in Chapter 3, most cases in the U.S. are first heard in trial court. Trial court judges preside at the trial and consider various trial motions. They act or "sit" alone. The Seventh Amendment of the U.S. Constitution provides a right to a jury at trial, in most cases. The members of the jury observe the presentation of evidence, weigh conflicts in the testimony and credibility of witnesses, consider the arguments presented by counsel, determine the facts, and apply the law—as instructed by the judge—to the facts to reach a decision. The facts of a case are litigated only at the trial court level.

Judges in the U.S. do not wear wigs, but do wear robes. Trial court judges are referred to as "Judge" or "Your Honor," rather than their first name. A lawyer stands if addressing a judge in court or if the judge is standing.

Judges sit behind a desk on a raised platform or "bench" in the courtroom. Next to the bench is an enclosed box with a chair, known as the "witness box." The judge's courtroom deputy clerk and court reporter sit to the side of the bench. At the other side of the room is an enclosed area with twelve or fourteen seats for the jury, known as the "jury box." Within view of the bench and the jury box are the counsel tables and a lectern. Lawyers must always remain behind the area marked by the lectern when addressing the judge or questioning a witness, unless they seek permission to "approach" the bench or the witness.

Behind the counsel tables is a half-wall or "bar." Most trials in the U.S. are open to the public, but members of the public must sit behind the bar. As noted above, judges and their staff also have private offices. Jurors meet in a private "jury room" when not in the courtroom. During a trial, lawyers are forbidden from communicating with jurors outside of the courtroom.

Practice in Appellate Courts

In the federal and most state systems, appeal is as of right from the final judgments of the trial court to the court of appeals. Appeals of non-final orders, known as "interlocutory appeals," may be allowed, but require the trial court and the appellate court to agree that it is efficient to address the issue raised by the interlocutory appeal without waiting for a final judgment. Courts of appeal judges sit in panels of three to hear and decide cases. As in the trial courts, intermediate appellate court judges are referred to as "Judge" or "Your Honor." Intermediate courts of appeal address trial court errors of law.

Appeals from the intermediate court of appeals to the court of last resort are discretionary. Judges of both the federal and the state supreme courts are addressed as "Justice." Justices of state supreme courts sit in panels of five, seven, or nine. The U.S. Supreme Court has nine members; Supreme Court justices sit as a body or "en banc." "Judicial review" allows the courts, especially the U.S. Supreme Court, to review legislative and executive action for constitutionality. Thus, the federal and state supreme courts play a crucial role in the development of the law.

Appellate courts do not review evidence, hear witnesses, or impanel a jury. The issues on appeal are raised in briefs filed by counsel for the parties. The judges review the briefs and hear oral argument by counsel in increments of 15 to 30 minutes. The judges sit behind the bench. Counsel stand behind lecterns to address the court. The purpose of oral argument is to highlight the main arguments in the briefs and respond to questions from the judges. Following oral argument, the court takes the matter "under advisement." The court later issues a judgment or order often accompanied by a written opinion on its decision. As discussed in Chapter 4, a judge agreeing with the result, but differing with the reasoning of the majority of the judges may write a "concurring" opinion. A judge disagreeing with the result may write a "dissenting" opinion.

Differences in State and Federal Court Practice

Most state trial courts handle all of the cases filed in a given jurisdiction. Handling such cases involves court personnel in interactions with lawyers, clients, jurors, witnesses, experts, and occasionally the media. As a result, the atmosphere of a courtroom in a state trial court may be chaotic. There may be lines for security clearance, lawyers negotiating in the hallways, and constant motion in the courtroom. Federal trial courts handle fewer cases; the atmosphere is generally subdued and formal.

Diversity and the Judiciary

Judicial diversity increases public confidence in the courts and assists in providing decision-making power to otherwise disenfranchised members of the population. Available figures indicate that, in the federal system, approximately 195 judgeships are held by African Americans, two are held by American Indians, 32 are held by Asian Americans, 116 are held by Hispanics, and three are held by Pacific Islanders. Women hold approximately 378 judgeships.

Available figures for state appellate and general jurisdiction trial courts indicate that the highest percentage of minority judges, 65%, are found in Hawaii. The states with the next highest percentages are Louisiana, New York, and Texas, where minority judges comprise approximately one-fifth of the bench. The states with the highest percentage of women judges are Florida, Hawaii, Maryland, Massachusetts, Nevada, and Vermont, where approximately one third of judges are women.

Analyzing the Role of the Associate

Let us return to you, as a new associate in an American law firm. What do you need to know about judicial culture and practice in the U.S. to succeed?

Of the client hypotheticals we have reviewed, one was set in federal court and involved free speech while others were set in state court and involved intentional infliction of emotional distress and various contract issues.

All of these cases that proceed to litigation, as opposed to an alternative method of dispute resolution, will begin in the trial court. You know that the trial court judge sits alone and that you must stand when the judge enters the courtroom. The judge will sit behind the bench, while his courtroom clerk and court reporter sit to the side of the bench. You or your supervising lawyer should "check in" with the courtroom clerk prior to the judge taking the bench. If a transcript of the proceeding is needed, arrangements should be made with the court reporter.

You must remain behind the bar, until after your case is announced or "called" by the courtroom clerk. After your case is called, you may sit with your supervising lawyer at one of the counsel tables in view of the bench. The supervising lawyer will stand behind the lectern when speaking to the judge. You will not be allowed to address the court, as counsel, unless you are a member of the bar.

The judge will be trained in the law generally, but not necessarily in any specialties. The judge may have legal experience, but it is not required. This could be the judge's first legal proceeding. The supervising lawyer may ask you to research the judge's professional background to assist in the preparation of written materials and oral presentations to the court. You may also be asked to prepare a memorandum on the law on the legal issue before the court.

The judge may rule on the matter from the bench or take the matter under advisement and write an opinion. You may be asked to prepare a letter or email communication to the client explaining the matter or to set up a counseling session. Depending on the issue, the judge's ruling may also influence settlement negotiations, a future mediation, a legal memorandum, or even transactional documents drafted for this or other clients.

Sample Documents

Document 1
The Multistate Practice Test

Now that you have completed your term in the global legal skills academy for foreign law students interested in U.S. practice and are well acquainted with the tools of the trade of the practicing lawyer, it is time for you to draft the sample documents.

The Multistate Performance Tests, or "MPT," are offered by the National Conference of Bar Examiners ("NCBE") and included in the bar exams of a number of states, including New York. The MPT is a 90 minute assignment designed to test a bar candidate's ability to use fundamental lawyering skills in a realistic client situation. All assignments include a File and a Library. The first document in the File is an office memorandum containing the instructions for the task you are to complete. The other documents in the file contain factual information about your case and may also include some facts that are not relevant. The Library contains the legal authorities needed to complete the tasks and may also include some authorities that are not relevant.

The MPTs for the period from 2004–2008 may currently be downloaded at www.ncbex.org. These tests also include the point sheets used by the examiners in evaluating the applicants' answers. Summaries of the MPTs from 2009–2013 are currently posted to the same website and may be purchased from the NCBE. Of those MPTs currently offered at no cost, MPT-2 from the February 2008 MPT exam provides an excellent opportunity to practice memo writing skills and MPT-2 from the February 2007 MPT exam provides a similar opportunity to draft a professional letter.

Conclusion

The study of global legal skills is a growing and exciting field of law. Lawyers around the world practice across borders, with increased exchange of ideas and comparison of techniques. This book is intended to contribute to this endeavor in a practical way. It presents a method for international students and lawyers to learn the practice of U.S. law, from the underlying principles of the common law and U.S. dual sovereignty, to the day-to-day work of the law firm and courtroom. We have included a variety of scenarios and sample documents that demonstrate U.S. legal practice skills in realistic settings. The References and Further Readings in the Appendix point you to texts that allow you to pursue each particular skill in the tool kit in a more detailed and specialized manner, according to your needs.

Perhaps the most exciting feature of global lawyering skills is the emerging consensus of best practices, while recognizing the unique nature and requirements of each nation's legal system. All effective lawyers make use of skills adapted to the jurisdictions and cultures in which they practice. Moreover, the most important skills—ethical and professional client representation—transcend national boundaries and enhance global legal understanding.

Appendix

References and Further Readings

Please note that many excellent books exist on each subject listed below; this list is intended only as an introduction. Further, many of the books listed in one category also include information on other categories.

Alternative Dispute Resolution and Negotiation

Roger Fisher, William L. Ury and Bruce Patton, *Getting to Yes: Negotiating Agreement Without Giving In* (Rev. ed. 2011).

X. M. Frascogna and H. Hetherington, *The Lawyer's Guide to Negotiation* (2nd ed. 2011).

John Garvey and Charles Craver, *Alternative Dispute Resolution: Negotiation, Mediation, Collaborative Law, and Arbitration* (2013).

Leigh Thompson, *The Mind and Heart of the Negotiator* (5th ed. 2012).

Citations

Colleen Berger, *ALWD Guide to Legal Citation* (5th ed. 2014).

Columbia Law Review, Harvard Law Review, University of Pennsylvania Law Review and Yale Law Journal, *The Bluebook: A Uniform System of Citation* (19th ed. 2010).

Comparative Law

John Head, *Great Legal Traditions: Civil Law, Common Law, and Chinese Law in Historical and Operational Perspective* (2011).

Oliver Wendell Holmes, *The Common Law* (1882).

Interviewing, Counseling, and Problem Solving

Robert Bastress and Joseph Harbaugh, *Interviewing, Counseling, and Negotiation, Skills of Effective Presentation* (1990).

Robert F. Cochran, Jr., John M.A. DiPippa, and Martha M. Peters, *The Counselor-at-Law: A Collaborative Approach to Client Interviewing and Counseling* (2d ed. 2001).

Roger Haydock and Peter Knapp, *Lawyering Practice and Planning* (3d. ed. 2011).

Stefan Krieger and Richard Neumann, *Essential Lawyering Skills* (4th ed. 2011).

Introduction to U.S. Law

William Burnham, *Introduction to Law and Legal Systems of the United States* (5th ed. 2011).

Tony Fine, *American Legal Systems: A Resource and Reference Guide* (2008).

Lawrence Friedman, *American Law: An Introduction* (2d ed. 1998).

Margaret Johns and Rex Perschbacher, *The U.S. Legal System: An Introduction* (2d ed. 2007).

Ellen Podgor and John Cooper, *Overview of U.S. Law* (2009).

Judicial Culture

Ruggero J. Aldisert, *Opinion Writing* (3d ed. 2012).

Law and Behavior

Edwin Scott Fruehwald, *Law and Human Behavior: A Study in Behavioral Biology, Neuroscience, and the Law* (2011).

The Legal Profession and Law Practice

Lisa Abrams, *The Official Guide to Legal Specialties* (2000).

Grover Cleveland, *Swimming Lessons for Baby Sharks: The Essential Guide to Thriving as a New Lawyer* (2010).

Bruce Davis, *Your Billable Life: A Law Firm Survival Guide* (2008).

Michael Downey, *Introduction to Law Firm Practice* (2010).

Mark Herrmann, *The Curmudgeon's Guide to Practicing Law* (2006).

James Kramon, *The Art of Practicing Law* (2013).

Nalini Mahadevan, *How To Start a Law Practice and Succeed:* Volume 1 (2013).

Nalini Mahadevan, *How To Start a Law Practice and Succeed:* Volume 2: Forms for Your Practice (2013).

Jerry Van Hoy, *Legal Professions: Work, Structure and Organization* (2001).

Legal Reasoning

David Romantz and Kathleen Vinson, *Legal Analysis: The Fundamental Skill* (2d ed. 2009).

Frederick Schauer, *Thinking Like a Lawyer: A New Introduction to Legal Reasoning* (2012).

Legal Research

Christina Kunz, Deborah Schmedemann, Ann Bateson, Mehmet Konar-Steenberg, Anthony Winer, Sarah Deer, *The Process of Legal Research* (8th ed. 2012).

Mark Osbeck, *Impeccable Research: A Concise Guide to Mastering Legal Research Skills* (2010).

Amy Sloan, *Basic Legal Research: Tools and Strategies* (5th ed. 2012).

Legal Writing

John C. Dernbach, Richard V. Singleton II, Cathleen Wharton and Joan Ruhtenberg, *A Practical Guide to Legal Writing and Legal Method* (5th ed. 2013).

Laurel Oates and Anne Enquist, *The Legal Writing Handbook* (4th ed. 2006).

Ann Sinsheimer, Kissane Brostoff, and Nancy Burkoff, *Legal Writing, A Contemporary Approach* (2014).

Helene Shapo, Marilyn Walter, Elizabeth Fajans, *Writing and Analysis in the Law* (6th ed. 2013).

Robin Welford Slocum, *Legal Reasoning, Writing, and Other Lawyering Skills*, (3rd ed. 2011).

Letter Writing

Thomas Kane, *Letters for Lawyers: Essential Communication for Clients, Prospects, and Others* (2d ed. 2004).

Litigation Process and Writing for Litigation

Kamela Bridges and Wayne Schiess, *Writing for Litigation* (2011).

Richard Freer, *Introduction to Civil Procedure* (3d ed. 2012).

Persuasion: Motion, Trial, and Appellate Practice

Mary Beth Beazely, *A Practical Guide to Appellate Advocacy* (3d ed. 2010).

L. Ronald Jorgensen, *Motion Practice and Persuasion* (2006).

Thomas A. Mauet, *Trial Techniques and Trials* (9th ed. 2013).

Michael Murray and Christy DeSanctis, *Advanced Legal Writing and Oral Advocacy: Trials, Appeals, and Moot Court* (2d ed. 2014).

Louis Sirico, *Persuasive Writing for Lawyers and the Legal Profession* (2d ed. 2002).

Professional Responsibility and the Attorney-Client Privilege

Ronald Rotunda and John Dzienkowski, *Professional Responsibility: A Student's Guide* (2013).

Vincent S. Walkowiak, Stephen M. McNabb, and Oscar Rey Rodriguez, *The Attorney-Client Privilege in Civil Litigation: Practicing and Defending Confidentiality* (5th ed. 2013).

Statutory Construction

Antonin Scalia and Bryan Garner, *Reading Law: The Interpretation of Legal Texts* (2012).

Transactional Law and Drafting

Cynthia Adams and Peter Cramer, *Drafting Contracts in Legal English: Cross-Border Agreements Governed by U.S. Law* (2013).

Scott Burnham, *Drafting and Analyzing Contracts* (3d ed. 2003).

Thomas Haggard and George Kuney, *Legal Drafting* (2d ed. 2007).

Richard Neumann, Jr., *Transactional Lawyering Skills: Becoming a Deal Lawyer* (2012).

Tina Stark, *Drafting Contracts* (2d ed. 2013).

Margaret Temple-Smith and Deborah Cupples, *Legal Drafting* (2013).

David Zarfes and Michael Bloom, *Contracts: A Transactional Approach* (2010).

Writing Style and Typography

Matthew Butterick, *Typography for Lawyers: Essential Tools for Polished and Persuasive Documents* (2010).

Bryan Garner, *The Redbook: A Manual on Legal Style* (2002).

Ian Gallacher, *A Form And Style Manual for Lawyers* (2005).

Richard Wydick, *Plain English for Lawyers* (5th ed. 2005).

U.S. Legal Skills in a Global Context

Teresa Brostoff and Ann Sinsheimer, *United States Legal Language and Culture* (3d ed. 2011).

Jeremy Day, *International Legal English* (2d ed. 2011).

Kevin Fandl, *Lost in Translation: Effective Legal Writing for the International Legal Community* (2013).

Craig Hoffman and Andrea Tylor, *United States Legal Discourse: Legal English for Foreign LLMs* (2008).

Debra S. Lee, Charles Hall and Susan Barone, *American Legal English: Using Language in Legal Contexts* (2d ed. 2007).

Deborah McGregor and Cynthia M. Adams, *International Lawyers Guide To Legal Analysis and Communication in the United States* (2008).

Mary-Beth Moylan and Stephanie Thompson, *Global Lawyering Skills* (2013).

Nadia Nedzel, *Legal Reasoning, Research, and Writing for International Graduate Students* (3d ed. 2012).

Jill Ramsfield, *Culture to Culture: A Guide to U.S. Legal Writing* (2005).

John Thornton, *U.S. Legal Reasoning, Writing, and Practice for International Lawyers* (2014).

Mark Wocjik, *Introduction to Legal English: An Introduction to Legal Terminology, Reasoning, and Writing in Plain English* (3d ed. 2009).

Index

citation, importance of, 102
client hypothetical, 98, 102–4
formulistic approach to, 98–99
issue formulation, 97, 99
issue resolution, 97, 100–101
outlining, 101–2
writing process, 101
office memorandum, 111–24. *See
also* objective legal analysis, organization of
client hypothetical, 112, 124
format of, 113–14
purpose of, 14, 112–13
short form memoranda, format
and discussion, 122–24
short form *vs.* long form memoranda, 111, 112
tone of, 97
traditional, components of,
113–14
traditional, discussion area and
analysis, 118–22
traditional, format of, 114–17
traditional, statutory analysis
in, 122
opinion letters, to clients, 214
opinions, judicial. *See* judicial opinions
opposing counsel communications,
211, 217, 236
oral arguments, in appellate courts,
21
oral deposition, definition, 18
organization
in drafting contracts, 250–52,
264–70
in emails, to clients, 231–33
in letter writing, 214

of objective legal analysis,
97–104
organization, definition, 6
of text book, 8–9

P
parol evidence rule, in contract
drafting, 248, 269
peremptory challenges, in jury se-
lection, 19
perjury by clients, 145, 146
persuasive precedent, 11, 49–50
possessors of rights, in contracts,
270
post-counseling memoranda, 199
post-interview memoranda, 186
precedent, 10–11, 43, 48–50. *See
also* stare decisis
preparation
for client counseling, 196–97
for client interviewing, 181
for negotiation and settlement,
307–8
pre-trial conferences, 19
privilege, in contracts, 270
problem solving approach, to negotiation and settlement, 305,
307, 313–14
problem solving skills, 165–68. *See
also* communication, with
clients
assessment/evaluation, of client
problems, 165–66, 168,
197–98
decision making, by clients,
142, 198, 308
multicultural considerations,
159, 166–67
problem solving, definition, 6